p. 149 Don't understand safety/
friendly state of indians
camped outside of the fort.

p. 158 American's calling for speed

p. 163 Break in  writing w/
sudden reference to cholera?
Trying to demonstrate its sudden
appearance.

p. 180 Validates a location by saying
important in character's life →
talks about Kit throughout story
finally begins to connect/explain
w/ to story.

p. 122 Makes a pt. to say I, myself
... wonder why

Other titles by Stanley Vestal
available in Bison Books editions

JIM BRIDGER: MOUNTAIN MAN

JOE MEEK: THE MERRY MOUNTAIN MAN

WARPATH: THE TRUE STORY OF THE FIGHTING SIOUX

TOLD IN A BIOGRAPHY OF CHIEF WHITE BULL

THE OLD
Santa Fe
TRAIL

BY

STANLEY VESTAL

INTRODUCTION TO THE BISON BOOKS EDITION
BY MARC SIMMONS

UNIVERSITY OF NEBRASKA PRESS
LINCOLN AND LONDON

⊚ The paper in this book meets the minimum requirements of American National Standard for Information Sciences—Permanence of Paper for Printed Library Materials, ANSI Z39.48-1984.

First Bison Books printing: 1996
Most recent printing indicated by the last digit below:
10   9   8   7   6   5   4   3   2   1

Library of Congress Cataloging-in-Publication Data
Vestal, Stanley, 1887–1957.
The old Santa Fe Trail / by Stanley Vestal; introduction to the Bison Books edition by Marc Simmons.
p.   cm.
Originally published: Boston: Houghton Mifflin, 1939.
ISBN 0-8032-9615-0 (pa: alk. paper)
1. Santa Fe Trail.   2. Frontier and pioneer life—Southwest, New.   I. Title.
F786.V56   1996
978—dc20
96-2238   CIP

Reprinted from the original 1939 edition by Houghton Mifflin Company, Boston.

INTRODUCTION

Marc Simmons

In 1821, Mexico, which then included today's American Southwest, broke away from mother Spain and launched herself on the stormy sea of independent nationhood. At Santa Fe in the old province of New Mexico, officials hurried to open the border facing the United States, displaying their approval of the change. The Spanish colonial regime had not allowed overland commerce between its subjects and the bumptious, business-minded Americans whose frontier was expanding westward from Missouri. But once the trade barriers were down, New Mexicans proved hungry for Yankee goods.

William Becknell, resident of the central Missouri town of Franklin, led the way. With five companions and a string of ware-laden pack mules, he headed for the Southwest in the fall of 1821, blazing a trail that would soon become a major commercial artery. With profits realized from this first venture, Becknell in 1822 outfitted three farm wagons and drove them loaded with merchandise to the New Mexican markets. When again he was amply rewarded, word spread through the borderlands community and men rushed to join this lucrative new enterprise. Historians of a later day would credit William Becknell as the Father of the Santa Fe Trail.

Around this, the first great American trailway in the Far West, there has accumulated over the years an enormous and marvelous history. Not only was the route to Santa Fe the oldest, but in the course of westward expansion it also became the most enduring, not closing down until arrival of the railroad at trail's end in 1880. That life of nearly three-score years contrasted sharply with the Oregon Trail whose heyday lasted a mere quarter century.

Among the many general accounts dealing with this historic road, Stanley Vestal's *The Old Santa Fe Trail* (1939) must be regarded as one of the most engaging and readable. Houghton Mifflin brought out four hardbound printings, and a single paperback printing (without the index) was released by Bantam Books in 1957. Its reappearance now as a

Bison Book, following a long period of unavailability, is certainly welcome.

Stanley Vestal was the pen name of Walter S. Campbell, long-time professor of English and director of courses in professional writing at the University of Oklahoma, Norman. Kansas-born, in 1887, he spent his youth in Oklahoma where he played regularly with Cheyenne youngsters, thereby gaining an affinity for Indians that never left him. As a Rhodes Scholar at Oxford and a captain of Field Artillery in France during World War I, Vestal saw something of Europe, but the focus of his attention as an author always remained fixed upon the Old West.

From his unwavering passion for writing came histories, biography, novels, short stories, articles, writers' manuals, and verse. Vestal's four novels and his verse, including the poem "Kit Carson's Last Smoke," which found its way into *The Old Santa Fe Trail*, can be charitably described as unmemorable. The biographies, on the other hand, although outdated still make lively reading, owing no doubt to the author's choice of stirring subjects like Kit Carson, Jim Bridger, Big-Foot Wallace, mountain man Joe Meek, Sitting Bull, and Sitting Bull's nephew Chief White Bull.

During the Depression years, university professors' salaries were extremely low, Vestal's being a scant $1,000 annually, according to his biographer, Ray Tassin. To make matters worse, Vestal was a self-admitted poor businessman who, despite his supplemental income from writing, could never quite pay all the family bills. Thus when he contracted with Houghton Mifflin in 1937 to do *The Old Santa Fe Trail*, he gave as a reason his acute need for money, saying that his creditors were hunting for his blood.

In his creative writing classes at the University of Oklahoma, Vestal taught his students the nuts and bolts of surviving as a freelance writer, which included steps for marketing their work. One year alone, thirty-nine of his class members sold ninety-four of their manuscripts to national magazines. For this success, the English department condemned Vestal, accusing him of commercializing the academic endeavor.

In part to escape the pressures in Norman, Vestal with his wife and two daughters retired to a summer house near Santa Fe when he was not teaching. The retreat also furnished quiet time for his own work. There he did research on *The Old Santa Fe Trail* and even interviewed a few aging men who could remember from first-hand experience the tag end of the glory days of the trail.

The book, although not without limitations, is probably one of Vestal's best. Early on, he decided against developing his subject chronologically, lest it bear the stamp of textbookishness and turn readers away. Instead, he resorted to a topical or geographical approach, treating distinct themes and places as they normally would have appeared to a traveler crossing the trail from east to west. It was a technique he would use again when he wrote his river history, *The Missouri*, published in 1945.

The Old Santa Fe Trail, therefore, ought not to be classified as a narrative history. Founder William Becknell, for instance, is scarcely mentioned, and a number of major episodes are left out entirely. What Vestal did was to take selected incidents that appealed to him and turn them into exciting reading, using the methods of the fiction writer, with which he was so familiar, and adhering to the rules of historical evidence as best he could. The result was a book that strongly attracted the reading public, one that still serves well as an introduction to the subject.

True writer that he was, Stanley Vestal worked right up to the end of his life. He died in harness on Christmas Day, 1957, at Oklahoma City. At his request, he was buried in the National Cemetery at Custer Battlefield National Monument.

In recent years, interest in the Santa Fe Trail has grown enormously, spurred by its elevation to the status of a National Historic Trail in 1987. Sites have been restored or marked, legions of visitors now drive the trail searching out points of interest, public events showcasing trail history are under development, and publishers continue to release a stream of new titles that expand our knowledge of the story.

Under the circumstances, the rerelease of Stanley Vestal's book on the 175th anniversary of the opening of the Santa Fe Trail seems timely, indeed. As happened more than fifty years ago, upon its original publication, the work should again find a receptive and appreciative audience.

Preface

A HUNDRED years ago three great highways diverged from St. Louis and the States into the wilderness of the Great American Desert — the Far West. All three were hazardous and long, highways on which danger and adventure lay in wait for all comers under the rainbow arch of romance. Yet each had a character and a traffic all its own.

The first route led up the winding, muddy Missouri some two thousand miles to the Continental Divide. It was a waterway, the route of *voyageur* and keelboatman, of the Mackinaw barge and the steamboat, and led at last to the rendezvous of the beaver-trappers and the fur-baron's lone stockade.

The second road ran overland up the Platte, over South Pass, and on to Eldorado and the farm lands beyond the ranges. Over that beaten highway crawled the covered wagons of the movers, slow caravans carrying the household goods and families of greenhorn pioneers seeking new homes across the continent. That was the one-way trail of the farmer — the Oregon Trail.

The third, the Trail to Santa Fe, was from the beginning a two-way thoroughfare of international trade. It too had its wagon trains, its ox-carts and laden mules. But those wagons and carts were seldom occupied by family parties. On the way west they creaked and swayed, crammed to overflowing with the precious wares of Yankee commerce; on the way back they groaned under corded bales of buffalo robes and beaver, and the rich metals of Mexican mines. That was the highway of the commerce of the prairies, the traders' road.

At times the Indians swooped down and levied tribute in hair and horseflesh. At times, Mexican officials over-reached themselves, mulcting the rich *Americanos* out of all reason. At times, combative Texans raided trains, forgetful of international boundaries. But all these found the Santa Fe traders old hands on the Trail. Their caravans were well organized and manned by veteran frontiersmen. Redskins and Spaniards, bandits and Texan raiders soon learned that the fighting merchants from the States were not easily intimidated or imposed upon.

Those hardy pioneers can hardly have foreseen the innovations which have broken up their plains: windmills, barbed wire, cattle, farms, irrigation. The prairie ocean they knew has vanished, their landmarks are forgotten. In one day now, by plane or motor, we can cover the length of their old Trail to Santa Fe. For us the magic of those Plains may well be lost.

But not if we ride, in imagination, with them. To help us do so is the object of this book.

To them the Santa Fe Trail was no mere line of ruts connecting two towns, two cultures. It was a perilous cruise across a boundless sea of grass, over forbidding mountains, among wild beasts and wilder men, ending in an exotic city offering quick riches, friendly foreign women, and a moral holiday. The Trail stood for adventure, travel, romance, danger, wealth, and the love of women. Let us try to recapture *the feelings, the sensations, the hopes and fears and humors which they knew.*

They were not conscious of dates and statistics, mileage and the march of destiny. They knew only darkness, fatigue, cold and sunburn, the insistent wind, the drenching downpour, the lone danger of guard duty while the wolves howled from the hills and the skulking Comanche fitted an arrow to his bowstring. They knew thirst and hunger, the feast and the carouse, the night attack, the dash after buffalo, the slow plodding through the clogging snow. If we are to know their Trail, we must know it as they did.

We can do that, for we have their diaries, their records, and the painful compilations of all that by later pens.

The method of this book, then, is to attempt to *recapture that experience*, starting at the port of embarkation in Missouri, and passing along the Old Trail, camping where they camped, seeing and feeling what they saw and felt. Here, statistical matter has been pushed back to the Appendix, *and typical historic events* have been given the center of the stage. That stage is a thousand miles of prairie, high plains, desert, and mountain; the time is the last century. Our curtain rises with the sun.

We must march, O Pioneers!

'Put out' on the Trail to Santa Fe!

Contents

PART VI
The Mountain Route

PART VII
La Fonda

Bent's Fort

Ox Team

Pack Mule

108°   106°   104°   102°

Denver

· Republ

ROCKY Mts.

BAYOU SALADE

So. Platte River

COLORADO

Pike's Peak

Colorado Springs

Big Sandy Cr.

K

Wild Horse Creek

Horse Cr.

Adobe Cr.

Arkansas River

· Pueblo

Bent's Fort

Big Timber

Salt Bottom

Pretty Encampm

Rio San Carlos

Ft. Lyon

Choute
Islan

Blanca Peak

Huerfano R.

Spanish Peaks (Wah-to-Yah)

Caddo Cr.

Antelope Cr.

Clay Cr.

Middle Spring

Rio Grande

Hole-in-the-Rock

Purgatoire R.

Timpas R.

Two Butte Creek

Willow Bar

Panil Cr.

RATON PASS

Upper Spring

Little Cimarron R.

Pueblo de Taos

San Fernández de Taos

Arroyo Hondo

Rayado R.

El Embudo

La Cañada

Wagon Mound Fort Union

NEW MEXICO

[TEXA

Santa Fé

Las Vegas

Cerro Pajarito

Pecos

Pecos River

Canadian River

108°   106°   104°   102°

TRAPPER   OSAGE   GOV'T. SCOUT   PAWNEE

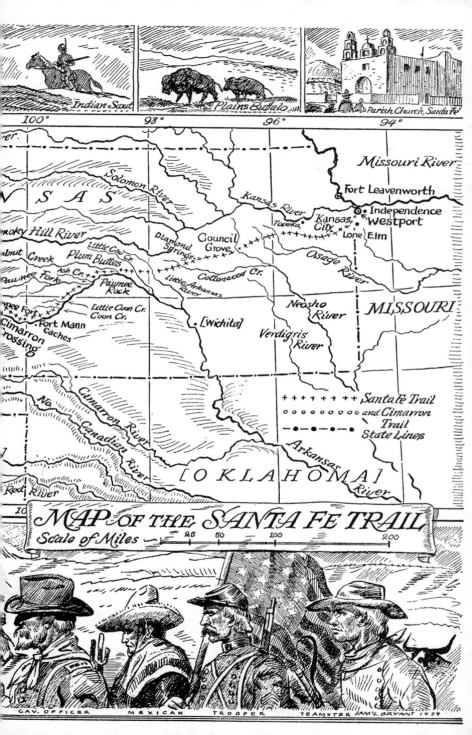

Indian Scout

Plains Buffalo

Parish Church, Santa Fé

100° 98° 96° 94°

Missouri River

Solomon River

Kansas River

Fort Leavenworth

S A S

Independence
Westport

Topeka

Kansas City

Lone Elm

Smoky Hill River

Diamond Springs

Council Grove

Osage River

alnut Creek

Little Cow Cr.

Plum Buttes

Ash Cr.

Pawnee Rock

Pawnee Forks

Cottonwood Cr.

Little Arkansas River

MISSOURI

Little Coon Cr.
Coon Cr.

[Wichita]

Neosho River

Verdigris River

nee Fort

Fort Mann
caches

Cimarron Crossing

Cimarron River

No

Canadian River

+ + + + + + + Santa Fe Trail
o o o o o o o o o and Cimarron
· — · — · — · Trail
                State Lines

[O K L A H O M A]

Arkansas River

Red River

MAP OF THE SANTA FE TRAIL

Scale of Miles — 25 50 100 200

CAV. OFFICER   MEXICAN   TROOPER   TEAMSTER SAM'L BRYANT 1939

PART I

The Prairie Ocean

CHAPTER I

Windwagon

THE TRAIL to Santa Fe led from Missouri almost a thousand miles across the Great Plains to the Spanish settlements at the foot of the Rocky Mountains.

Those plains were like the ocean, a region of magnificent distances, of desolate and barren wastes, strange, solitary, unexplored. Sometimes that ocean was a sea of grassy hillocks, sometimes level with the flatness of dead calm, oftener rolling in long swells to the far-off horizon, green, tumultuous, tossing its waves of grass under the driving winds, changing shape and color as swift cloud shadows sped over the uneven surface.

Like the sea, those plains were swept by masses of living things: vast shoals of shaggy bison, antelope, and other game, which appeared and disappeared without warning. Birds, sometimes even gulls, flapped and soared above it. And like the sea, the plains were subject to violent storms, sudden variations of temperature, terrific gales, cruel frosts, tornadoes, and drenching cloudbursts. Here and there that empty sea was broken by buttes like islands, sterile promontories.

The emptiness, the loneliness, the pathetic solemnity of the region oppressed some men, and all women, to the verge of madness. Many, on first emerging from their familiar woodlands, became physically sick. Even Coronado's hard-boiled Spanish troopers were terrified by a country where one could see the sky under a horse's belly.

But for those hardy tempers who could love great spaces, where one spot was no more important than another, experience of the sea of grass was glorifying. On the Great Plains a man of strong identity stood always at the center of his world, a king of infinite space.

Today we think of the Santa Fe Trail in terms of wagons: wagons creaking up long prairie slopes; wagons rolling down hills; wagons grinding through heavy sand, sucking through sticky mud, swishing through tall grass; wagons with locked wheels plunging down steep river-banks; wagons snaked through clinging quicksands, or jiggling over ribbed sand-bars rough as cobblestones; wagons hauled yard by painful yard up the forbidding rocks of the Raton Pass, two slow miles a day; wagons corralled against the attacks of treacherous redskins; wagons broken down, abandoned, stranded by the loss of animals stolen by raiding savages; wagons burned in prairie fires; wagons warped and shrunken by the heat and drouth. Wagons crammed with rich furs, Mexican silver, gold bullion.

But in the old days, travellers on those plains spoke habitually of 'making port,' urged Congress to enact navigation laws for the 'prairie ocean.' Their covered wagons, appropriately dubbed 'prairie schooners,' were in fact watertight boats mounted on wheels, rising high at prow and stern. They thought of the plains in terms of seafaring, and felt the glamour of them as a magic of the sea. They named the jumping-off place in Missouri Westport!

In Westport, fittingly enough, a company was actually formed to navigate the uncharted plains in wagons rigged with sails and steering-gear.

One spring day in 1853, the citizens of that frontier town were amazed to see a light vehicle steering down the street, driven by the wind which filled its white sail. Horses reared and ran away, women and children fled into their houses, dogs scuttled for safety, and the men of Westport stood with open mouths, watching that strange craft come sailing in.

Its pilot lowered the sail, locked his brakes, and rolled to a stop before the entrance to the Yoakum Tavern. He disembarked, and the startled citizens gathered to inspect his bark and question him.

They learned that his name was Thomas, that he had come from somewhere east, and that his sole cargo consisted of a compass, a water butt, and a carpetbag. He walked like a seafaring man, and they suspected that he was tattooed under his faded monkey jacket. Was he a whaler, had he ever struck a fish? They could not tell, for Thomas wasted few words in telling of himself. He announced that he had come as the Navigator of the Prairies, and invited them to join with him and form a company to engage in the Santa Fe trade!

In Yoakum's Tavern, leading citizens split a bottle with him, while he diverted them by explaining his plan. He proposed to build — with their backing — a fleet of large prairie clippers to carry cargo to the cussed Spaniards. The advantages of wind-power were numerous, according to the nautical stranger. Speed, economy, freedom from the expense of buying and the trouble of feeding draft animals, freedom to leave the Trail along the Arkansas River (since there would be no animals requiring water) and sail on the high prairies by compass. Westport was the outfitting place for all travellers bound west; it would be easy to have the wagons built there. Injuns would be scared of the strange craft. And there would never be any lack of wind to drive them.

But the men of Westport were not to be taken in by any clever Yankee. They dubbed the stranger Windwagon, hooted at his scheme for a 'dryland navy,' and kept their money in their pockets. And so, when the bottle was empty, Windwagon left the Tavern, not at all cast down by their ridicule. 'I'll l'arn ye,' he declared. 'I'll sail to Council Grove and back. Then maybe you'll listen to reason.'

With that, undaunted and imperturbable, he embarked in his wagon, hoisted sail, and left the staring citizens of Westport in his dusty wake. Once beyond the town, he tacked out upon the open prairie, and laid his course to the setting sun. The wiseacres returned to the Tavern, laughing at his folly. It was close upon one hundred and fifty miles to Council Grove. They thought they had seen the last of Windwagon Thomas.

His coming might have remained a nine days' wonder, had he not come sailing into port again before the nine days had elapsed, bringing with him a letter from a well-known man, who managed the blacksmith shop at the Grove. Once more he cast anchor before Yoakum's door, rolled into the Tavern, and proceeded to talk turkey to the men of Westport.

That same day the men who had made fun of him chipped in and financed the building of a super-windwagon. The Overland Navigation Company included among its members and directors Doctor J. W. Parker, a leading physician; Benjamin Newson, the Indian agent; J. J. Mastin, a young lawyer; Henry Sager; Thomas W. Adams, and the inventor, Windwagon. Under his supervision, the first ship of the plains was built and launched.

The result was a mammoth wagon, constructed after the fashion of a Conestoga prairie schooner. It was fully twenty-five feet from stem to stern, seven-foot beam, and mounted upon four huge wheels, each twelve feet in diameter, with hubs as big as barrels. The sides of the wagon-box, or cabin, rose to the top of the wheels, and above that was the deck. The craft was rigged like a catboat, with the mast stepped well forward, and carried only a mainsail.

Specifications for the steering-gear are lacking, but it is certain that the craft was intended to move backwards; that is, the tail-gate of the wagon was the prow of the ship, and the tongue was brought up and over the stern to serve as tiller. When the craft was completed, the directors gathered in Yoakum's bar and fortified themselves. Then they adjourned to witness the inventor's demonstration.

Two yoke of oxen hauled the huge contrivance out upon the open prairie, and the directors of the Company — with one exception — climbed aboard. Doctor Parker, who knew what broken bones meant, preferred to watch the maiden voyage from the hurricane deck of his saddle mule. Windwagon Thomas, elated by his importance, and perhaps by his potations, took his place on deck, hoisted the mainsail, and grasped the helm.

Slowly, the wagon creaked into motion. A strong wind caught the sail, and away it went, rolling high over all obstacles, scooting over hill and dale, tacking and veering over the plain. The passengers were at first amazed, then delighted, and at last alarmed at the speed of their craft. Doctor Parker, who had thoughtfully filled his saddlebags with necessaries for any accidents, whipped his mule into a run, and lumbered after. The windwagon made the wagons drawn by oxen seem like snails.

The directors shut up in the cabin were frightened, unaccustomed as they were to anything faster than a horse and buggy. They dared not abandon ship, and began to call upon the pilot to shorten sail.

But Windwagon Thomas was riding the waves. He paid no heed to their clamor, steering before the gale. Instead of obeying his partners, he began to show his seamanship, and yelled down to his helpless passengers, 'Watch me run her against the wind!' He put the helm over, and the heavy craft came round grandly.

But then, somehow, something went wrong. The wind caught her, and in spite of all the pilot could do, the windwagon went into reverse. Doctor Parker and his mule narrowly escaped being run down, and had to turn and fly before the monster. The steering-gear locked, and the craft went sailing round and round in a circle a mile wide.

By this time the passengers, thoroughly scared, decided to abandon ship. High as they were above ground, the jump was risky. But they risked it, rather than stay in that crazy ship with its confused hunk of a sea-captain. One by one they dropped to the ground, miraculously unhurt except for a few bruises and considerable fright.

But Windwagon Thomas was made of sterner stuff. He was evidently determined to go down with the ship, colors flying. He remained on deck, clutching the useless helm, until the mammoth wagon jolted him off as it brought up against a stake-and-rider fence on the bank of Turkey Creek.

Nothing Windwagon could say would induce the Company to build the rest of the fleet. The lubbers had no heart for prairie seafaring. They went back to their shops and their offices, put the venture down to profit and loss, and thanked heaven that they were still alive and sound. What else could be expected of men who had halted on the edge of the sea of grass?

But Windwagon remained undaunted. He embarked once more in the small, light craft in which he had come to Westport, made sail, and vanished as swiftly and mysteriously as he had come. History has no more to tell of him.

Maybe he sailed away to shoot buffalo from the after-deck, or harpoon redskins daring enough to run afoul of him on their cruising ponies. Perhaps he ran hard aground in some deep valley or ravine, where no wind came to fill his sail, and no bull-whacker blundered in to haul him out upon the windy plain. Perhaps the cussed Injuns found him thus becalmed, and hung his hair upon some pony's bridle. There are legends among the Indians of a vehicle seen on the prairie, a wagon that was bigger than any wagon, which moved without horses or oxen to draw it, and carried a white 'flag' as tall as a tipi. What became of the Navigator of the Plains will never be known.[1]

But, in two respects, his story is significant, showing us how men of those days thought of the Plains, with all the beauty and mystery of the sea, and also illustrating the dauntless character of the men who crossed them, made them their home.

For the Great Plains of the West were man's country. Women and weaklings shrank from the vastness, the sameness, where there was nothing to give shelter, no bower of trees, no security, no nest. The women either persuaded their men to halt and build at the edge of their familiar woodlands, or scuttled fearfully across the prairies to the snug forests of Oregon, the cozy valleys of California. Even later, when those plains were settled, and lone nesters dotted the grass with sod houses and dugouts, women still hated the lonesome, wind-bitten land. Everything there was different, strange, and frightening. Many and many a settler's wife went crazy on the plains.

But not the men. Not men of the old North European stock, hard-drinking, hard-fighting warriors and wanderers, gamblers and explorers. They loved those plains, delighted in vague, receding horizons, in the loneliness, the sand and the silence, the independence and chancy emergencies of that romantic country. There was Valhalla come to earth, a region where men might do impromptu battle, and ride away to fight again some other day. The moods of the plains were moods of violence, and the men who loved them shared that moodiness. Not since the day of the Vikings had the virile white man found a country so congenial to his heart's desire.

CHAPTER II

Outfitting for the Trail

OLD JOE ROBIDOUX was an Indian trader. His rival in the market for the Pawnee furs was foxy Manuel Lisa. Each tried to get as many pelts as possible. Fur traders, as a rule, were not squeamish as to the ways and means to their profits. Therefore the two competitors were suspicious of each other, and often quarrelled. Their trading posts were close together.

But one day, so the story goes, when each one felt sure he could get the best of the other, the pair made a truce: each pledged himself to be 'loyal,' and not try to take advantage of the other, next time a band of Indians rode in to barter. During this armistice, each one kept his eyes skinned, watching the other.

Finally, the day came. Runners arrived, and announced that the Pawnee camp was dragging in, dogs, babies, camp-kettles, and all.

Old Manuel went into action. He secretly brought out all his goods, and displayed them, then hastily sent for more. Having set his trap, he strolled over to the rival warehouse, to watch Robidoux. Manuel thought old Joe would hardly dare to make preparations for trade while he was present, and he was burning with curiosity to see what old Joe was up to. Robidoux made Manuel welcome. Both of them put on a show.

Robidoux was idle, apparently making no preparations for the Pawnees. Instead, he offered to split a bottle of champagne with Manuel, to drink to their mutual success in the trade. Lisa was thrown off guard, and agreed. Old Joe complained that his gout made it painful for him to stoop, and asked Manuel to go down into the cellar and fetch the bottle.

Lisa obligingly raised the trapdoor in the floor and went down the steps into the cellar. Joe quickly let the trapdoor fall, rolled a heavy cask upon it, and called down to his prisoner that he could come out after the Pawnees had gone. Old Joe had the trade all to himself that day.²

Robidoux's trick was a mild one, as the fur trade went. From the start, that business had been monopolistic. Rival companies and rival traders left little undone in their competition for the furs; beyond the frontier there was no law, and regulation of business was hardly dreamed of then, even in the States. Some of the men engaged in the trade resorted to slander, bribery, smuggling, bootlegging, intimidation, theft, and even murder, in their lust for fur. The profits were enormous; a fortune could be gained in a single good season. Some of these men set up as dictators in their lonely posts, and ruled all comers with floggings, fines, and killings from ambush. Their own memoirs offer ample evidence of the unscrupulous methods common in the trade.

The emporium of the fur trade was St. Louis. And travellers to the Far West generally came through that town. There they assembled, there they often outfitted, there they formed companies, since no man dared to cross the Plains alone. They had to buy their supplies from men trained in the traditions of the business in which Lisa and Robidoux made their fortunes. They had to keep their eyes peeled, and get up early in the morning, to get the best of traders in St. Louis. The merchants in Missouri in those days were experts in *skins!* They advised the greenhorns that they would find prices much, much higher farther west — at Franklin, Independence, or Westport.

Most travellers reached St. Louis by water: down-river from the Falls or down the Ohio from Cincinnati; up-river from New Orleans. Fleets of steamboats lay tier on tier alongside the narrow wharves of that busy little city, then the growing metropolis of the West.

Disembarking, the stranger fought his way through a mob of hotel runners, put his baggage into safe hands, then went into the town to enter his name on the books of the principal hotel, the Planters' House.[3]

A few hours sufficed to explore the city, to inspect the shot-towers, to wander through the shabby lanes of French Town, Carondelet — better known as Vide Poche, because of its empty pockets — or prowl along a back street past the open windows of the Rocky Mountain House, the rendezvous of the trappers.

There a fandango was likely to be in full blast, and the greenhorn could watch shaggy, long-haired mountain men in blackened elk-skins, prancing with French belles to the scraping of fiddles and twanging banjo, and introducing steps learned in far-off Cheyenne camps, while some stentorian mountaineer roared out an Injun chorus, thumping his belly to jerk out the vocables more forcibly.

There the stranger might match his skill at Old Sledge, with men whose leggings were fringed with Comanche hair, squatting on a buffalo robe over a greasy deck of cards and an old wool hat full of silver dollars, playing them close to the hair on his chest. There, over horns of potent Monongahela, he might fill his ears with tall tales of glass mountains and man-eating buffalo, or hear profane yarns of 'hard scrapes,' *coups*, scalps, and 'fixes,' yarns spiced with half-comprehended words of French, Spanish, Injun, and mountain American lingo.

Though the residents of St. Louis numbered scarcely more than two thousand, there was a large floating population of many races and types: sallow French Canadian *voyageurs*, gay and improvident; lank Missouri teamsters in homespuns and checked woolen shirts; dark Spaniards under tall peaked sombreros; rich merchants in high beaver hats and ruffled shirts; sturdy emigrant farmers in their blue jeans; self-reliant Delaware hunters, blanketed squaws, naked brown children, negroes, and the degraded Indian beggars of the settlements. Packers, wagon-masters, bull-whackers, soldiers, mule-skinners, roustabouts from the steamboats, and keelboatmen swarmed up and down the muddy streets in the spring sunlight. Among them strode sun-browned trappers in worn buckskins, and the Santa Fe traders in frock coats of black broadcloth, which showed the creases of long disuse beyond the frontier.

From these, or from the pages of some manual of the trails like Captain Marcy's *Prairie Traveller*, the greenhorn learned what he required for his long cruise across the sea of grass. He went about the purchase of his equipment with serious purpose, for there was no place on the Trail where he could be sure of obtaining supplies, once he had left the last settlement behind him.

Accordingly, the greenhorn traded: for arms, for cloth-ing, for provisions, for medicines; for saddlery, cutlery, and kitchenware; for ammunition, harness, wagons, carts, bedding, and animals; sometimes for tents, carriages, and camp furniture. His health, his comfort, even his life might depend upon the right choice, the proper outfit.

All his notions of armament he found brushed aside as of no account. The long rifle of the woodsman, with its light charge and small bore, was rated no good in a country where buffalo and grizzly b'ar took the place of deer and turkeys; flintlocks gave way to percussion caps; double-barrelled fowling-pieces were here loaded with buckshot, ready to do heavy execution in a night attack. Breech-loaders, first used on American soil by the British in the Revolutionary War, were gaining ground. Single-shot weapons were steadily losing it.

He was impressed by the respect shown by old-timers for the Indian's short buffalo bow, with which the savage could fire so rapidly. 'Happen an Injun slips one arrer betwixt your ribs, he'll slip four,' was the maxim. And the 'muzzle velocity' of the bow was also incredibly greater than that of most guns; he heard yarns of how Injuns had been known to shoot entirely through two bison! Old-fashioned pistols were therefore discarded for the new-fangled revolving pistol invented by Samuel Colt, with which the Texas Rangers and Kit Carson's band of trappers had done such bloody work against Comanches and Kiowas. Colt's was the only weapon able to match the Indian's bow. The greenhorn rotated the cylinder with curious fingers, while the gunsmith persuaded him to buy an extra one, and keep it loaded — in spite of the printed instructions of the manufacturer pasted on top of the case, which warned of the danger of removing the loaded cylinder from the pin. Fitted with percussion caps, such a cylinder, if dropped or struck, was deadly as a bomb! With two loaded cylinders, the gunsmith explained, a man would have twelve shots to spend before recharging![4]

Of course, unreconstructed veterans of the beaver stream scoffed at the new weapon, and pinned their faith to the muzzle-loading rifle, with which their gnarled hands had made a heap of redskins 'come.' The greenhorn who bowed to their experience let the new models alone, went straight to Hawkins' gun-store, and bought a regular mountain rifle: a piece of 'very heavy metal, carrying thirty-two balls to the pound, stocked to the muzzle, and mounted with brass; its only ornament being a buffalo bull, looking exceedingly ferocious, which was not very artistically engraved upon the trap in the stock.'[5] With such a weapon, he was told, a practiced hand could pour, load, ram, and fire five times a minute by the clock! With it, he would acquire an extra wiping-stick of hickory, a supply of fine glazed Du Pont powder and Galena lead, patches, and bullet-mould. Give an old-timer his Hawkins and powder-horn filled with sure-fire powder 'to make her crack,' and with a Green River blade at his belt, he was ready for Injuns galore! Wagh!

The most fashionable costume for the prairies was a fustian coat furnished with a multitude of pockets in which to carry extra tackling. Backwoodsmen clung to a linsey or buckskin hunting shirt, teamsters wore flannel-sleeve vests over hickory shirts. Horsemen bought short, stout coats, boots big enough to contain the trouser-leg, for riding; those who intended to walk, looked for shoes with broad, heavy soles, in which the toes had free play. Broad-brimmed, low-crowned hats of soft felt, sometimes gaily painted against the rain, were popular. Calico and linen shirts gave way to blue or red flannel.

Greenhorns generally inclined to buy buckskins for the Trail. Most greenhorns had a secret craving to wear that historic costume of the frontier — colorful, fringed, and heroic. Buckskins, they argued, would turn sharp winds, and nothing else would break the sharp bill of those big Plains mosquitoes. Caravans started, as a rule, as soon as the grass was high enough to feed the stock in spring — and that was the wet season on the prairies. Mosquitoes were bound to be bad; buckskins would be just the thing!

But old-timers, who wore trousers of thick, soft woolen goods, reinforced inside the leg with leather, shook their shaggy beards. 'Buckskins in the rainy season? Wal, I reckon the green will rub off afore long.'

Heavy cotton drawers, woolen undershirts, cotton and woolen socks, colored silk handkerchiefs, extra shoes, with perhaps a waterproof poncho, completed the outfit. The fastidious also carried razors, towels, comb and brush, toothbrush, Castile and bar soap, and a whetstone for their shining belt-knives.

Caution dictated the purchase of a 'housewife' — a

small, waterproof package containing strong needles, stout linen thread, a bit of beeswax, extra buttons, a paper of pins, and a thimble. But veterans of the Trail got along with a bundle of buckskins, a sharp awl, and a few shreds of dried sinew for the mending of moccasins and hunting shirts.

His trading over, the greenhorn was likely to go straight back to his room at the Planters' House, tired, excited, but happy. There he divested himself of polished boots, high hat, and frock of broadcloth, packing these away in his trunk, to be held against his return — in case he did return!

After that, he would stand — as if by accident — before his mirror, and somewhat self-consciously pull on his red flannel shirt, his 'leather-stockings,' and his beaded moccasins. Then, although he might never have killed anything more dangerous than a chicken, he buckled a belt, heavy with long sheath-knife and revolving pistol, around his hips. Over his shirt, he put on the long-skirted buckskin hunting-coat, dripping fringes, gay with beads, and decorated in small black diapers of velvet running in horizontal bands all around — a swagger garment. Then he faced the mirror, squarely, to knot the silk scarf about his white neck, and tilt the broad-brimmed low felt hat jauntily across his sleek soap-lock. With powder-horn and shot-pouch slung over his shoulder and a new rifle in the crook of his arm, he felt at once manly — and embarrassed!

It was all a little histrionic. Yet Adventure, and the heavy drag of the weapons at his belt, seemed to justify a masculine love for fine feathers. Vaguely, he sensed the instinct of his sex: that a young man of spirit should go handsome and debonair to his rendezvous with death. Then as now, the West seemed to demand something colorful, romantic, bizarre. The vastness of the country compelled a man to assert himself, make himself visible. Though now he felt uncomfortably conspicuous, he took comfort in the thought that every man on the Plains frontier had, inevitably, been, in the beginning, a greenhorn, tenderfoot, or dude.

It was only later, after some experience of the Trail, that our greenhorn discovered that his fantastic outfit was, in reality, devised on strictly practical lines. For the present, he took a deep breath, threw out his chest, and went downstairs, looking every man straight in the eye, truculently daring him to laugh.

Having sent his baggage to the wharf, the stranger hurried to the levee, crossed the landing-stage to the boat, located his cabin, and then took his place at the rail, puffing a long Havana in affected nonchalance.

On the boat were Santa Fe traders, professional gamblers, adventurers of many kinds, and the deck below was jammed with a motley, polyglot crowd of emigrants bound for Oregon or Californy, with mountain men, negroes, and blanket Indians. Some were heading west to make a fortune, acquire free land, or merely to seek excitement. Some went out of curiosity, or sheer restless love of travel. Others, taciturn and watchful, were fugitives from justice, deserters from the Army, or misfits who could no longer endure conditions in the States: pioneers who found new settlements crowding around their familiar clearings, and had moved on to be rid of that unwelcome pressure; writers and artists looking for new worlds to conquer; explorers; runaway boys headin' west to kill Injuns; embezzlers, thieves, murderers, madmen.

In the cabins were always a few invalids afflicted with chronic liver complaint, dyspepsia, lung fever, or rheumatism, or fleeing from epidemics of yellow jack, smallpox, or Asiatic cholera; or men, who, having been given up as hopeless by the doctors at home, preferred to meet death suddenly under the scalping knife of the redskins rather than endure the slow tortures of incurable disease. Life on the prairies was said to effect remarkable cures.

With these was a sprinkling of foreign sportsmen in white shooting jackets of dandy cut, trousers of shepherd's plaid, and Panama hats, who had crossed the Atlantic to enter what was then a hunter's paradise.

The steamboat was so heavily loaded that water broke over her guards continually.

Her upper deck was completely covered with big Pittsburgh and Conestoga wagons with blue beds and bright red wheels, all laden with precious goods for the trade with Mexico. Below was a band of horses, mules, oxen, and stacks of saddlery, harness, boxes, bales, trunks, bedrolls, carts and carriages, and assorted packages of every kind. At last everyone was aboard.

At the third tolling of the bell, and in obedience to the signals of the high and mighty pilot, the steamboat swung away from the levee, and was soon stemming the yellow waters of the Mississippi.

A few miles brought the craft to the mouth of the Missouri, where undercurrents projected the muddy waters of the swifter stream far out, to boil up to the surface of the more transparent river in surprising eddies. The steamboat nosed into the Missouri River. Then the greenhorn drew a long breath of satisfaction. He was on his way.

The trip up-river might occupy a week or more, and half the time the steamboat was sure to be hard aground on a sandbar somewhere in the shifting channel of the fickle stream. The pilot faced many hazards. Half-submerged fallen trees, borne down and then released by the swift water, rose and fell, earning the name of 'sawyers,' and threatening to rip the bottom of the boat in two. Snags — dead and broken tree-trunks firmly planted in the mud — projected dangerously from the water, or lurked beneath its surface, always facing down-stream, thickly planted as a military abattis, and menaced the planks of the wallowing craft. Great trees fell suddenly into the water, undercut by the current playing upon the soft mud banks. New islands choked the channel, cloaked with the tender green of young cottonwood and willow. Everywhere were boiling eddies, hidden bars. Travellers did not find the journey dull.

The first travellers to follow the Trail made Franklin, county-seat of Boone's Lick County, their jumping-off place. Founded in 1816, only five years before Captain William Becknell opened the Santa Fe Trail, Franklin was soon the second town in the Territory, with a booming trade and a land-office. Local boosters bragged that 'the public square contained two acres; the principal streets' were 'eighty-two and a half feet wide' — and nearly as deep in mud; the town afforded 'an agreeable and polished society' — a society from which the bound boy, Kit Carson, gladly ran away on September 1, 1826, two years before the town-site was washed into the river!

After Franklin vanished, Independence, with its toy courthouse and four clanging blacksmith shops, became the prairie port, as steamboats gradually learned their way farther up the river; to Fort Osage, Blue Mills, Ducker's Ferry, and on to Independence. First begun in 1827, the town took first place in 1832, and held that place until the forties. There many from Tennessee and Kentucky made their homes, there the Mormons lingered, and from that town thousands started for the West.

But Independence had its disadvantages, especially in the spring rainy season, when most travellers set out. Then the prairies to the west were miry, and the Blue River was hard to ford or ferry. And when the steamboats found a good landing *above* Blue River at Kansas (now Kansas City), Westport sprang up near by, and won most of the outfitting trade from Independence after 1840. Westport held that trade until the first locomotive rolled into Santa Fe, forty years later. There were reasons!

Westport had plenty of good grass for teams, a fine spring,[6] groves ample enough to provide shelter and fuel for any number of wagon trains, and a rocky ledge near the landing which supplied abundant building stone. Besides, sandbars had formed down-river which made landing at Independence difficult.

But whatever town the traveller made his starting-place, he found much the same life, much the same scenes, the same people.

There was much to do, before the caravans moved out on the long Trail!

CHAPTER III

Preparations for the March

THE PLAINS were horseman's country. A man's first
thought, on reaching a prairie port, was to obtain an animal
to carry him to Santa Fe.

English-speaking people had always been horsemen.
Their primitive ancestors lived on horseflesh, and worshipped the white horse, as the Plains Indians worshipped
the albino buffalo. The English language has more words
for horse than for any other creature; the white horse was
flaunted upon the banners of the Anglo-Saxons who came to
settle Britain; and today the English national holiday is a
horse-race, the Derby. Men of that breed felt only half-
grown, half-alive, afoot. The Englishman's house is not,
and never was, his castle: the Englishman's house is his
stable.

That tradition, that feeling, was even stronger in America, if only because of the distances to be covered here. To
this day, a man born and bred on the Plains is ashamed to
be seen walking. A cowboy will go a mile to catch his horse
and saddle up, so that he can ride across the road.

As everyone knows, the great weakness of the horse lies
in his feet, and the chief enemy of his feet is moisture. Keep
a horse dry-shod, with plenty of forage, and the world is his
paradise. Such a paradise was furnished ready-made for
him on the high, grassy, semi-arid Plains of the Far West.

There, man and horse became one. The animal was no
longer a tame creature of stall and barnyard, but the com-

panion of his wandering master, a friend in need, indispensable in war or peace — something precious that a man must risk his neck in guarding; something irresistible, worth a man's neck to steal or capture.

Many a man was hanged or shot for horse-stealing on the Plains; many a man perished miserably from famine, in prairie fires, or under the scalping-knife, when left afoot. Many a man broke his neck in a tumble from the back of his horse. The saddle was, of all places, the most dangerous — yet also the happiest.

But, as with arms and clothing, the greenhorn found that he had everything to learn, when it came to buying a saddle animal.

Horses bred in the States did not stand up well under prairie conditions. With nothing but grass in summer and cottonwood bark in winter to feed on, they lost flesh and spirit alarmingly. The first run after buffalo was likely to leave them stove up. The smell of Indians terrified them. Rattlesnakes bit them, wolves nipped their heels, mosquitoes drove them frantic; their thin, silken coats left them unprotected against the chill rains and freezing blizzards on the open prairie. Their courage deserted them, and they fled back to the settlements and their familiar pastures, their comfortable stalls, at every opportunity.

But the horses native to the Plains were a hardy breed, descended from the barbs brought over by the Spanish conquerors.

It used to be thought that the mustang was the progeny of animals which had run away from the *caballadas* of the Spaniards: from Cortez, Coronado, or Oñate. But historical research has pretty well punctured that legend, since very few horses did get away, and wild horses were seldom found later in the regions where those few escaped.[7] The fact seems to be that, principally during the twenty years following the Pueblo Revolt near the end of the seventeenth century, when all the Spaniards had been killed or driven away, the Indians of New Mexico took to trading horses to the nomads of the Plains. Santa Fe, Taos, and other towns became horse-markets, and for many years thereafter supplied the Indians — sometimes by trade, often by theft — with the animals which multiplied like rabbits and spread all over the grasslands. After all, it is hardly likely that a wild Indian could learn to manage a runaway horse just by watching a Spaniard do it. At any rate, the type of their horsegear is proof enough that the Plains Indians learned to manage horses in the Southwest. . . .

The greenhorn was apt to be disappointed on seeing his first Indian pony. The mustang was not, as a rule, a handsome, dashing steed like his Arab ancestor. He lacked the size, bone, and general conformation of an American saddler, or of the carefully bred Spanish horse of Northern Mexico, the slender legs, the long body, the white star and stockings.

The hardships of wild life had stunted and changed him, the severe winters had taken their toll. Indiscriminate coupling in Indian camps or wild bands had flared and blotched his hide fantastically with white and many colors. He was small, tough, deer-legged, big-barrelled, with mulish hocks, slanting quarters, and often carried one 'glass' eye to show the devil latent in his heart. His coat was thick and staring, his mane fell to right and left indifferently, and his tail was full of burrs. He was wary and self-sufficient as a coyote. Yet no stable-bred horse from the States could match him for sheer service.[8]

Once broken, the mustang showed as much sense as a mule, as much endurance as the wolves that pestered him, and he had a 'hard' stomach that enabled him to stand an incredible amount of riding, and to go without grass and water for long periods. He could dodge an angry buffalo — or a man's snaring rope; he would buck and kick and bite.

But he could go, and go, and go. When his white master had abandoned him as 'used up,' a Mexican would ride him all day and leave him for dead. Then an Indian would ride him for a week — clear into the Happy Hunting Grounds!

As likely as not, his name was Paint. The greenhorn who bought him, merely because he looked western and bizarre, soon found that he had an animal with any number of good points — and a mind of its own.

There were those, of course, who preferred mules.

These were men who had lived much in the mountains, where mules were more sure-footed than horses, or men who had become accustomed to riding mules in Mexico, where most of the mules in use on the Trail originally came from. Mexican scrub mules were unequal to the heavy work of drawing freight wagons, and in the attempt to replace them with bigger animals for the Santa Fe trade, the Missouri mule was invented. Those who rode mules lauded their staying qualities, the way they endured heat, and the certainty with which they gave warning when they whiffed Injuns. 'Mules,' they claimed, 'are knowin' critters — next thing to human, if it comes to that.'

The United States Army once tried out camels as a means of transportation on the Great American Desert, and Captain Marcy, with military thoroughness, recommended oxen as saddle animals. In Africa, he reports, they were so used, and could be guided by means of a stick thrust through a hole in the nose. But, if any traveller on the Santa Fe Trail ever voluntarily rode a camel or an ox, record of it has been lost. The notion never 'took.' Even Captain Marcy admits that such a means of locomotion would 'probably be regarded by our people as a very undignified and singular' one! Americans either rode horses, or mules — or walked.

A man on foot was little better than a captive or a slave, plodding wearily along the ruts, lugging his heavy arms and other plunder — plunder for which there was no room in the

groaning wagons. The man on foot dared not wander from
the Trail, he could not hunt buffalo, or toll antelope; he
missed most of the fun and dangers of the trip. He was almost a part of the wagons he accompanied. He was welcome, since he might stand guard at night, or help shoulder
wagon wheels through the mire, or fetch buffalo chips for
the fire in his blanket, or carry water from the river. And,
if his boot-soles did not become so slick from walking on
grass that he went lame, he would eventually arrive at his
destination. But nobody who could afford a saddle animal,
nobody who had a carriage, or was free from the duty of
driving a team, would walk of his own volition.

True, the Mormons, spurred on by religious fervor, not
only walked, but shoved push-carts ahead of them. But
Santa Fe traders questioned whether Salvation was worth
the trouble.

On that Trail only hirelings walked, goading their sullen
oxen, lashing their stubborn mules. Invalids and women
and old men rode in Dearborn carriages or spring wagons.
But free men, healthy men, rode horseback, or on mules.

Horse or mule, they had to have a saddle. And that
saddle, by almost unanimous agreement, was the California,
made by the cussed Spaniards across the mountains. It
had no iron in its composition, but was tied together with
buckskin strings, so that it was a simple matter to take it to
pieces for mending or cleaning. The tree conformed to the
animal's back, distributing the burden over a wide surface.
It was covered with rawhide — put on green, and stitched
— which, in drying, bound the whole thing tight together.
The horn — a regular snubbing-post — was large as a
saucer, but not very high, and the stirrup leathers hung so
that the rider sat nearly erect, in a position to use his gun or
control his horse. The whole saddle was covered by a large,
thick sheet of sole-leather, with a hole in it for the pommel,
and wide skirts to cover the animal's hips, and support

saddlebags. In camp, this sheet could be spread down as a foundation for the blankets of a bed. The girth was a single cinch of hair six inches wide. In short, it was the primitive model for a modern center-fire range saddle.

The stirrups, in those days, were uniformly of wood, broad and flat for the thin soles of moccasins, with huge *tapaderas* covering them.

With a California saddle, a hemp picket-rope (wolves gnawed ropes of leather), and hobbles, the horseman had only to buy his bridle, and his outfit was complete. A few also carried hair ropes, or rawhide ropes boiled in grease, or plaited leather lariats suppled with oil, for roping animals.

So equipped, the stranger rode out to the wagons which he was to accompany, and made friends with the men belonging to them.

There he would see Mexican ropers, in their tight-fitting leather costumes, performing miracles with graceful lariats which seemed to be as much a part of them as the filament of a tricky spider, snaring a horse or a mule, in preparation for breaking them to harness. Once noosed, the mules would be snubbed up to a wagon wheel, choked down by the ruthless rope, while their labored breath came *whoof, whoof* through straining throats, tied there, with a bare two inches of rope, and left to starve for a day and a night, until they were subdued enough to endure the harness.

Then Blas or Vicente or Pedro would grab the ribbons, lash the frightened team into lunging and rearing activity; the big wagon would roll and rumble behind them, scaring their eyes almost out of their heads as they lurched away; and so, after an hour's exhausting flogging and yanking, the bewildered mules stopped kicking and plunging, and pulled the locked wheels after them in sober earnest. That done, they were pronounced 'broken to harness,' and ready for the Trail. It was an unflinching discipline.

Oxen were broken in a manner equally picturesque. The

teamster would snare them with a rope, drag two of them to
a snubbing post, yoke the pair, and tie the tails together.
Then he released them and stood laughing as they charged
toward the prairie or threshed through the brush. By this
method, they soon became accustomed to the yoke and to
moving together. Tying their tails together prevented them
from breaking their necks.

Meanwhile, men had been greasing the axles with a mix-
ture of tar, rosin, and tallow. And evening found them
making camp under the shelter of wagon sheets stretched
out from the side of a big Pennsylvania wagon. Invariably,
while they could enjoy the shelter of such an improvised
tent, the weather would continue fine!

There they spread down their bedding: the poor man, his
single Mackinaw blanket; the canny stranger, his pair of
them; the old-timer, his buffalo robe and Navaho rug, tattered, greasy, and burned with holes where sparks from
long-dead campfires had lodged; the lover of luxury, his
painted canvas sheet, his two blankets, comforter, pillow,
and waterproof coverlet.

Little cook-fires sprang up, dancing in the twilight, as the
men of each mess gathered about the camp-kettles, coffee-
pots, and spiders. Afterward, for a time, there would be
only the sound of steady mastication, as mess-pork and
bread went into their gullets. Sighs of content followed, and
the loosening of belts.

Then, when the old-timers had cleaned their knives by
thrusting them into the earth a few times, and had cleaned
the grease off their fingers, Indian-fashion, by wiping them
on their long hair, could be heard the click of flint on steel,
pipes began to glow, and there would be tales to tell.

Those tales, naturally enough, generally had to do with
the cussed Injuns — a subject on which the greenhorns had
a yawning curiosity to be satisfied. And the veterans of the
Trail were ready to give them their bellyful. . . .

'Nope. Injuns is sociable critters. Happen you see one, thar's allus another'n not fur away — and more'n likely a dozen. Fact is, you ain't likely to see none atall, lessen they want you to see 'em, and that means they figger they got everything their own way. . . .

'Sure, the Injuns air brave — accordin' to their lights. In a corner, they'll scrap like so many wildcats, and die to the last man afore they'll give in. But they don't aim to git in no corner; they aim to git *you* in one. And if they do, and know it, 'tain't no use shakin' hands and makin' peace with 'em. Might makes right with them, every time.

'Take Carafel — trader used to work with the Assiniboine. Him and a fellow named Ramsay was a-ridin' to camp, when all of a suddent, fifteen Sioux warriors come up over the hill, spang in front of 'em. The Injuns cut loose all together, and Carafel caught it in three places. Down he went, and Ramsay lit out, tight as he could go.

'When Carafel dropped, his horse dropped too, and his gun went under the horse. The horse was dead, and he couldn't git it out. So he was helpless to fight, and his foot was all shot to pieces, so he couldn't run nuther. Leastways, not fast.

'He got up and tried, all right. But his lame foot made him clumsy, and he caught his toes in a tangle of grass and tumbled again. They war right on top of him then, and when he jumped up, one of 'em stuck his rifle in his face and pulled the trigger.

'Howsomever, Carafel grabbed the muzzle and shoved it away, so it didn't kill him. But then the rest of the varmints war all around him, beating him down with the butt-ends of their rifles. Well, he thought he was gone then. So he says to them, "It sure takes a lot of you Sioux to kill one white man!" And down he goes. He thought he war done for. He could feel the prick of the scalp-knives on his yaller hair already. But lo and behold, they all quit then, and run off as if he'd had the smallpox. Then he fainted dead away.

'When Carafel come to, the Sioux war clean gone. Nary one in sight nowhars. So Carafel he crawled home to the fort in a pretty fix, all covered with blood, and his foot torn to pieces. He'll allus be lame, I reckon....

'How come they didn't finish him? Why, when they heerd him say he was white, they seen his yaller hair and blue eyes, I reckon, and they knowed he warn't no Chippeway half-breed, like they thought he was. They thought he war dead, *sabe?* So they skipped, for fear somebody would find out they had killed him. You see, he war married to one of their women. Lucky for Carafel! Lucky for Ramsay, too. Ramsay *war* a half-breed Chippeway sure enough!' [9]

'Wagh! Injuns are the most onsartainest varmints in all creation, and I reckon they're not more'n half human. For you never seed a human, after you'd fed him and treated him to the best fixin's in your lodge, jist turn around and steal all your horses, or ary other thing he could lay hands on. No, not adzackly. He would feel kinder grateful, and ask you to spread a blanket in his lodge if ever you passed thataway. But the Injun don't keer shucks for you, and is ready to do you a heap of mischief as soon as he quits your feed.

'Nope. It's not the right way to give 'em presents to buy peace. But if I war Governor of these yeer United States I'll tell you what I'd do. I'd invite 'em all to a big feast, and make believe I wanted to have a big talk. And as soon as I got 'em all together, I'd pitch in and sculp about half of 'em, and then t'other half would be mighty glad to make a peace that would stick. That's the way I'd make a treaty with the red-bellied varmints; and as sure as you're born, that's the *only* way.

''Tain't no use to talk about honor with them, nohow. They hain't got no sich thing in 'em, and they won't show fair fight, any ways you fix it. Don't they kill and sculp a white man when-ar they git the better of him? The mean varmints, they'll never behave theirselves until you give 'em a clean out and out lickin'. They can't understand white folks' ways, and they won't l'arn 'em; and if you treat 'em decent, they think you air afeard. Nope, you kin depend on it: the only way to treat Injuns is to thrash 'em plenty first. Then the balance will sorter take to you and behave theirselves....'

Then the old-timer would gravely put up his pipe, roll into his blankets, and cock one wary eye at his disturbed listener, waiting for the inevitable question. When it came, he had his answer ready:

'Wal, no. It's been some time since they cut up any right *yereabouts*. But you never kin tell.... *Sure* I'm a-goin' to sleep. I'd ruther be sculped sleepin' than stay awake and be sculped anyhow. Happen *you* don't feel thataway, keep yore eyes peeled. That's all!'

Such was the horror of Indians among greenhorns, that many a stranger, after hearing such yarns and opinions, valid as they might be on the high Plains, found himself unable to sleep after hearing them, until the stentorian snores of the mountain men, drowning the hum of mosquitoes, made sleep impossible anyhow!

Yet it was close upon two hundred miles to the nearest Indians who could be called hostile!

CHAPTER IV

The Trail to Council Grove

THE TRAIL to Santa Fe was like a long rope flung carelessly across the Plains — an old rope, loosely twisted, so that here and there the strands parted, only to join again. At either end, the rope frayed out into several strands, several routes. At the Missouri end, trails led from Fort Leavenworth, Independence, Franklin, Kansas, and Westport — to name no more. But all these united to form the main Trail before reaching Council Grove.

All these prairie ports were also outfitting places for those bound to Oregon or Californy, and in them play and drinking were the order of the day. Caravans for Santa Fe were organized by experienced, responsible men. But the wagon trains on the Trail to Oregon and the goldfields were, all too often, composed of greenhorns without the faintest notion of what they had to face. Gold fever, the promise of free land, seemed to have stolen away their senses.

The farmer, bound for Oregon, commonly overloaded his wagon with household furniture, heavy farm implements, and miscellaneous plunder, lashed a chicken coop on behind, and slung a heavy iron kettle underneath. Behind, in a trailing cart, rode his sturdy wife and numerous children, while a small, barelegged girl in a bonnet bestrode an old mare and kept the milchcows moving. It was no use telling him that he could not fight off redskins with a bullwhip; that his animals would go lame and have to be replaced — if the Indians did not stampede them; that wolves would gnaw his ropes and harness to bits; that his load would shake his wagon to pieces, or prevent him from crossing the mountains; that, before he reached South Pass, he would have to saw his wagon into two carts and abandon everything except his family.

The goldseekers were even more reckless than the farmers, every man confident that he would soon return with fifty thousand dollars in dust, though he might be flat broke at the moment. Once across the ferry, he thought he would have no need for cash; as for redskins, he went heavily armed — with weapons he barely knew the use of.

Some of these men were less sanguine. They were the ones who had tried to hurry off while the grass was still too short to maintain their animals, and had wrecked their teams, trying to push them to make twenty miles a day, instead of the regulation fifteen. Now they were back in town, their outfits gone, busted, hanging morosely around the bars, or gambling with what they had left, trying to gain a new stake. Old-timers were apt to laugh at them.

But not always.

One day a dazed man dragged wearily into Westport with a single yoke of oxen, and two forlorn children peering out from under the wagon sheet. In the blankets behind him lay the body of his wife, which he had brought back to the settlements for burial. . . .

Sometimes the caravans of the Santa Fe traders were organized at one town, sometimes at another. But the final organization was, as a rule, perfected at Council Grove, beyond which buffalo and Indians might be encountered, and strict discipline had to be enforced. It was therefore not unusual for small parties to set out from the settlements as soon as their preparations were completed there, and to await their companions on the march at Council Grove, nearly one hundred and fifty miles west of Independence.

While waiting for the wagons to be repaired, greased,

and loaded, travellers found time on their hands to explore
the near-by settlements, to visit the log house of the hospitable and universally helpful Colonel Chick, head man at
Kansas Landing; to take a horn at Vogel's dramshop,
look for friends in Yoakum's Tavern, or lay in supplies at
Boone's grocery, in Westport.

Carefully avoiding the heels of the shaggy, barefoot
Indian ponies tied along the racks and fences, and passing
among the colorful calicoes and turbans of Shawnees and
Delawares, the shaved heads and painted faces of Sac and
Fox, and Wyandots dressed like white men, they would
finally find the grocer's counter before them, and place their
order for the journey.

The grocer would sell every man his necessary ration of
fifty pounds of flour, fifty pounds of bacon, ten pounds of
coffee beans, twenty of sugar, and a small quantity of salt.
With the prospects of a long separation from the familiar
diet of the settlements before them, many were tempted
to buy supplies of tea, rice, dried fruits, crackers, a case or
two of claret, peppersauce, beans, a few live fowls, and a
bottle of citric acid and some essence of lemon, to prevent
scurvy.

Scurvy was a great curse on the Plains — for greenhorns,
soldiers, and all who lived upon superfine flour, salt pork,
and even red meat. The medical science of those days pre-
scribed lime-juice and dried fruit, never taking any account
of the fact that Indians and mountain men, who lived upon
nothing but meat most of the year, never suffered from
scurvy. The rare greenhorn who was curious and enter-
prising enough to ask questions was likely to be read a hard
sermon, on the concise text: 'Meat's meat!'

'Injuns do it,' the old-timer would snort, indignantly.
'Who keers what the sawbones says? Do you reckon a
cussed Injun kin do anything *I* cain't do?'

And then, maybeso, the old-timer would proceed to dilate upon the merits of a diet of strict prairie and mountain origin, beginning with such mouth-watering delicacies as painter-meat; then beaver-tails, biled; unborn buffalo calves afore they hair over; rattlesnakes, like a long chicken neck — only whiter; skunks; and goats. 'Then, thar's buffalo. I mean the *hull* critter, mind you — barrin' hide, hair, horns, and hoofs. Red muscle meat will do for you in the settlements, maybeso, whar you kin git plenty greens and vegetables. But on the perairie, you'll eat the cow's insides for choice: marrow, lights, heart, and tongue; warm liver spiced with gall; best of all guts — plain *guts*, and raw at that!

'Makes your stomach turn over to think of it now, but the time's comin' when it will make your mouth water. You stay on the perairie long enough, and you'll forgit all about lemons, and quit dreamin' about sugar, and biscuits. You kin live without salt, and like it, just the same as me. And then you'll know it's the truth I'm tellin' you, when I say thar's only one meat better'n buffalo, and that's dog — Injun dog. You eat animiles like them — the insides too, like all meat-eatin' animiles do — and you'll never git sick with the scurvy. How come? *Quien sabe?* All I know is, try it!

'Who do you think is the best judge of meat, anyhow? Them as eats a little piece cut acrost the grain and burned in a pan oncet a week, or them as eats nothin' else and all kinds the year round, as often as they kin git it?

'What to do for fresh meat on the prairie? You'll find plenty of that on the hoof. All you have to do is kill it!'

With this admonition in mind, a man soon tired of the clatter and bang of the blacksmith shops, the bustle in the stores, the palaver in the taverns, and the slow-moving emigrants. Even the occasional lady between the twinkling wheels of her carriage, or the more frequent buxom girl, seated — there is no other word — on her sturdy horse, and shielding her sunburned cheeks with an old umbrella or faded parasol, soon failed to hold the eye. The greenhorn could not forget the heavy pistol dragging at his belt, the heavy rifle in the crook of his arm. He was anxious to get off alone somewhere, and have a little private target practice. It had begun to dawn upon him that he was now absolutely on his own hook. And he was already painfully conscious of the fact that 'those Kentucky fellows,' and most others on the frontier, loved a joke. If he missed his first shot at a buffalo, he knew he would never hear the last of that.

A miserable log bridge led out of Westport, and from it an equally bad road led the determined hunter into the woods, now fresh and green in their spring foliage, bright with sunlight, and enlivened by a multitude of birds. Blue jays and orioles flashed from tree to tree, squirrels darted about. The grass was just pushing its tender shoots from the good earth, wild-apple trees hung with blossom made the air fragrant, and vines, unable to conceal themselves under their scanty young leaves, twined among the trunks, giving promise of purple fruit.

In the midst of all this, the traveller would begin banging away, terrifying the families of the Shawnee and Wyandot farmers in the neighboring clearings, maybe killing a razorback ranging the woods, but more probably killing nothing but a stray woodpecker or jay! The charging of a muzzle-loading Hawkins seemed to consume hours of time, during which the hunter could imagine the prick of scalping-knives in his hair, or visualize buffalo disappearing over the distant rim of the horizon. And the Colt's revolver, in his unfamiliar clutch, seemed not to be loaded with ball. At the end of an hour's practice, he was likely to go back to camp for his scatter-gun, to shoot plover on the prairie.

There, like as not, he found the wagons gone to the Landing for their cargo just arrived by steamboat, no wagon

sheet to shelter him, and a shower falling. By the time the
wagons returned, he would be wet and miserable, in cold,
clammy buckskins that felt like the skin of a man drowned
two days, and made the poor greenhorn sick at his stomach
when he touched or looked at them.

Like as not, too, the rain had melted his sugar and salt,
perhaps his flour as well. And he found the teamsters would
not make room for his bacon at the bottom of the wagon,
where it would be kept cool on the march. No sirree! Those
wagons were ready for the Trail, snugly packed, with bales
and boxes so expertly stowed away that no jolting could
work them free, no friction damage their precious contents
on the long journey of more than two months. Why, those
wagons held a fortune in goods: cotton goods, coarse and
fine cambrics, calicoes, domestic shawls, steam-loom shirt-
ings, handkerchiefs, cotton hose; woolen goods, blankets,
stroudings, super-blues, pelisse cloths and shawls, crêpes,
bombazines; velvets, silks, and silk shawls, ribbons; iron
worth a dollar a pound to start with, and precious hardware
made from it; traps, knives, pocket-knives, axes, hatchets;
lead, powder, trinkets, writing-paper, hats, and looking-
glasses. Over all were stretched two huge Osnaburg sheets,
covering the wagon bows, the cargo, and coming far down
the sides of the bed to prevent any rain from reaching the
goods within. Between the wagon sheets was spread a pair
of Mackinaw blankets as added protection — and in a convenient hiding-place for those contraband articles, when the
Mexican customs should be reached. The teamster made
room at the top of the load for the greenhorn's supplies.
And the greenhorn crawled under the wagon bed out of the
rain.

Those big Pennsylvania wagons (Pittsburgh or Conestoga) were originally built high off the ground for a country
infested with stumps, built with curves to hold goods stowed
within perfectly steady on hills, and watertight, so that the

bed could be used as a boat in floating cargoes across flooded streams. White-oak, hickory, and *bois d'arc* went to the manufacture and repair of those sturdy frontier wagons, woods well seasoned for whiffletree, tongue, reach, hounds, and bolster, felloes, hubs, and spokes. The ponderous wheels had tires five or six inches broad. Stay-chains and traces were of iron — short, thick links. Rising high at prow and stern, the prairie schooner, under its white tilt, which soared and sank with the curve of the bed, was an impressive vehicle, and when loaded for the Trail moved with slow majesty behind its laboring oxen, or eight plodding mules. And it became even more impressive as it came to be built larger and larger as the trade with New Mexico increased, so that teams had to be increased to as many as twelve animals. The traders to Santa Fe were men with big ideas; they liked a swagger wagon. Besides, there was an import tax of five hundred dollars on every American wagon entering Santa Fe, and it was good business to haul the freight in big ones. They soon crowded the pack train out, as the usual means of transportation for traders.

The Conestoga wagon, built to be drawn by the strong breed of Conestoga horses, was the streamlined vehicle of its day. It expressed the American love of bright color, size, noise, and movement. Painted bright red and blue, it was the ancestor of the gaudy steamboat, the painted Pullman, the garish circus-wagon. At the beginning of the trade with Santa Fe, such wagons were usually drawn by six horses large as fire-horses or brewer's draft animals, and the harness they wore was in keeping with their impressive dignity.

The back-hands of their harness were commonly fourteen inches broad, the hip-straps twelve, and a heavy black housing — usually a bearskin — covered the shoulders of the horse clear down to the bottom of the hames. Bridles were adorned with loops of red trimming, fringes, and shining buckles. Over all swung a set of finely toned bells, cone-shaped, and large as small dinner-bells, fixed on wrought iron bows above the tops of the hames.

On the Plains, horses soon gave way to mules, and mules to oxen. But horse or ox or mule, the teamsters remained much the same: bull-whacker, mule-skinner — all were men accustomed to hard labor, excitement, responsibility, and inspired by an insane love of their animals and their privileges. Profane, combative, tough as rawhide, they knew how to wield whips or fists equally well. They had as much pride in their teams and their work as a locomotive engineer.

Therefore, the greenhorn did not argue the matter. He crawled under the wagon, glad of that broad shelter against the cold drizzle of spring, dragging his blankets.

But his shelter, he found, was not merely broad; it was high above the ground. The wind carried the rain under it to him. And when at last the rain stopped and the wind subsided, water continued to drip into his sodden blankets from axle-trees, wheels, and chains, washing down with it considerable quantities of mud, grease, and tar, as it came. The ground under his bed collected water, yet was no whit softened thereby. The prairie pushed hard against his unseasoned bones. He did not sleep well, what with wet, cold, and mosquitoes.

Somehow, finally, the interminable night came to an end. The wind sprang up, the sun rose, and the mosquitoes quit singing, giving place to the spring chorus of the happy frogs. The men gathered disconsolately around a smoky cook-fire. Those who had forgotten to buy a coffee-mill smashed their coffee grains with a stone on a wagon-tire, and had breakfast.

On such a morning, exercise was imperative. And every man who had a horse naturally wished to ride, to be on his way. The wind would dry their buckskins, the sun would warm their backs, and they would be rid of the half-contemptuous company of the hard-boiled wagoners. Two or three, having assured themselves that no hostile tribes ranged within a week's journey, stowed their firearms in the wagons, or in one of the Dearborn carriages, and having saddled, clambered stiffly up and jogged on ahead of the creaking, lumbering wagons. Rifles and revolvers seemed heavy plunder to lug along on a pleasure jaunt.

Up-hill and down-dale they rode. And then the inevitable happened.

Sooner or later, for one reason or another, the party would become separated. A hill or valley would intervene, or one of the party would turn back to get his pipe or to see how the train was coming along through the mire. And then, without warning, two or three Indians, with shaved heads and nodding roaches, would appear on horseback. Let one of the travellers tell it:

' . . . I noticed two Indians coming out of the prairie toward the road. I knew them not to be Shawnees by their dress, and therefore watched them more closely. After reaching the road between me and the train, they stopped, and the foremost Indian uncovered his gun. This called me to a dead halt immediately. They started toward me on a gallop. In this dilemma, prudence became the better part of valor. Being . . . wholly unarmed, I at once turned my horse and took the back track toward my company, about a mile and a half distant. Being well mounted on a blooded race mare, I had no fears if the question resolved itself into one of speed. The race was kept up until we came in sight of my company, when the Indians at once slackened up and remained in our rear for two or three hours. We were all imprudent, for with the company I found but one pair of pistols. Our number forbade, however, any hostile demonstration. . . . The Indians proved to be Osage. . . .' [10]

Such incidents were typical. The Osages were not at war with the whites. But a lone traveller, unarmed, with a horse and saddle, offered an irresistible temptation to young warriors. Osages, Kaws, and other 'friendly' Indians were always to be found on the trails leading to Council Grove, begging, hunting, looking for stray animals to recover for the reward, or sell; a lone white man was lucky if he escaped with his skin, after losing everything else he possessed. . . .

After one such adventure, the greenhorn realized that his weapons were not useless trappings, but a necessary part of his equipment, even among peaceful tribes. He formed the habit, thereafter, of carrying them with him horseback or afoot, and of keeping them loaded and ready for use. Only when with the wagons was it safe to dispense with them. . . .

But as the sun thawed out the traveller's bones, and his jogging horse pumped the blood into faster circulation, a new irritation bothered him. The wind and the sun dried his buckskins, and he found himself encased in stiff leather armor, which did not fit. The wrinkles became hard as wood, and chafed his body. Then the woolen shirt became abrasive, itching where the buckskin had rubbed him raw. The wet sinews of his moccasins worked loose, and he found his toes sticking out. The fringes, so soft and graceful before, were now like dangling icicles along his legs and arms. The whole suit was stretched out of shape and monstrous, so that his legs and arms were too short, or too long, and the bottoms of his leggings flared out like the nether garments of a sailor.

On his return to the wagons, he was sure to be greeted with guffaws and witty comments. Only greenhorns, he was told, would be fool enough to wear buckskin britches in the rainy season. And it dawned upon him as a great discovery that buckskins were simply the working clothes of the penniless frontiersmen, who — once they got into Indian country — preferred civilized fixin's to Indian dress, not merely because they were more practical, but because they cost more, and so gave them more prestige among the savages.

Perhaps he dashed back to Westport and bought a more sensible outfit. Perhaps some old-timer took pity on him, showed him how to limber up his buckskins by rubbing and beating them into something like flexibility. Maybeso he was taught how to smoke his clothes brown over a fire of willow twigs, and so make them retain their softness, even after a severe wetting. Like as not, he went on wearing them until he wore them comfortable again!

The wagons made slow progress over the miry prairie. Teams were not accustomed to working together, grass was short as yet, and animals lost flesh if pushed too hard along the trails. There were repairs and accidents, and a general lack of discipline and co-operation among the teamsters and other men with the train. A man was seldom refused permission — if he asked it — to join a train, since there was safety in numbers. The result was a gathering of strangers, many of whom were suspicious of their fellow-travellers, and not without reason. Occasionally somebody disappeared, and with him a good horse, a rifle, or some other prized possession.

In that region of many creeks, and patches of timber, camp could be made almost anywhere, for fuel, grass, and water were plenty. No two wagon trains camped in identically the same spots on the first stages of the journey. Delaware Spring, Lone Elm, Round Grove, Bull Creek, and other names were given these halting-places, as the wagons passed them in slow, rumbling march towards the dreaded bogs of the Narrows.

The Narrows, also known as Willow Springs or Wakarusa Point, was a narrow ridge between the waters of the Kansas and Osage Rivers, where Wakarusa Creek and Ottawa Creek flowed away to join the larger streams. There the mud was black and deep, with a surface which often appeared firm and dry. But once a heavy wagon ventured upon that deceptive surface, down went the wheels to the hub, and the train bogged for the rest of the day.

Then teams were doubled and tripled, and all hands put their straining shoulders to the wheel, standing waist-deep in mud and water. The long lines of oxen, each weighing fourteen hundred pounds or more, would lower their heads, hump up their backs, and with tails sticking out behind straight as a whipstock, they spread their legs and heaved against the heavy yokes. Slowly, their hoofs spread, while the mud spurted and curled up between their toes. The long chain tightened, the wagon tongue stopped whipping from side to side, and men and animals put forth every ounce of strength to move the heavy load. The mud and water gurgled, the spindles chucked against the thimbles of the wheels, the long whips cracked like rifles, and the bull-whackers filled the air with their cries, '*Hua! Vaya!* Gee-up! Woha!', and made the air blue with profanity. Slowly the wagons budged, then one by one were dragged through the bog. The men lost patience, the oxen and mules lost weight, and the wagon train lost a day's time. But at last the train passed the danger spot, and rolled into camp — in the rain!

There was rain in plenty, day in and day out, at that season: sometimes a fog, or slow drizzle, sometimes a steady, prolonged downpour, more rarely a deluge. Then came sharp and incessant flashes of lightning, such stunning and continuous thunder as men from the seaboard had never heard before. The landscape was blotted out by sheets of rain, that shot down diagonally like a waterfall, with a heavy roar, and rose in spray from the ground. The slopes were slick and greasy after that; and the streams rose in a few minutes, so that it was next to impossible to ford them. Old buffalo wallows filled to the brim with water, frogs were singing everywhere, and the flower-spangled prairie — which looked so green and inviting — was actually an inch deep in water under its squashy coverlet of green.

Saddles got wet and sticky; blankets never dried, and sometimes became fly-brown and maggoty, until they reached the limits of the blow-fly's range at Turkey Creek. Clothing was always wet, mosquito bars became dank and mouldy, cooking was difficult, and the lurching wagons sucked and gurgled through mud and slush when they moved at all. But the worst trouble was with the animals.

Horses, mules, and oxen alike set their heads to return to the settlements. They missed their grain, they missed their stables, their comfortable fenced pastures, their easy labor on good roads. Mosquitoes, horseflies, and buffalo gnats kept them twitching and itching, stamping, rolling, and tossing their heads day and night, so that men had to drape spare articles of clothing over the wretched creatures, in order to give them enough peace of mind to graze a little. There were no trees to shelter them. Thunder and lightning frightened them. The small, cozy world they had known was now replaced by a region fit for giants, with enormous fields hedged by colossal fringes of timber along the streams. At the first opportunity, they broke loose and headed back. And the soil was so wet that it was an easy matter for a restive animal to jerk up his picket-pin and be gone.

So, day by day, the animals disappeared, dashing from the Trail into the brush, from the cavayard of spare animals behind the wagons; making off without ceremony, when turned out to graze; or pulling up their picket-pins under the very noses of their exasperated masters.

And then, sometimes, they simply stampeded in a body!

CHAPTER V

Stampede

STAMPEDE!

Nothing to match that disaster could be met with on the Plains, short of absolute massacre by Indians. And nearly every train had at least one such experience, whether it was using oxen or mules. The danger was well understood, and bull-whackers took precautions. On the first stages of the journey, oxen were turned out to graze still carrying their yokes, in the hope that these would impede their escape. But as often as not, they ran off anyhow.

Even during the day, they were apt to go. But after dark was the time to be watchful. The ox was a whimsical critter, nervous as a cat, and would take fright at almost anything — or even, apparently, at nothing at all. A sudden shout, a bolt of lightning, a dried tumbleweed rolling along the ground in ungainly bounds, a deer passing by, the howl of a lone wolf, a sudden movement by one of the oxen themselves, or even the jingle of their own yoke-irons was enough to send them rushing away into the night. And when marauding Indians, prairie fires, thunderstorms, or a blizzard frightened them, nothing could prevent the stampede.

Blind with terror, they swept away like an avalanche, and left their owners to tumble out of their blankets, catch up a horse, and follow at a desperate pace. Then the herders would plunge headlong through the darkness, trying to get ahead of the maddened animals, waving their coats, shouting, firing pistols, trying to turn the leaders. In the rain, in the darkness, over strange ground, where badgers or prairie-dogs had pitted the earth with deadly holes, the horsemen urged their animals along. Sometimes a horse went down, and its rider was trampled to death by the thundering hooves of the cattle. Sometimes the rider broke his neck before the oxen touched him. Sometimes he was brushed aside and left raging, as the herd swept by. In a storm or a blizzard, he might get lost, and never find his way back to the train at all.

The worst disaster of the kind was perhaps that of the wagon train which — with fifteen hundred oxen — was returning to the States, approaching Council Grove from the west. It was autumn, and a sudden norther struck the train one night, blinding man and beast with its flying particles of frozen snow. Away went the herd, with the roar of hooves and rattle of yokes, vanishing into the whiteness. In a few seconds they had disappeared as though they had never been. The men were helpless to follow, as it would be death to stray from the wagons into that blinding smother. Not an animal was left to them.

Next day, when the sky was clear again, they wandered around, searching for their cattle, nowhere to be seen. At last one of the search party let out a yell, halting on the edge of a ravine. The others hurried up, lined the rim of the gulch, and stared down in silence, while their freezing breath formed a cloud about their red faces.

The gulch was filled to the top with frozen carcasses, hundreds of oxen piled up level with the surrounding prairie, where they had been trapped in their headlong flight and plunged to their death. 'For years the festering mass of hair, hides, and bones, even after the flesh had decomposed, polluted the air for miles around, and ... myriads of carrion birds and droves of ghoulish wolves' [11] gathered there. Literally tons of bones lay there, gradually crumbling into the ground. Perhaps some of them remain to this day in that little gulch near Diamond Springs.

A stampede of mules was, if anything, even worse. Few Indians cared for oxen: the flesh was not to their taste, the mere sweetish smell of the animals made some buffalo-eaters physically sick; and the redskin had no use for oxen as draft animals. But mules were valuable: the Indian could use them, sell them, give them away, or claim a reward for their return. And so the owners of mules kept their eyes skinned, and made haste to follow the trail of the runaways. Mules, moreover, had a habit, in buffalo country, of running off with the shaggy herds. And as the beat of a thousand hooves obliterated their trail, they could seldom be recovered. Even in the first stages of the trip, mules were hard to follow, harder to catch, because of the patches of timber, numerous creeks, constant rains, and the speed with which they hastened back to the settlements.

Careful wagon-masters kept their herders always saddled up, armed, and ready for action. Proprietors kept fast horses ready saddled all night, tied to a wagon wheel *inside* the corral, so that — in case of a stampede — there would be a mounted man to follow. The picket-pin of the bell-mare was usually a strong one, three or four feet long, driven deep into the earth. For mules would follow the bell-mare through hell and high water, swarming after her like bees about their queen. Once she broke loose, there was no stopping them until she had been captured.

On those dismal rainy nights, after a hard day's labor with the wagons in the mud, it was human nature for the bull-whackers to roll up in their blankets, let the animals graze, and trust to luck. All too often they found Luck an untrustworthy old bitch, and wakened to hear the roar of galloping mules vanishing into the pitchy blackness.

Then the wagon-master would jerk out a word of instructions to some man he could trust, telling him to keep his pistols handy, and take care that none of the men ran off during his own absence, carrying the outfit with which they had been provided on credit, and everything else they could lay hands on.

The wagon-master, in too much haste to don his coat, or boots, would rush off after the faint jingle of the bell of the lead mare, splashing through buffalo wallows, stumbling over hill and dale, running his heart out to keep that fading sound within earshot. If he did not slip and strain a muscle, or break a leg, or drown in some flooded creek, or halt, spent and winded, he might at last hear the bell growing louder, more intermittent, as the animals stopped to graze. He might be able to approach the lead mare, gently grasp the strap from which her tinkling bell depended, fasten his rope around her jaw, climb aboard, and round up the herd, turning them back to the stalled wagons.

It might be days before he came up with the mules. It might be that some other train had corralled them for him, or some Indians had found them. Or it might be that some of them were never seen again. The wagon-master returned at last, worn out, cold and wet, shivering, with his moccasins full of cactus spines, and a mouth full of blistering maledictions for his feckless bull-whackers.

Thereafter, for a time, mules and oxen would be securely hobbled, picketed close to the train, and guarded relentlessly.

Immediately, the bull-whackers would be fighting one another over grazing rights!

Some men resented staking out their animals, saying that they could not get enough grass at the end of a rope, that they did not like to graze in the bottoms where the wagons generally corralled, but preferred the shorter, juicier grazing on the hill slopes and high prairie. They resented getting up during the night to shift the picket-pins. And, being good Americans of the old school, and bull-whackers to boot, they resented being told what to do.

Touchy as so many porcupines, and ready to fight at the drop of a hat, or the hat's shadow, each of these men laid claim to every inch of ground extending outwards from his own wagon for a hundred yards or so. Whoever carelessly allowed his animals to encroach upon that sacred domain was in for a fight with its overlord. And since a good many men with the train had no wagons, but were horsemen, and naturally preferred to keep their animals staked close to the train, combats and quarrels for this cause were numerous.

Moreover, when a train was first organized, corrals were apt to be formed in a clumsy manner. One side would be flat, the other side round, or the whole thing would be heart-shaped, or oval, or ovoid. Then the area belonging to one man would obviously overlap that of another. Bruised knuckles and bloody noses were common.

And when there was nothing else to fight, there was always a stubborn mule, a fractious horse. Animals tied up to picket-pins for the night grazed more steadily than those which had the whole prairie for a pasture, and could therefore pick and choose, nibble and pass from one bunch of grass to another. If an animal was not well fed, he was logy and sluggish on the Trail next day: whereas, if he had filled his belly on good grass, he would be hard to rope, mean to saddle, and wary as a wolf. He would neither lead, drive, nor follow; his principal object was to break loose, or buck his master off.

Garrard tells us of his own experience, which was typical: 'My large beast, Diabolique (for never mule gave more trouble) was refractory owing ... to the unusual quantity of good grass the preceding night. After repeated vexatious trials, I succeeded in roping her. Holding the lasso in one hand, and two other mules by their bridles, I led them toward camp, jumping over an intervening mud-hole, expecting them to follow. But no such thing! Instead, astern flew their heads, and flat went I in the puddle. I then en-

deavoured to drive them over, but they backed their ears
preparatory to kicking the hindsights off the first man that
struck them. With a running noose over Diabolique's nose,
and a "heave-ho," I pulled lustily, but she held stiff her
elongated neck and head, planted firmly her feet in front,
and with strained eyeballs stood provokingly patient. How
exquisitely malignant does one feel the "mounting devil in
his heart" in such a position! But for the want of her as a
riding animal, a bullet would have been the reward of her
stubbornness. Nor is this uncharitable feeling peculiar to
myself; for there is yet the first amiable mule rider to be
seen, as the best mule, at times, will become refractory, and
to refrain from clubs and curses is a moral impossibility.' [12]

Not every man was as gentle and forgiving as Garrard.
One night on Black Jack 'one of the trappers, on arriving at
the camping-place, dismounted from his horse, and after
divesting it of the saddle, endeavoured to lead his mule by
the rope up to the spot where he wished to deposit his pack.
Mule-like, however, the more he pulled the more stubbornly
she remained in her tracks, planting her forelegs firmly, and
stretching out her neck with provoking obstinacy. . . . After
tugging ineffectually for several minutes, winding the rope
round his body, and throwing himself suddenly forward
with all his strength, the trapper actually foamed with passion; and although he might have subdued the animal at
once by fastening the rope with a half-hitch round its nose,
this, with an obstinacy equal to that of the mule itself, he
refused to attempt, preferring to vanquish her by main
strength. Failing so to do, the mountaineer, with a volley of
blasphemous imprecations, suddenly seized his rifle, and
levelling it at the mule's head, shot her dead.' [13]

As the train plodded on through sun and shower up the
long, gradual slope to the west, the traveller had time to
become acquainted with his mess-mates, and with other
men who marched and rode with him. Each of them, by

precept or example, or both, taught him something of the plainscraft which was the secret of their success in the Far West.

He was instructed in hobbling his saddle animal, and heard learned discussions of the advantages and disadvantages of the *fore-hopple* — a strap or rope connecting the forelegs — and of the *side-line* — a hopple connecting a fore and a hind leg. The latter, he was told, was better for most animals, since it really prevented speed; whereas the fore-hopple, once a horse got the hang of it, was hardly any good at all. The horse so manacled simply learned to throw both fore feet along together, and could go ahead nearly as fast as he could run without it.

The Mexicans taught him the rudiments of the use of the rope, lariat, or lasso — as it was then called; taught him how to splice a *honda* at one end, and knot the other; taught him how to build a loop, how to spin it, how to throw it across an animal's back, since at first he would be quite helpless to cast it around the neck of his beast. To his joy, the green-horn discovered that a horse which had been frequently roped would stop and stand the moment it felt a rope lying across its back or shoulders, even though the noose had missed its head.

And what the ropers could not teach him, they showed him: how to spin a rope, in vertical loops, overhead and around the body, while they jumped in and out, and were apparently as much masters of the trick with one hand as with the other. They let him ride by and snared the feet of his mount in obedience to his shouted demands: a fore foot, a hind foot; fore and hind together, head, or tail. They could noose two, four, six, eight horses together. And they displayed the marvellous teamwork of man and roping horse in catching, throwing, and tying the animals in a moment of time. It was magical, and the poor greenhorn acquired a new humility and a new ambition as he watched them.

In all likelihood he bought a fine, supple, rawhide lariat, and rode off to one side to practice with it, oblivious of Indians and of time.

He learned something of the tracks made by a horse in the mud — the mud made the first lessons easy: how to distinguish the long strides and single prints of a running animal from those shorter strides and doubled imprints of one trotting or walking. How to tell a mule-track from that of a horse or an ox. If quick and clever, he might even learn to know the tracks of his own animal, and to distinguish them from those of others.

He learned to help drive the loose stock into the corral of a morning, how to snare his own mount, how to saddle up, mount, and ride, how to stick on when the mule or mustang bucked and reared. And he learned that a horse makes for water after feeding, which saved him much leg-work when his animal strayed.

By the time he had eaten all the honey in the rawhide bag brought from the last Indian cabin, he had settled down into a steady routine, his muscles had gained tone, his face had browned perceptibly, and his beard — if any — gave him the appearance of Robinson Crusoe.

By the time he reached Big John Spring, that clear, cool, gushing fountain flowing from the hillside, after two weeks' 158 mi journey, he felt himself fit to play his part with others on the long Trail ahead. Big John Spring was one hundred and thirty-eight miles from Westport.

Far behind were the log cabins of the Shawnees and Delawares, the bark lodges of the Kaws, the loaf-shaped Osage dwellings. Just ahead lay the real beginning of the Plains. Just ahead was Council Grove!

Preceded by a rising wave of grasshoppers, and flanked by plover running with their teams, the wagons rolled down to the creek, hub-deep in the yellow blooms of sensitive plants, white primroses, wild tea, and gooseberry bushes.

They passed a pile of rocks, with its long pole leaning mournfully, which marked the grave of a pioneer murdered there by Osages. Then, sobered by that monument, and by the long day's labor, the men and animals swung into the corral for the night.

PART II

Council Grove

CHAPTER VI

The Start

COUNCIL GROVE, the point at which caravans organized for their long cruise to the Mexican settlements, was one of the most agreeable stopping-places on the Trail. It consisted of a continuous strip of timber nearly half a mile wide, extending along the valley of a small, running stream known as Council Grove Creek, the principal branch of the Neosho River. Along this stream were fertile bottoms and beautiful upland prairies. The Grove itself contained many fine old trees: ash, oak, elm, maple, and hickory, festooned with enormous grapevines, and it covered altogether about one hundred and sixty acres. Its dense shade was delightful after the glare of the sunburned plains. Its name was gained from a council held by Osage Indians in 1825 with a party sent out by the United States government to mark a road from Missouri to Santa Fe.

The Grove was the last stop on the outbound Trail where hardwood could be obtained and wagons repaired. There was a blacksmith shop, and every teamster took care to cut an extra wagon tongue, spare axle-trees, and rough out a hickory ox-bow, to be slung under his wagon. At this point everyone stopped and made camp while day by day the wagons rolled in from the east preparatory to organizing for the trip across the plains.

While they waited, the men were kept busy repacking the wagons and drying out all goods wetted by the rains. Everyone unshipped, overhauled, and repaired his equipment.

Wagonloads of trunks and boxes, bundles and bags were scattered about and their contents spread abroad in great confusion.

Fires crackled under iron kettles, water boiled and bubbled, and nearly everybody did his washing, or went to work with needle and thread to mend his clothes, sew on buttons, or darn his socks. Others kneaded bread and baked it in the spider, or Dutch oven. Some prowled through the brush with their shotguns, trying to knock over a prairie hen or a rabbit for the mess. The woods were lively with the wings of catbird, bluebird, wild turkey, brown thrush: the prairies with quail, grouse, and curlew.

The men who assembled at Council Grove to make their way westward, sweating, swearing, singing, fighting, plodding through the mud, riding through clouds of dust, groping through fog, were of all kinds and of many races, typical Americans: Indian hunters whose job it was to supply the caravans with fresh meat — Delawares, Shawnees, Sac and Fox, Potawatomies, with long hair or shaved heads, armed with powder-horns and flintlock rifles; swarthy French Canadians, carefree, given to song, and no friends of labor: Mexican muleteers; trappers from Tennessee or Kentucky, lank and narrow-chested, wearing fur caps or battered wool hats to top off old elk-skins, black with grease and smut; Kanakas; negroes; vigilant traders with new two weeks' beards and the bearing of men of wealth and authority, conscious of their reputation among the greenhorns for violence and sharp practice; sometimes untidy soldiers going along as escorts against the Indians, Texans, or Mexican bandits, or heading for 'the Halls of Montezuma' and the Mexican War; men of all sorts rushing west to the goldfields of California, heavily armed, alternately arrogant and panic-stricken, distrustful of strangers, unable to hide their inexperience. With these, an occasional lady in her full skirts of silk or cashmere, farmwives in cottons; French or

Mexican women with blue-black hair and instinctive coquetry; sometimes a squaw, wife of a trader or mountain
man, in her colorful, practical costume. Oddly sorted as
these were, they were already melting together in the face
of a common exposure to the emptiness and dangers of the
plains, like shanghaied seamen on a windjammer.

Yet the association of these seamen of the prairies was
entirely voluntary. No sooner had the various outfits gathered in the Grove than organization was thought of, and the
great American game of politics reared its lovely head.

In the early days of the Republic, a candidate for office
made a personal canvass of the voters, and the spoken vote
was given face to face with the candidates for office. These
sat side by side under a tree, whose generous shade was
thrown over an open whiskey barrel from which every
citizen might help himself. One by one the voters approached the election officials, and each cast his vote in a
loud voice, whereupon the approved candidate would arise
and publicly thank him. No secret ballot then. What with
whiskey, inflamed partisanship, and the intimidation practiced by loyal supporters in the heat of the campaign, such
a gathering was likely to be turbulent.

It was in this spirit, as often as not, that caravans were
organized beneath the stately Council Oak (still standing)
at the Grove. First of all, the men would elect a captain of
the Caravan — some man of experience and standing, in
whom the travellers had confidence — such a man as
Charles Bent (grandson of Captain Silas Bent, leader of the
Boston Tea Party), afterward first American governor of
New Mexico, who commanded the caravans of 1828, '29,
'32, and '33. Under him might be a lieutenant, sometimes a
second lieutenant; a clerk; a court, for the trial of offences,
consisting of three judges; a pilot or guide; and a commander and four sergeants of the Guard. The Commander
of the Guard was, after the Captain, the man of most

authority, since every able-bodied traveller was a member of the guard.

Some caravans boasted a chaplain, who, if the train rested on a Sunday, could hold services before an altar made of a mess-chest or a couple of trunks covered with a blue blanket. In early days it seemed that clergymen were almost as numerous on the plains as buffalo. Though marriages and baptisms were rare events on the Santa Fe Trail, burials were all too common. The whole way from Council Grove to the Mexican settlements, that Trail was lined with the bones of horses, oxen, and mules, and among these the skeletons of men shovelled into a shallow hole, only to be dug up again by the wolves.

The train had no surgeon.

Physicians seldom ventured from the settlements, and those who went were commonly so incapable that travellers usually preferred amateur treatment by experienced traders and mountain men, or placed themselves, when possible, in the care of Indian medicine men. Most travellers, even soldiers, had to doctor themselves, as a rule, with the result that gunshot wounds, Indian arrows and lances, typhoid fever, scurvy, smallpox, Asiatic cholera, chills and fever, tuberculosis, and mere exposure left many gaps in the ranks. No one has written a history of frontier medicine and surgery. It would make a thrilling story.

So the caravan was organized.

Such an organization tightened steadily as the caravans progressed through the Indian country, and loosened again as they approached the Mexican settlements. The Captain and his Commander of the Guard had many problems.

First of these was the keeping of a vigilant watch over the property and lives of the men, the regulation of the order of march, and defence against raiding Indians. Once out of danger, on the far side of the Indian country, travellers were likely to leave the caravan and ride ahead to Santa

Fe, packing their goods on muleback. To prevent this, an agreement was sometimes entered into at the Grove providing that no man should leave the caravan until it had arrived at its destination. In spite of this, some men carried pack-saddles ready for use in their wagons; others, particularly in the early days of the trade, used pack mules instead of wagons the whole way.

A Mexican muleteer was paid from two dollars to five dollars a month. He lived on beans and corn and such meat as he could get. Each man cared for six or eight mules, making fifteen miles a day. In spite of the cruel pack-saddles and packs lashed mercilessly tight, in spite of gall-sores which sometimes exposed the ribs of the unfortunate animals, even barefoot mules generally survived the summer trip better than oxen — but they were far more expensive. Good mules, big enough to haul the heavy wagons, each carrying from twenty-five hundred to seven thousand pounds of goods, cost two hundred dollars a pair. Oxen were much cheaper, and endured cold better, but suffered dreadfully from tender feet, and so were often broken down and worthless at the end of the trip. Few men knew how to shoe them properly. Whether mules or oxen were used to draw the wagons, teamsters had to take along enough spare animals to replace all their teams.

Oxen were plenty in Missouri, rare in New Mexico; whereas Missouri had few mules: westbound trains therefore were likely to have more oxen than mules; while trains outfitting in Santa Fe used mules more often than oxen.

A caravan might consist of twenty to one hundred wagons with three times as many men, hundreds of mules, oxen, and saddle horses, a few Dearborn carriages, and a small cannon or two mounted on wheels. About the time of the gold rush, iron axles came into use, with rings fastened in their ends to which ropes could be attached when the teams bogged down. Some of the gold-rush outfits were admirably equipped, with provisions for nine months, clothing for two years, extra saddles, harness, ox shoes, mule shoes, scythes for cutting grass, a complete set of blacksmith and carpenter tools, and plenty of powder and lead.

Dogs sometimes were taken along, though usually a source of quarrels between the owners and men who had been snapped at. Watchdogs helped guard against Indians, and would drive buffalo away.

Having elected their officers, the men of the caravan gathered into messes of six or eight men each. Naturally, birds of a feather flocked together; Indian hunters messed by themselves, teamsters with those belonging to their wagons, traders and genteel travellers with each other, French Canadians or Mexicans by themselves. A married man, like James Magoffin, lived with his wife in her tent. However, tents, camp furniture, and elaborate equipments were rare. Experienced traders, having acquired something of the Indian's lack of care for the morrow, were apt to neglect such comforts and rely upon their wits and courage, taking things as they came.

Mountain men — and most of the traders were old mountain men — looked with scorn upon all such fofurraw and civilized fixin's!

The first action of the newly elected Captain of the Caravan was to demand from the various proprietors a list of their wagons and men. In the beginning there were many proprietors, each with a few wagons. But, as usual in the history of American business, as the trade to Santa Fe became better organized, the number of proprietors grew less as the number of wagons increased. The enforcing of this order of the Captain's entailed some trouble, since the traders, like other Americans, were independent as hogs on ice, and likely to treat the order as a mere request.

Once the Captain had the list in hand, the Commander of the Guard proceeded to make up a roll-call, or roster, for

guard duty. The cook of each mess was relieved of this
duty, as was every *bona fide* invalid who could summon the
energy necessary to present his excuses. All others, whether
old-timers or greenhorns, laborers or genteel idlers, had to
serve. For though the traders generously fed everyone who
chose to attach himself to the caravan, they were relentless
in their demand that these hangers-on take their part in
protecting the wagons. In those days, many young men on
the border took a trip or two to Santa Fe before settling
down, as young men since have gone to sea, joined the army,
or ridden the rods.

The Commander of the Guard divided the night into four
watches between sundown and daybreak. This meant that
each member of the guard was on duty every other night
or so.

When these details had been arranged, the last ox-bows
smoothed, the wheels greased, and harness repaired, the
wagons were formed into a hollow square or corral, forming
a horseshoe or circle on the prairie with wheels interlocked
and tongues all pointing outward, each supporting the har-
nesses or yokes of its team. Then the teamsters, in their
homespun pantaloons, sturdy high boots, fur caps, and
checked wool shirts, rounded up the oxen. Each had a whip
with an eighteen-inch stock and sixteen-foot lash. Cracking
this, they drove the bulls into the corral ready for the start
next day. The prairie resounded with their loud 'Wo-ha!'

The lingo of these bull-whackers has left its mark upon
the language of the West even to this day. Old-time Plains
Indians still use the words 'wo-ha' for beef, 'goddam' for
wagon. You may still hear some old Cheyenne describe a
wagon bogged down in the quicksands of the river in these
words: 'Goddam stick fast; wo-ha swimmin' all aroun'.'

That last night at Council Grove was a sore trial to the
greenhorns on guard. They had little confidence in their
marksmanship or plainscraft, and therefore feared guard

duty worse than anything. The old-timers, on the other hand, who knew that their wagons and their scalps would soon be under the protection of those same greenhorns, were in haste to teach them their duty. 'Break 'em in quick,' was their maxim. Accordingly, that last night at the Grove gave the greenhorns their initiation, their baptism of fear. . . .

One by one men tapped the dottle from their pipes, and rolled up in their blankets under the stars. The fires shrank and faded into heaps of gray ashes. The animals grew quiet. Only the distant yapping of a coyote or the snuffle and clapping lips of a pony browsing the prairie could be heard. The Big Dipper swung halfway round the sky. The guard changed for the second time. The tired men snored.

Suddenly the crack of a rifle split the silence.

Men sat up in their beds, fumbled for their weapons. From the prairie west of the corral the pulsating terrible war-whoop rattled on their frightened ears, and the guard on that side screamed and howled as if he were being torn to pieces.

Dogs rushed from their warm nests in a fury of rage, vanishing into the darkness towards the nearest timber. Someone raised the cry of 'Injuns!' Another rifle cracked, then came the dull boom of a smooth-bore.

'Git your gun, they're comin',' a gruff voice commanded.

All round the camp men were jumping up, running from their blankets, throwing themselves prone under the wagons or outside them ready for the attack, silent as so many stones.

The crouching greenhorn, staring blindly into the night, felt his heart rise into his throat as a heavy hand struck him between the shoulders, knocking him flat. 'Git down thar! Lay your ear to the ground. Cain't you hear 'em comin'?'

Guns banged all around the corral, like Christmas, or the Fourth of July. Men rushed forward a few paces, then flung themselves down, ready to fire. A dog returned snarling, unhurt, with hackles bristling.

Then the sergeant of the Guard was heard calling men back. 'Come back! Come back! False alarm!' His voice sounded choked and strangling, as he kept his laughter under. The greenhorns sneaked back to their blankets, shaking with excitement.

Then old-timers had the laugh on the strangers. 'Shucks! Thar ain't no hostiles closter than Walnut Crick,' they bantered. 'The boys were jest trying you out. L'arnin' you suthin' about night attacks. Good for you. Make your heart strong. Maybeso next time you won't be so all-fired quick on the trigger!'

Men snuggled into their blankets again. After that, it seemed hardly time for one good snore before they heard the Captain shouting, and opened their eyes to a fathomless gray sky. The call was repeated.

'Turn out! Turn out! Hooray for Santy Fee!'

CHAPTER VII

Diamond Springs

THE moment the Captain of the Caravan roused the sleeping men with his loud 'Turn out!' the wagon corral became a scene of almost frantic activity. Every man was on his feet rolling and tying his blankets, tossing them into the wagons. This was hardly done when they heard the second command: 'Catch up! Catch up!' The men hurried after their animals, repeating the call up and down the valley, while others yipped and whooped in Indian fashion, in the enthusiasm and confusion of getting started. Every man went quickly to work throwing the harness on his mules, urging his oxen under the yoke, in the midst of a great clatter of bells, and rattle of yokes, and jingle of harness. Ropes uncoiled through the air, saddles were swung upon the backs of restless horses, and the bustle of preparation was accented by good round oaths, in French, Spanish, and plain English. Each teamster fought to be first in getting ready, and within an incredibly short time, the first one straightened up and sang out, 'All set!'

Some of the men had to hitch a team to the halter of an unusually stubborn mule, or ox, and drag him into position. But at length the teams were all hooked up, and the last sweating teamster reported himself ready. His call was echoed from every side, and the Captain, rising in his stirrups, bellowed the final command, 'Stretch out!'

It was an impressive sight to the greenhorns, the way that double file of great, hulking wagons rumbled away to the west behind the eight-mule teams and rolling oxen. With them went the carriages and horsemen of the Captain and his mess, the ponies of the Indian hunters, the mountaineers' saddle mules and pack animals, and the mob of spare animals shambling along behind. The boy who wrangled this herd of miscellaneous animals — lame oxen, extra saddle horses, sore-backed mules, broncs, mares with foals, and milch cows, no longer required the help of Mexican ropers to keep them moving. By the time the outbound train reached Council Grove, few of the animals cared any longer to attempt a run back to the settlements.

The first camp west of Council Grove was one of the best on the trail. There a large spring flowed into Otter Creek, named by the Government Survey of 1825 'the Diamond of the Plain,' but known more commonly as Diamond Springs. This generous fountain gushed out from the head of a hollow in the prairie from which game trails radiated. The spring supplied a large flow of clear water that was also really *cold* — a rare treat. Some benefactor of mankind had set out mint roots around the four-foot basin of the spring, and after 1840 they provided a bountiful supply of leaves for all who passed that way. Old-timers always had mint juleps at Diamond Springs.

Nearby was a gulch filled with the remains of stampeded oxen lost in a blizzard, as described above. Two miles east of the springs, in a gully, some nameless caravan came to its end — whether by fire, Indians, or stampede, no man can say. Teamsters who needed chains, bolts, or wagon irons of any sort could find them there.

The Springs had also more heroic memories. In 1852 a troop of cavalry encamped one autumn day on the high prairie east of the Springs to recruit their horses, which were in poor condition. It had been frosty, and the grass was very dry. Kaw Indians had been seen hanging about all that day, but the soldiers did not expect an attack. Two hours before sundown, the boys had just finished eating dinner when all at once fire broke out in a circle around their camp just out of rifle range. There was a strong south wind, and before they knew it, the tall grass was blazing furiously — the flames leaping twenty feet high, coming on the run!

In desperate haste the troopers set a counter-fire all around their camp, beating out the flames nearest it with grain sacks and saddle blankets. The men knew that their animals and their lives were at stake. For fifteen minutes they fought like demons, blinded by smoke and ashes, their hands and faces blistered by the flames. Colonel Percival G. Lowe, who was present, says the men were utterly exhausted; hardly one could speak: 'My hands and face were blistered in several places; my mustache and whiskers — the first I had ever raised — were utterly ruined. I could not wash on account of the wounds, and dipped my face and head deep down in the lovely spring of water and held my hands under to relieve the pain. My experience was that of most of the troop. Fortunately we had quite a quantity of antelope tallow, which was warmed and applied gently to our sores.

'Undoubtedly the Kaws had set fire to burn us out. . . . The troops were notified at retreat roll-call that we would start at daylight. The guards were doubled and we rested as best we could.' It is pleasant to know that the troop went on to the Kaw Agency and there recovered some stolen horses. They were eager to avenge their ruined whiskers. A fight was barely averted near the mouth of Big John Creek. . . .[14]

From Diamond Springs to the Big Bend of the Arkansas River, the Grand Arkansas (a distance of one hundred and five miles), the Trail crossed a series of small streams cutting the prairie from north to south, each one more difficult than the last. These creeks were narrow, but muddy, with steep banks.

A march of fifteen miles from Diamond Springs brought caravans to uninviting Lost Springs, which had gained its name from the fact that it sometimes went dry. All that day and the next day's march of twelve miles to Cottonwood Creek was over a level prairie covered with tall, rank grass. On this desolate portion of the trail, travellers observed zigzag strips of grass, denser and taller than the rest, which amateur natural philosophers explained as a result of lightning, that, striking there, had made the earth more fertile. Some elaborated their guess into a scheme for irrigating the plains with electric fluid, by means of lightning rods or an iron forest!

On the way, the train was sure to be mired down, and so 'doubled out,' at Mud Creek, otherwise known as the Devil's Hind Quarters. The teamsters cut grass to bridge the mud; but even so they lost half a day. Here the first antelope might be seen.

Cottonwood Creek was still worse, with its deep mud and steep banks. The crossing there was always difficult. It was hard to keep a wagon from turning over, as it slid down one bank on top of its team — in spite of the locked wheels and a yoke of oxen behind holding back. But, if getting down was bad, getting up again proved worse. Moreover, this heavy labor came always at the end of the day, when everyone was tired, cross, and profane. For, on the Santa Fe Trail, it was the rule to ford any stream before making camp. Otherwise, there might be a cloudburst during the night, filling the creek from bank to bank, and causing a delay of days or weeks.

The Cottonwood Fork, when not in flood, was clear and clean, and caravans sometimes halted here to wash their clothing.

All this region was barren of trees. And from the Cottonwood on, the vegetation changed. Cottonwood, elm, boxelder, and willows took the place of ash, burr oak, black walnut, blackjack, sycamore, buckeye, pignut hickory, and maple. Wild plum was seen, and goldenrod abounded. Buffalo grass hugged the ground; tall grass, except in the bottoms, was left behind. The crumbling bones of buffalo were seen occasionally.

At Turkey Creek, twenty-five miles beyond, men found good grass and water, but not a stick of timber, not even a twig as thick as a pipestem. Here the traveller learned to gather the round, dry buffalo chips scattered in profusion over the prairie. When dry, these burned easily, and quickly provided hot embers on which to cook. Wet, a chip fire was only a stinking smoke, into which a man was glad to stick his head at night, in the vain hope of snatching a few hours of rest from the torment of the mosquitoes. Without that smudge, a man soon learned why the Indians, in their sign language, dubbed the mosquito Bites-through-blanket! But wet or dry, a chip fire kept a man busy gathering fuel to keep it going.

In the three forks of Turkey Creek fishermen caught sun perch and catfish. Along its banks, bright with scarlet flowers, they found *pomme blanche*, tumble-bugs — and rattlesnakes! The bleaching bones of long-dead bison began to be seen more frequently now.

Seventeen more miles brought the caravan to the Little Arkansas, at a point some ten miles below its source. Here the stranger had his first mass encounter with the buffalo gnat, which filled the air, and drove human victims and their animals half mad with pain and vexation.

The buffalo gnat was a small black insect. It not only attacked the bare face and hands, but even got under the clothing, fastened itself, and remained until sated. The bites caused intense irritation and swelling, and soon made a man look as if he had the smallpox.

Some travellers carried mosquito nets to sleep under — and then found no sticks on which to prop them! Others wore green veils over their heads, running the risk of not being able to see where they were going, and so colliding with the business end of a mule! Men unprotected sometimes were ready to break down and cry from vexation. The gnat was worse than the mosquitoes, which were found chiefly along the streams. Men from the woodlands, used to making camp in valleys, had to learn that on the prairies the place to camp, in summer, was on the uplands.

Disused buffalo wallows, full of water, and ringed with golden coreopsis, scarlet mallow, and silver-edged euphorbia, began to show themselves. The blow-fly was behind now, and blankets soon lost their maggots, even in the wet. Antelope were seen more often now, but as like as not the hunter's gun was so wet that his powder would not explode. Crows began to be replaced by ravens. The water-fowl were everywhere. And puff-balls, large and white as so many human skulls, dotted the damp prairie. Purslane and lamb's quarter abounded, and the air was filled with swallows, doves, blue jays and kingfishers, and the whirring quail.

The Little Arkansas was only a small creek five or six yards wide, but its bed was so miry and its banks so steep that men were always sent ahead with axes, spades, and mattocks, to dig down its banks and cut willows to bridge the quagmire. If the caravans crossed that stream without breaking a wagon-tongue or injuring draft animals, oldtimers considered it a miracle.

Land turtles began to be a lively feature of the ruts, lizards darted about, and crawfish scuttled into the pools as the men advanced. In the distance Plum Buttes showed themselves, crickets hopped about big anthills, and beyond Cow Creek a large village of prairie-dogs studded the plain with mounded holes.

Cow Creek, twenty miles beyond the Little Arkansas, was even worse. As Gregg put it: 'After digging, bridging, shouldering the wheels, with the usual accompaniment of whooping, swearing, and cracking of whips,' they got safely over and encamped in the valley beyond. All the streams in this part of the Trail had slippery, treacherous crossings.

Treachery on the Santa Fe Trail was not confined to the streams and mud-holes. It is true that, at least within the territories of the United States, the caravans of the traders were seldom annoyed by bandits, but occasionally some crime was committed on the Trail. The most notorious of these was perpetrated on the Little Arkansas, early in 1843.

Don Antonio José Chavez, a member of a distinguished New Mexican family, set out from Santa Fe on his way to Missouri, in February of that year. He had five servants and more than fifty mules. His two wagons contained furs, and upwards of ten thousand dollars in specie and bullion. It was a bad time of year to make such a trip, and dangerous for so small a party at any season. By the time he reached the Little Arkansas, the weather had accounted for all but five of his mules, and he had had to abandon his wagons.

At that time, the citizens of Texas were very bitter against the Mexicans, because of the harsh treatment given by Salazar to the members of the Texan Santa Fe Expedition, two years before. John McDaniel, who claimed to hold a commission from the government of Texas, had got together fifteen ruffians in Missouri, and started west, declaring that his purpose was to hold up Mexican caravans. It appeared that a certain 'Colonel' Warfield, holder of a similar commission, was already active on the plains in the same enterprise. McDaniel set out to join him.

Naturally, the government of the United States could not tolerate the organization of such an expedition on American soil, and sent a troop of dragoons riding on McDaniel's trail. But before the dragoons could overtake them, the desperadoes met Don Antonio and his five servants. There was no resistance, and all the Don's property fell into the hands of the bandits. The crime was committed on territory belonging to the United States.

Having divided the loot, the party split up. Seven of them turned back towards Missouri. The remaining eight led poor Chavez off the trail a little way and, in cold blood, shot him to death. Dead men tell no tales!

The citizens of Missouri were outraged, and when the ruffians turned up, ten of them were captured. Of these, eight were fined and put in prison. John McDaniel and his brother, David, were hanged.

American citizens travelling with west-bound caravans could take pride in the prompt justice of their government in this affair, when they passed the scene of this crime, heading for the Grand Arkansas.

PART III

Grand Arkansas

CHAPTER VIII

Buffalo Fever

Pushing steadily on, the wagons reached the valley of the Arkansas River, the Grand Arkansas. The Trail struck the stream at the top of the Big Bend, south of Cheyenne Bottoms, at a point some two hundred and sixty-five miles from Independence. Thereafter it followed the river one hundred and twenty-two miles to the Cimarron Crossing, where the Desert Route turned southwest; and, if the Mountain Route was chosen, followed it another one hundred and forty-three miles to Bent's Old Fort.

The Arkansas River, seldom less than a quarter of a mile in width between its low, barren banks, flowed shallow and turbid over broad bars of sand, which rose here and there into small, shifting islands set thick with stunted, short-lived cottonwoods. The banks were vertical, but the water ran only three or four feet below the level bottoms, so that a careless man might almost walk into the stream before he saw it. No trees marked the banks, except here and there, where a lone elm or hackberry or a few cottonwoods had survived the prairie fires under the protection of some slough or sand dune. The hills on either side the broad bottoms were equally bare. And the river itself, often dividing into several winding streams, was seldom more than knee-deep.

For all that, the sight of the Grand Arkansas roused the heart in every man who came with the rolling wagons from the eastward. Everyone felt that, on reaching the river, he had emerged into a new region. Far behind were the gentle, fertile prairies, the luxuriant grasses, the gay flowers, and timbered creeks. Here began the Great Plains. Bright green in spring, the short grass turned a greenish gray in summer, browned to buffalo color as autumn came on, and showed faintly blue in winter, matching the delicate tint of the sky above.

That was the heart of the buffalo country. Far and wide, on every hand, the sign of those majestic animals was to be seen, and at all seasons. Everywhere the short grass was dotted with dried buffalo chips. Everywhere the turf was criss-crossed by narrow trails leading to and from the river. Everywhere bleaching bones, broad skulls, and hoary, flaking horns marked the sites where savage hunters or more savage wolves had thrown their prey to earth. Everywhere the soil had been scooped into shallow, saucer-like depressions by wallowing bison.

These wallows were indestructible, unmistakable from their circular shape — though they varied in size from four or five to fifty feet across. In spring the rains filled them, and their round mirrors were ringed with lush greenery, haunted by snipe and killdeer, inhabited by small aquatic animals, offering water to man and beast, so that one could camp anywhere at that season. In summer the plants around the wallows withered, the blossoms of the wild mallow vanished, the water evaporated, and the mud cracked into hard, dry, geometrical plates. In autumn the wallows became miniature dust bowls, and in winter showed only as round depressions under the snow, or harbored a tilted drift under the northern rim. But in any season, those wallows were an unfailing sign that buffalo ranged the country. And now, as gray wolves were seen insolently trotting along the ridges, everyone knew that the herds could not be far off. Every man in the caravan felt his blood begin to heat with buffalo fever.

Many of those men had come West with no other ambition than to shoot buffalo. Most preferred the flesh of the bison to that of any other creature. And after long weeks of subsisting on salt sowbelly, all were eager to feast upon fresh meat — or, as the trappers called it, fat cow!

Those men's imaginations were filled with the buffalo: buffalo marching in long, majestic files to drink at the river; buffalo grazing far as the eye could reach, covering the plains as with one great shaggy robe; buffalo wallowing in the mud, smearing their ample shoulders with wet clay, an armor against their insect enemies in fly-time; buffalo rolling in the dust in summer; buffalo blocking the Trail, trampling down tents, oversetting wagons, stampeding mules, as they rushed furiously away; buffalo rooting with bleeding noses for the grass beneath the crusted snow; buffalo cowering together in some snug canyon during a blizzard, or milling on the open plain, each one trying to force his way into the midst of the herd, out of the bitter wind; buffalo crossing a river on a mile-wide front, so that the splashing of their headlong rush into the water made a sound like some gigantic waterfall; buffalo blinded in a prairie fire, to blunder and wander and fall a prey to merciless wolves; buffalo pacing round a grazing herd on sentry duty; buffalo with heads down and tossing horns, forming a ring about their calves, shaking their shaggy heads at the wolves which leaped and loped around, their red tongues lolling; buffalo bawling and roaring in the rutting season; buffalo pawing up the earth, gouging the prairie with angry horns in savage, jealous rage; buffalo fighting!

Summer was the season of their fury. And after the calves were big enough to travel with the herd, and the bulls had rejoined the cows, that fury knew no bounds. Hundreds of battles went on in the same herd, at the same time, and the prairie was rent and channelled, and showed like a plowed field, where those titanic struggles had taken place.

The bulls, fat and saucy with good living, stood and pawed the ground, shaking their heads, tossing tall plumes and banners of sand into the sky, so that bits of earth fell all around like hail. Then those mighty champions, each weighing a ton or more, standing above six feet tall at the top of their humps, charged, rushing together with a terrific impact and thud of broad foreheads, and stood braced and straining, thrusting hard, clashing their tough black horns, moving back and forwards with cracking sinews and foaming jaws, until the muscles of their thighs stood out like huge welts. So they would struggle, their small, dark eyes rolling in their stubborn heads, until one gave way, pushed to his knees, and suddenly found himself across the other's horns, ripped open. Then the victor, wheeling, trotted off, driving the cow, cause of the dispute, before him.

All during the season they raged, and every bull, so long as he remained in the herd, found, wherever he turned, a fight on his horns. But in the end, the younger, lustier bulls prevailed, and drove the old fellows, with their wrinkled, splintering horns, out of the herd. Hunters preferred cows, and bulls far outnumbered them. And each season, as the disparity in numbers increased, the fury of the bulls mounted.

The greenhorns had much to learn about the animals, and there was time for the lesson, as they eagerly approached the range: in the saddle by day; with the crawling wagons; in the corral during the long noonday halt for breakfast; or, better still, sitting around the campfire at night, listening to the tales of Indian hunters and mountain men.

Old-timers never tired of arguing about the number of bison on the Plains. Some had very definite opinions, estimates for which they were ready to fight, if need be: forty million, twenty million — or, as one insisted — exactly seventeen million, the precise number needed to maintain the species! But all agreed on the vast numbers they had seen. Herds that took days and weeks to pass a given point; herds that blocked the Trail, compelling men to corral their wagons about their excited livestock; herds that, grazing slowly forward, devoured every blade of grass in their path, so that oxen and mules were left without forage until they had cleared the trail of the buffalo — perhaps after a march of forty miles! Such a herd might be two hundred miles long, fifty broad. Where it had passed, the water was so fouled that men who tasted it sickened, and even oxen and mules refused to drink. The buffalo had a habit of standing and staling in the water, and after a man had had to quench his thirst on such 'buffalo tea' for a few days, he acquired a hatred for the animals, a grudge which goes far to account for the wanton killing of the shaggy beasts.

A lone horseman, finding himself in such a herd, had to keep moving all night, or fell trees around his camp to fend off the buffalo. Then, all night long, he could hear the ceaseless tramplings of that marching multitude, feel the heavy logs about him shiver as the huge creatures rubbed past, and in the morning find his shelter brown with their shed wool!

There was always danger, in passing through a vast herd, of starting a stampede, in which wagons and teams might be injured or swept away. For the buffalo had an ingrained dislike for being headed off, and would not willingly cross a trail behind the wagons. If the herd was heading in somewhat the same direction as the caravan, it would insist on passing ahead of the lead wagons, and as the bulls in the rear had to run to catch up and pass the oxen, it was natural that the whole herd should get to running, and start a stampede. Indian hunters sometimes took advantage of this peculiarity of the buffalo to guide a herd to a bluff, or even near their village. For the leaders of the herd would always incline towards any riders advancing on one flank in a parallel course — if not too close. Thus, by sending

flankers riding on either side, alternately pressing forward
and dropping back, the herd could be steered, sometimes,
in the desired direction. This accounts for the fact that
Indian medicine-men were able to lure buffalo over the
plains to the corral where they were to be destroyed.

seen as miracle?

If the wagons had already passed, the buffalo, on coming
to the ruts, would often stop, snuff the trail, and then jump
quickly over, like sheep jumping over a stick. They did not
like the odor of white men and cattle, nor the sound of
Indian drums. The creature had very definite traits and
characteristics. And when disturbed, the bulls bravely
turned and walked 'into the wind,' in order to avoid being
approached from leeward. This fact saved many an old-
timer's life on the Plains. When he saw a buffalo, or a bunch
of them, moving against the wind, contrary to the general
direction of the migration, he knew that Injuns had been
after them, and took steps to protect his scalp. The lore of
the buffalo was a matter of practical value to the frontiers-
man. His life might depend upon his observation of their
habits. Besides, he had a natural curiosity, and watched
the herds, hoping to see something of which his comrades
were ignorant. Such curiosity was not unrewarded: there
were men who swore that they had actually seen buffalo
mating, though most hunters were utterly sceptical, and
said that it never happened by daylight.

The plainsmen, who had hunted buffalo season after
season, prided themselves upon their knowledge, and were
as touchy as though the animals had been their own personal property. They were always ready to talk, and once
a man got to talking about buffalo, he never wanted to stop.
The lore of the bison was without end.

The greenhorn, naturally enough, compared the bison
with tame cattle in the settlements. His mentor soon
showed him the superiority of the buffalo. They were, it
seemed, altogether hardier and more enduring than domes-

tic cattle. They did not drift in storms, or have their tough horns split open, even by the cruellest frost. They ate less and fattened faster, seemed never to require salt, and were never known to eat loco-weed, which was always to be seen standing, untouched, after they had passed. When they lay down, they never got wrong-end-to on a hillside; and when they got up, they got up front feet first, like a horse — though they got up so swiftly that some old hunters swore that they sprang up on all fours, like a jack-in-the-box! They would fight anything in defence of their calves, and once started, would not turn aside for any danger. They would jump off a bluff that a horse or mule would wheel from. And in the spring, when the ice on the Stinking Water grew treacherous, they marched out upon it, following their leaders, crashing through, until the stream was clogged with their bloating bodies, and the whole country stunk to heaven for miles around. It was the same in bogs: men had counted as many as seven thousand bulls mired on the banks of one river.

Yet hunters did not consider them stupid — 'smarter'n a hoss — if it comes to that!' Speedy, too. Wonderfully keen sense of smell, though not much for eyesight. They were long-lived, too, because they had better teeth than a cow, more ribs, could graze closer to the ground, and had a hump to store their fat on. And when a buffalo lay down, it tucked its feet up under it, where the heel-flies could not bother. As for the meat — there could be no comparison! Beginning with Cabeza de Vaca, every traveller in the Southwest had declared that buffalo meat was 'finer and fatter' than the flesh of cattle.

When it came to fighting qualities, the buffalo had backers galore. No Spanish bull could match him, so they said.

On that point, the bull-whackers took issue. And they had a story to support their opinion. At Fort Union, mouth of Yellowstone, a thoroughbred bull was used to drag an old two-wheeled ox-cart, to bring in wood. Nigger named Joe drove the bull, and never had no trouble with him. One summer they went up-river a spell, to bring down firewood, and the bull was gentle as a lamb, like always, poking along between the shafts. Might of been an ox, the way he acted. But all of a suddent, a buffalo bull come charging out of the brush, dragging a mess of vines that had got caught in his horns. Nigger Joe yelled to scare him off, but the buffalo kept on coming. Right there he put down his horns and stuck up his tail and went for that bull. Nigger Joe jumped out of the empty cart, and flew up a tree. He thought that bull war a goner, sure.

But no such thing. The thoroughbred put down his head and went spang into the buffalo. Joe always said they hit so hard that the ground shook, and he could feel it clean up in the tree-top. The bull war jumping round like a cussed Injun in a fight, and the way he whirled that cart around war a caution. The cart went over on one side, then on t'other, bam, rattlety-bang, slap! The bull had an idee he didn't want that buffalo to poke its horns in his ribs, and met him head-on every time.

Nigger Joe thought his bull would be killed for certain, what with that cart tied to him, and all. But the bull didn't seem to mind it, nor the harness nuther. And sure enough, oncet in a while the buffalo would git round and go for the bull's haunches, afore he could turn the cart and meet him horn to horn. But if the cart slowed him down some, it helped him too, 'cause the buffalo's horns war too short to reach him, when it butted its head agin the shafts. The buffalo turned the bull over two-three times, but never could gut him. But the bull's horns war long and sharp, and he gouged the buffalo plenty. Come sundown, he got his horns between the buffalo's ribs and shoved one of 'em into his heart, I reckon. The buffalo went down, and the thoroughbred tromped him. And when Nigger Joe come down out of his tree, it took him till dark to git the bull to leave the buffalo and go back to the fort. The bull warn't satisfied; he kept trying to git the buffalo to git up agin and fight some more! [15]

'Wal,' the mountain man spat into the fire, 'maybe the buffalo war feelin' puny! A tame bull ain't made to match a buffalo, anyways you fix it.'

'Why not, I'd like to know?'

'I'll tell you. Yore tame bull shuts his eyes to charge, and a buffalo keeps his'n wide open.'

'How do you know that?'

The mountain man swelled up like an angry adder. 'Buffalo bull l'arned me, on Cheyenne River. He come after me, and I could mighty near feel his horns in the small of my back. So I tried to dodge. Side-stepped him, and whirled round to see him bust by. But he turned quicker'n scat, and knocked me clean into the river.'

The bull-whacker grinned. 'Feelin' puny that day, war you?'

'Maybeso. But I done got over it. How do *you* feel?'

But before hostilities could follow, a peace-maker would step in. 'Hold on thar, boys! You cain't do yoreselves justice, fightin' on sowbelly. Hold on till ye git some bull-meat under yore belts! Thar's buffalo a-runnin' on Arkansas.' . . .

Then, inevitably, the talk would turn to extraordinary buffalo, and of all these, the white buffalo, rarest of animals, came first. Few men had ever seen a white buffalo, 'one in a million, I reckon.' The Omahas, and the Crows, too, had white buffalo hides — sacred, kept in a bundle by the medicine-man. George Bent, though, claimed to have seen five. One of them was silver-gray in color — white tips on the ends of black hair. Another one was clear white. One was a claybank — dark cream, a three-year-old cow. One, a two-year-old heifer, was dappled gray. And a two-year-old bull was a yellowish fawn color.[16] Injuns claimed the white buffalo war the chief of the herd. He come first, like white daybreak comes afore sunrise. And they thought the albino led the others out of the cave in the Black Hills, Wind Cave, where you can look into the mouth of Mother Earth, and feel her breathe in and out, and see her stone teeth hanging down from the top, and stickin' up from the bottom.

The old-timer would claim he had seen a white buffalo running in a herd — a sure-enough snow-back. Others would scoff, and say he had merely seen an ordinary cow covered with alkali dust. And when that dispute ended, someone would tell the tale of the famous double-toothed, man-eating bull, which chased the Cheyennes up and down the country, busted right into their camps, and devoured men whole. That, of course, was many years behind! The critter had teeth on both jaws, so they say. 'And if you cain't swaller that one, maybeso you will believe that the Sioux killed a cow at Slim Buttes, and when they come to butcher out the calf, it turned out to be human. Calf-woman, they called it. That war in 1850.'[17]

Then there would be stories of buffalo that spoke to men, of buffalo with four horns, of ghost buffalo. And the green-horn would sit gaping and listen to stories about Indian hunters: of how, in old times, the redskins had lured or driven bison over a bluff, to fall broken and maimed into a log corral; of how they would swim into a herd crossing the Missouri, and knife them in the water; of how they ran alongside on snowshoes and lanced buffalo wallowing through deep drifts; of Big Ribs, who jumped from his horse to a bull's back and buried his knife in its flanks; of the Flathead who killed buffalo by throwing stones, cracking them between the eyes; of men who could shoot through one, or two, or even three buffalo with a single arrow; of men who killed buffalo on foot, blinding them with a blanket, and then cutting their throats; of the Indian who lanced a bison, lost his lance, and finally *strangled* the animal! That yarn was vouched for by Father De Smet himself!

But the best story was that of the Arapaho hunter, Circle Runner. He had a white horse, mighty fast, but the Arapaho didn't want him to run buffalo on it. Everybody knows that a white horse is bad medicine in a buffalo hunt. Buffalo don't like white horses, and anyway, they can see one miles away. So the chiefs wouldn't let Circle Runner hunt with the other hunters, unless he would ride a horse of a different color. It was time for the tribal hunt, up near the Big Horns, and it was agin the Injun law for a man to go off alone and hunt on his own hook. Fact is, the Injun soldiers — kind of camp police — had orders to soldier-whip any man caught hunting alone. And soldier-whipping is no joke, you bet.

But Circle Runner was a stubborn man, and needed meat, and he wouldn't give in. He made up his mind to ride his fast horse, soldiers or no soldiers. And so he told his old woman to slip out of camp with him, and away they went, hell-bent to kill meat. Each of them rode a pack-horse, and Circle Runner led his fast-running horse. It was summertime, when bulls are mean. Circle Runner had an old brass-mounted pistol, and a horn full of powder.

He rode up the crick, trying to get the start of the other hunters, and told the old woman to hide in the brush. He left his pack-horse with her. Across the crick was a bunch of bulls.

'First thing, he picked out a fat bull, and banged away. Dropped it, too, and the others hung around, snuffing at the blood on the dead one. That give him time to reload, and he tried another shot. "*Thit!*" the bullet smacked into the bull. The herd began to move. So Circle Runner poured some powder into his pistol, stuck the muzzle to his mouth, and spit a ball into the barrel. Then he smacked the butt on his saddle-horn to sock her down tight. By that time the white horse war alongside the bull. But afore he could shoot, the bull whirled on him.

'The white horse war too quick for the bull, and stayed clear of his horns. The bull war facing him, and Circle Runner got a good look at it. First off, he thought the bull war blind. Thar warn't no eye on the off side — and when he looked at the t'other side, he couldn't see no eye thar nuther. But that bull warn't blind — not a mite. And when that Injun saw how it war, he just about fell off his pony. He pretty near fainted. He war so scairt, he mighty near lost his heart out of his mouth.

'That bull had just *one* eye — and that war spang in the middle of his forehead! And when he turned that eye on Circle Runner, the Injun saw death in that eye.

'The horse must of seen it too. For that white horse whirled round and lit out, tight as he could go. And the bull right after him, with its horns in his tail, you might say. That horse war racin', and Circle Runner didn't try to stop him, you bet. It was the tightest race he ever run. No matter how he dodged and turned, the bull stuck to him. And every time the Injun looked back, he saw that big eye on him. He quit trying to shoot then, and just rode that horse, prayin' like mad.

'Lucky for the old woman, the horse didn't head for the crick. It went straight for the river. Circle Runner didn't know where it war headin', and didn't care. All he wanted war to git away from that One-eye. But he couldn't. The bull war always right thar, stickin' to him like a burr. Sometimes it come fast, and agin it slowed down a mite. But it never quit. And pretty soon that white horse begin to play out. And Circle Runner war too scairt to load his pistol. He thought he war gone, sartain. He let the horse go, and the horse went — lookin' for company.

'He got to the river, but that never stopped him. He went on acrost, as if it had been a puddle. He hardly even wet his feet, he went so fast. But the bull war faster. And then Circle Runner saw a bunch of men horseback — and he knowed they war the Injun soldiers! And he couldn't fool them that he warn't huntin', because he had brung the buffalo right along with him! He knowed they would beat him and kill his horse. He war scairt to death.

'But he war more scairt of the bull than he war of the soldiers. So he headed straight for 'em.

'When they saw him comin', and the buffalo after him, they unlimbered their bows and grabbed a handful of arrers, and come a high-tailin' for that bull. They aimed to kill the meat first, and knock the hindsights off of Circle Runner afterwards. And the bull never stopped. Afore you could say scat, arrers were flyin', stingin' that buffalo.

'"*Chit . . . chit . . . chit!*" they hit him — and that bull stopped suddent like, and stood thar groanin' and heavin', with the feathered ends of the arrers stickin' out of his ribs, movin' his head from side to side, lookin' at the cussed Injuns. And they set thar and looked at him, you bet, with their mouths wide open and their eyes bugged out. And thar he war, swayin' and gruntin' and weavin' from side to side, till all at oncet he lurched, and his knees buckled, and down he went, dead as a nail, and all four legs stiff as yore wipin'-stick. But that big *eye* war still open, and *watchin'!*

'Wal, you bet them soldiers never touched *that* buffalo! They stood around and looked at him. And then an old man spoke up, and they got out some paint, and some red cloth, and some white shells, and edged up and dropped 'em alongside that dead bull. Then they got on their horses and skipped, and clean forgot to go huntin' that day. That's a *fact.*

'Nope. They never whipped Circle Runner. He war big medicine after that. Maybeso they thought he'd been punished enough a'ready. . . .'[18]

Such were the tales of the Trail — those that have come down to us. And when, at length, the old-timer put away his pipe and rolled into his blankets, the greenhorn followed suit, only to lie blinking at the glowing planets and the twinkling stars, wondering and hoping and longing for the chance to try his hand at throwing the biggest game on the prairie.

It would not be long now. The howling of the wolves spoke a promise: the herds were not far off.

CHAPTER IX

Running Meat

Wɪᴛʜ every mile, more and more wolves were seen, trotting along the ridges, following the caravan in packs; for the wolf was a clever creature, and much preferred devouring meat killed by hunters to killing his own. Indians claim that wolves would lead them to game for this very purpose. However that may be, they certainly trailed hunters, both red and white, in order to share in the kill. In those days, they were called 'white wolves,' though a dirty gray in color, except in extreme old age. And as the men had opportunity, they shot at them — not yet having any buffalo to shoot at.

In those days of muzzle-loaders, loading a gun was a slow process for most men, and as a result, they carried their weapons loaded. Teamsters, having their hands full with their long whips, and tiring of toting heavy weapons, commonly stowed them in the tail of the wagon, or under the tilt up front. And all too often, knowing that a gun resting on its barrel might damage the sights, they put the gun into the wagon butt first.

As a result, accidents were common, and almost every caravan of which we have record had one or more men injured by gunshot wounds. The classic story of this sort is that told in Gregg's *Commerce of the Prairies:* an accident that befell a man named Broadus.

In his haste to bring down a particularly large wolf, which was making off over the prairie, Broadus ran to the tail of his moving wagon and began to pull his gun out by the muzzle as he ran. Somehow or other, the gun went off, and the ball shattered the bones of his forearm to bits.

The Captain halted the train, and enquired if there was a surgeon in the caravan. There was none.

Then Charles Bent and the wagon-master urged the injured man to let them amputate, telling him that otherwise it was only a question of days until he would be a dead man.

But the man with the broken arm would not consent. His nerve was shaken, and he refused point-blank to let green hands experiment upon him. And so they made room for him in one of the carriages, and the train moved on. They all regarded him as a dead man. The caravan moved slowly on, until Broadus himself knew that death stared him in the face.

The train halted for a day. Broadus was going to die, they agreed. His arm was so gangrened that spots had appeared well above the place where the amputation should have been performed. The poor fellow, who had suffered agonies as he jolted over the rough prairie trails, and hoping against hope, now began to plead with his mess-mates to perform the operation which he had refused to permit before. It seemed no use to them. It would only kill him outright, and they wanted no hand in his death. But he was so urgent, so persistent, that at last volunteers were called for.

Broadus lay on the buffalo grass, sick with terror and pain, begging the men not to let him die, arguing, crying, pleading, while they stood around and looked on, stirring uneasily, looking at each other, chafing at their inability to help, curious, pitiful, nervous. Kit Carson, then just a boy, was first to offer his services.

Following his lead, shamed out of their inaction, two or three of the men undertook to amputate the arm, assuring each other that they did so only to gratify the dying man. After that there was no delay.

A skinning-knife was whetted to razor sharpness. One of the teamsters brought out an old rusty handsaw from his toolbox, and the back of this was filed to a fine set of teeth. A small fire was built, and the king-bolt of one of the wagons laid upon the coals to heat. When all was ready, they placed the patient on his back on the grass, and a dozen men held him fast while the amateur surgeons went about their terrible deed of mercy.

A tourniquet prevented bleeding. The whetted knife quickly opened the arm to the bone; the bone was immediately sawed off; the white-hot bolt seared the raw stump, taking up the arteries more swiftly than ligatures could have done, had they had any. Then a coating of cool axle-grease was laid over the wound and covered with improvised bandages. The patient was carried to his bed in the shade of one of the wagons. Next day the caravan moved on. The arm healed rapidly, and long before they reached Santa Fe the patient was sound and well.

The operation was performed on Walnut Creek.

Next day about noon the men of that caravan had the usual experience. They heard a confused, dull, murmuring sound, which seemed to come from a distance, and grew louder as they advanced. Not long after, dark masses showed on the Plains ahead, and the cry of 'Buffalo! *Bison! Cibola!*' rang out along the train.

Under the cracking of impatient whips, the wagons rolled along more swiftly, and swung into the circle of the corral, for the midday halt. On every side men were rounding up the loose animals, tightening their girths, reloading weapons, mounting, dashing away. Everywhere was bustle, shouting, laughter. Now they were through with hard bread and salt sowbelly. Now they would feast upon dark-red fresh meat, sweet fat, hump-ribs, marrow, and tongue!

At that season the bulls were fatter than the cows, and much preferred, if not too old. They were sleek and lively, in color (to quote Audubon) 'between a dark umber and a liver-shining brown' back of the hump, and forward bushy with black manes and beards and frontlets. Having shed the wool behind, and retained their long hair before, they looked perfectly ferocious. But they could not run so fast as the cows, now lean and rangy.

As the hunters approached the herd, the nearest bull turned suddenly to face them. The others, too, raised their heads and stood motionless together, staring. Then, as if pricked with a knife, they whirled as one, and lunged away. Immediately, the fright was communicated to the others, and the whole herd was in motion. They rushed off in a mass, shouldering each other, moving in a curious rocking gallop, much like the frantic flight of a bunch of gigantic hogs.

To kill buffalo in the chase, or 'run meat,' as old-timers called it, a man had to have a trained buffalo horse, a sure seat, and skill in using weapons on horseback. An untrained horse would not willingly approach a bison, and — if he did — was likely to be caught unprepared, if a wounded bull jerked round to hook him. An animal unused to fire-arms might also take fright, jump, and destroy his rider's aim, as the gun went off. And even a trained horse had to be swift, and able to endure a run of miles. A speedy cow might lead a man a chase of ten or twenty miles before he could come up with her.

Many of the best buffalo-chasers were Indian-trained, and old-timers preferred them. They could generally be recognized by their split ears — a mark by which Indians distinguished such animals on the Southern Plains. These horses were rarely used for ordinary purposes — but were pampered and maintained only for hunting — or war. Horses had no grain on the prairie, and their strength and spirit had to be conserved. Their master's dinner — and even his life — might depend upon their speed and agility.

In the hurly-burly of the chase, a sure seat was indispensable. And a sure seat meant more than the ability to stick to a saddle. Old-timers often unsaddled and rode bareback after buffalo, in order to make their horses as quick and agile as possible. They also dispensed with bridles, using only a halter, or a rope knotted about the lower jaw, with which to stop the horse. They had no need of reins to guide him, for a trained pony knew his work; such animals, when turned loose, would haze buffalo over the prairie for the fun of it, as a cow pony will haze cattle, even without a rider. Such control as was needed was exercised by the pressure of the horseman's knees, or by leaning his weight towards the side to which he wished the horse to go. Riding in that way, a man could anticipate the movements of his horse by the feel of his muscles, and the two became, in effect, one creature.

Such bareback riding at the dead run in a smothering cloud of dust, over unknown ground, among dog-holes and across gullies, while loading and firing and anticipating the movements of the horse as it charged warily among the frantic bulls, was no pastime for amateurs. Jogging along the Trail beside the wagons, or going for a canter in the park, proved poor training for the buffalo hunt. To run meat, a man had to be able to *ride*.

More, he had to handle weapons dexterously. For the buffalo, big as it was, was hard to kill, and unless hit in the heart or spine, seemed indifferent to bullets, as to weapons of any kind. The lance — a six-foot stave with a three-foot blade — was quicker, but demanded expert hands, a stout wrist and arm. The Mexicans preferred this weapon — which was 'always loaded!'

The Indian's short bow was excellent for the purpose, and many white men, who had lived with Indians, used it on occasion. Made of horn, *bois d'arc*, or hickory — the hope of capturing a hickory ox-bow was a major incentive for attacking wagon trains — the bow was tough, strong, and short enough to be handled with ease in the saddle. Indians were right-handed, as a rule, and therefore shot to the left, and so mounted their ponies from the right side. They were incredibly quick, as anyone who has timed an old hunter killing buffalo or cattle can testify. A skilled hunter could loose an arrow once a second, for he had no need to aim at close range. The quiver was slung under his left arm, handy to his right-hand fingers, but he often grasped half a dozen arrows in his bow-hand for greater speed. Good bowmen sometimes dropped a dozen buffalo before their horses were winded — and each with a single arrow!

White men generally used firearms: rifles, carbines, repeaters — light weapons for choice, with large bore and short barrels for close work, throwing heavy slugs. Those who used muzzle-loaders never bothered with ramrods, but carried powder loose in their coat-pockets, and the bullets in their mouths. At such close range, the size of the charge did not count. So they poured in the powder by guess, dropped the wet bullets on top, and sent the charge home by striking the butt on the horn of the saddle. A wet bullet was supposed to stick to the powder, for the muzzle was not depressed until the moment of firing. A dry ball, however, would roll towards the muzzle, and if it did, an explosion followed, which might maim or kill the hunter or his horse. The famous mountain man, Fitzpatrick, earned his name Broken Hand in such an accident.

But the Colt's revolving pistol, Dragoon model, was the favorite weapon for running meat. It gained adherents everywhere, from the time of the Mexican War on. Unlike the old-fashioned pistol, it could be cocked at the moment of firing, by pulling back the hammer with the thumb as the weapon was thrown down to fire. This prevented many an accident, and also allowed the hunter to use his left hand to control his mount.

Thus, a seasoned hunter, tossing his hat off, and tying his long hair with a handkerchief around his head, would jump on his Split-ear, and bending his knees, push them under the lariat tied loosely about the animal's barrel. In that position he was securely fastened to the bare back of the horse; yet, if he wished to dismount, or free himself in case of a fall, he had only to straighten his legs, and the rope released him instantly.

Riding so, or with shortened stirrups, and armed with a lance, rifle, or revolving pistol, he was ready to 'make meat come,' and in one day provide food for a whole wagon train. He and his horse were a team of trained acrobats, who thought and acted as one. A daring young man.

Giving rein, such a rider trusted to his horse. The pony, with ears set back and long tail flagging the wind, knew his business perfectly, soon laid his master alongside the racing buffalo, and held the pace — not ten feet distant — until the hunter, without aiming, and trusting only to his trained sense of direction, fired down and forward, trying to pierce the bull's heart, or smash his spine.

The buffalo was a vital creature, hard to kill, and even when shot through the heart might run on a hundred yards or more before he fell — records of the hunt are full of such cases. Therefore, the hunter had to *know* where his ball struck. Then, knowing he had made his kill, he could swing his weight slightly to one side, the pony would catch the signal and veer in that direction, bring his master alongside a new victim, and the two made another kill. Experienced men did not waste time, or get too near wounded animals, unless these required another shot to finish them. It was wise to kill quickly, before the horse tired — not merely to spare the animal, but because the moment a bull began to tire and lag, it was likely to turn and attack its tormentors.

The greenhorn might, or might not, be instructed in all this theory before he reached buffalo country. But theory and practice are two things. And when the novice asked the old-timer about hunting, and casually inquired as to the dangers of the 'sport,' he was likely to be taken aback at the candid reply:

'Runnin' meat dangerous? Wal, yes. I reckon it is, if you come right down to it. Specially if thar's a greenhorn along. Fact is, the greenhorns are more dangerous than the bulls!'

That statement was true, though the greenhorn himself might think it a joke. One day Will Comstock, the famous scout, was watching a flock of greenhorns chasing a lone bull along a crawling caravan, and proposed to a comrade that they join the chase and put the bull out of his misery — afore the greenhorns scared him to death!

The greenhorns, galloping wildly over the prairie, and firing even more wildly from a distance of fifty yards behind, filled the air with their flying lead. Will's pardner, watching this performance from the wagons, expressed the opinion that joining such a chase would be too dangerous.

Will snorted. 'Wagh! Come on. The closter we are to the bull, the safer we'll be.' He rode swiftly out, fired a single shot, and dropped the animal. The greenhorns, riding up, were amazed to learn that only one bullet could be found in the huge carcass, and spent the rest of the day arguing as to which one of them had fired it!

Too often, the greenhorn rode an untrained horse, and exhausted it before he reached the herd, instead of getting as near as possible at a walk, before spurring into a gallop. Even if trained, the horse would be nervous, uncertain what to make of the unfamiliar signals of its master, and excited by the nervousness of the man as well, to say nothing of being overloaded with a heavy California tree and Spanish bridle. A horse unused to buffalo and the sound of firearms would never close on the buffalo, and long-range shooting was apt to prove ineffective.

Shooting from the saddle of a running horse at a moving,

doubling, dodging mark was novel and hard for the beginner, and the size of the buffalo offered such a broad target that he was apt to forget that his lead would be thrown away unless he placed his shots with care. The result was that he commonly dashed away the moment he saw a herd, with his horse in a trot and himself in a gallop, brandishing a deadly cocked pistol, a menace to every living thing within range — except the buffalo he was after!

Such men met with a variety of adventures. Here follow typical examples:

He blazed away, time after time, throwing his lead into the huge bulk of the bull, astonished that it did not fall, unable to hit the vital spots. The greenhorn was naturally sensitive to ridicule, and he knew well how the men would laugh at him if he returned unsuccessful. He had come hundreds of miles to kill buffalo, and he intended to do it, now or never. And so he kept going, spurring his weary horse after the herd, mile after mile after mile, until the pony, exhausted, overheated, and used up, played out completely, and stood covered with lather, heaving, utterly stove up. Too late the greenhorn realized that he had ruined his horse! Sadder — if not wiser — he would set out afoot to plod all those weary miles back to the Trail, where he would be told that 'the idee is to *shoot* buffalo, not run 'em down!' He would have time to ponder the lesson as he plodded all the way to Santa Fe.

Sometimes, of course, the greenhorn, though new to the Plains, was nevertheless a shot and a horseman. Such a man would place his shots, and find his mark. Then, if not dropped in its tracks, the wounded bull might whirl, quick as lightning, and throwing its horns under the belly of the horse, toss him over and down, gore him, trample him, and his rider also. The neck of a buffalo bull was quite strong enough to lift a horse in the air, and its horns were sharp and deadly. If the bull confined its fury to the horse, the man was lucky, and lucky too, if the falling horse, in its somersault, did not crush him. Sometimes he staggered to his feet, bruised and shaken, with a broken gun, and no cover, only to find himself on the horns of the furious buffalo. There could be only one end to such an incident.

Even the best of hunters had falls. Frémont tells how Kit Carson's horse 'fell headlong, but sprang up and joined the flying herd. Though considerably hurt, he had the good fortune to break no bones; and Maxwell, who was mounted on a fleet hunter, captured the runaway after a hard chase. He was on the point of shooting him, to avoid the loss of his bridle (a handsomely mounted Spanish one) when he found that his horse was able to come up with him.' To avoid the loss of the horse, some adopted the custom of the Indian warrior, who tied one end of a lariat about the horse's neck, the other about his own waist, and carried the slack coiled and tucked up under his belt, where it would play out in case of a fall and stop the horse. Either way, when a horse went down, there was always a chance of smashing a thigh, or a pelvis — injuries for which there was no remedy on the Plains.

But Kit Carson never found running buffalo half so dangerous as the greenhorns did. They were their own worst enemies. Theodore R. Davis tells of a hunt he witnessed in the Arkansas Valley not far from the Santa Fe Trail, in 1869.[19] The inexperienced hunters had wounded a savage bull, which turned and charged one of the party. The greenhorn's horse, without waiting for instructions, wheeled and raced away with the bull right at his heels. The wind caught at the brim of the greenhorn's hat. He felt it going. His left hand was busy with the bridle reins. In his right hand he held a cocked pistol. Instinctively, he put up his right hand to hold his hat. The pistol discharged. The hat went one way, the pistol the other, the horse jumped with fright, and the rider tumbled forward upon the animal's

neck, and began slipping to the ground. In this predica-
ment, tragedy was averted by one of the greenhorn's friends,
who stopped the bull with a single shot. Fortunately, the
pistol bullet had hit the hat, not the greenhorn's skull.

In the snow, running meat was even more hazardous.
Palliser tells how he killed a cow and a bull, and then rode
after 'an uncommonly fine fat cow. She gave me an awful
chase, turning and doubling incessantly. My little horse
. . . began to show symptoms of distress; but I could not
manage to get a broadside shot. At last, making one
more push, I got pretty close behind her, and raising myself
in my stirrups, fired down upon her . . . the bullet breaking
her spine. My horse, unable to stop himself, rolled right
over her, making a complete somersault, and sending me,
gun and all, flying clean over both of them into a snowdrift.
I leaped up, ran back to my horse, which I caught without
much difficulty and was glad to find no more hurt than myself. My gun was filled with snow, of course, but otherwise
uninjured.'[20]

But the greenhorn was not content with unavoidable
adventures like these. He had a knack for putting himself
afoot, and regularly did it in a way of his own. The method
seems strange, yet it was common, however surprising to the
man who used it. The greenhorn did not lose his horse — he
shot it!

Wild with buffalo fever on his first chase, half-choked
with dust, half-blinded by the gravel and dirt flying into
his face from the heels of the scurrying bison, trying to
manage his frightened horse, keep his seat and his stirrups,
watch the buffalo, take aim, fire, and remember all the
advice he had been given, the poor fellow had too much to
handle.

Perhaps his horse stumbled, or dropped suddenly down
the side of a gully, or scrambled up the other side. In either
case, the greenhorn was thrown off balance, felt himself

slipping, and grabbed wildly at the mane, or clutched the slippery saddlehorn, thinking only of hanging on, forgetting the cocked pistol in his hand. Without knowing how he did it, he pulled the trigger — and blew out the brains of his horse!

With startling suddenness, the horse vanished from beneath him, he parted with his saddle, lost his gun, and sailed through the air. That moment of calm surprise ended abruptly, as he felt himself mauled by a heavy blunt instrument — the earth. Looking up in amazement he might see a dead horse falling on him from the sky, and only escape by rolling his bruised body out of the way. If not killed, or seriously injured, he would get up then, and stand with shaking knees, watching the buffalo disappear over the horizon in a cloud of dust. At length he came out of his daze, collected his wits, gathered up his pistol, hat, and bridle, and started on his walk back to camp. Perhaps he was able to recover his saddle as well, and lug it along. In that case, he might hope to buy another mount for the long trip to Santa Fe.

On reaching the wagons, worn out and shamefaced, he was sure to be gravely approached by a tall Santa Fe trader. Without batting an eye, the trader would courteously inquire whether the greenhorn had brought in any buffalo hides to sell.

Shamefaced, the greenhorn would answer, 'No.'

'Too bad,' the trader would reply. 'You see, at present there is no demand for horse-robes. Of course, there will be. There's bound to be — if *you* stay on the Plains long enough!'

The chorus of guffaws that followed taught the stranger something of the hearty, but not unfriendly, elaborate humor of the Southwest. . . .

Another common experience while running buffalo was to get lost. A man used to the woodlands found himself literally all at sea on the plains. However skilful he might be in his woodcraft, he found it useless there. None of the rules for lost men applied. He could not follow the streams down to the river — for no streams were visible, few of them having any timber to mark their courses. He could not look for moss on the north side of trees, and so determine the points of the compass, for there were no trees. He could not take his bearings from the landmarks, for no landmarks existed. He could not, as a rule, even follow the trail he had made in reaching his lost position — for the grass and the wind left few traces to be seen. On the boundless flat plains of western Kansas, when a greenhorn was lost, he was *lost!* He had left no more trail, it seemed, than if he had flown to the spot!

On a cloudy day, or after night came on, his sense of direction would desert him, and he might wander in a circle during the hours of darkness. The level grassy plains curved regularly, like the sea, and a lone man could be seen for only a few miles in such country. Firing his gun seldom helped, in a region where the wind was always blowing. His friends were far away, and could not hear; while, in Indian country, his enemies might be nearer, within earshot. The grass might as well have been water. All around there was nothing. Only the grass and sky. And — of course — the lost greenhorn.

If he had friends, they generally found him. If he kept his head, he might remember whether he had ridden north, or south, from the Trail, wait for sunrise, head back, and find his wagons again. But sometimes he lost his head. Then, it might be, a tragedy followed. In the nature of things, the details of such tragedies are hard to come by. But, if nothing else happened to the tyro on his first hunt, he was almost sure to have a good scare! Running meat was a ticklish business.

But there was another method of killing buffalo, and one

more congenial to men from the woodlands, who were accustomed to shooting deer on foot. This was known as approaching, still-hunting, or stalking, and consisted in taking advantage of any cover the country afforded, and crawling up-wind to some point within easy range of the grazing herd. It was better adapted to broken country than to the level parts of the Plains, and to other seasons than summer, when the bulls were rutting. The fellow who was handy with a rifle, free style or layin' to a chunk, was certain to prefer approaching to firing off-hand from the saddle. But if the country was sufficiently broken, a man might even stalk buffalo on horseback.

It was best to advance straight towards the herd, up-wind, and slowly. The buffalo's sight was none of the keenest, and when grazing, the thick thatch of hair on his head interfered with it anyhow. A buffalo was much less likely to notice a man coming directly towards him than one moving across his line of sight. The chief danger in approaching buffalo was that a man's horse might run off, leaving him afoot. Hunters therefore took good care to hobble their animals before beginning their crawl towards the meat. Once in a blue moon, there would be something — a bush or stone — to which the horse could be tied. But such things were mighty scarce on the buffalo plains.

Once within range, the greenhorn might take aim at his leisure. But even here, he had something to learn. Ruxton has put it best:

'The first attempts of a greenhorn to kill a buffalo are invariably unsuccessful. He sees before him a mass of flesh, nearly five feet in depth from the top of the hump to the brisket, and consequently imagines that, by planting his ball midway between these points, it must surely reach the vitals. Nothing, however, is more erroneous than the impression; for to "throw a buffalo in his tracks," which is the phrase for making a clean shot, he must be struck but a few inches above the brisket, behind the shoulder, where alone, unless the spine be divided, a death-shot will reach the vitals. I once shot a bull, the ball passing directly through the very center of the heart and tearing a hole sufficiently large to insert the finger, which ran upwards of half a mile before it fell, and yet the ball had passed completely through the animal, cutting its heart almost in two. I also saw eighteen shots, and half of them muskets, deliberately fired into an old bull, at six paces, and some of them passing through the body, the poor animal standing the whole time, and making feeble attempts to charge. The nineteenth shot, with the muzzle touching his body, brought him to the ground. The head of the buffalo bull is so thickly covered with coarse matted hair that a ball fired at half a dozen paces will not penetrate the skull through the shaggy front-lock. I have frequently attempted this with a rifle carrying twenty-five balls to the pound, but never once succeeded.'[21]

Hard to kill — that was the only word for a buffalo, and the greenhorn was likely to believe, after expending a dozen shots, that there was something in those Injun yarns about ghost buffalo! For, if the hunter remained concealed after firing, the buffalo might remain standing, offering him a plain target for one shot after another.

Many have described their experiences in approaching the bison; the best account is that given by Francis Parkman, who encamped on the Arkansas River for some time to shoot buffalo, on his return from Bent's Fort to the settlements:

' ... We had nothing to do but amuse ourselves. Our tent was within a rod of the river, if the broad sand-beds, with a scanty stream of water coursing here and there along their surface, deserve to be dignified with the name of river. The vast flat plains on either side were almost on a level with the sand-beds, and they were bounded in the distance by low, monotonous hills, parallel to the course of the

stream. All was one expanse of grass; there was no wood in
view, except some trees and stunted bushes upon two
islands which rose from the wet sands of the river. Yet far
from being dull and tame, the scene was often a wild and
animated one; for twice a day, at sunrise and at noon, the
buffalo came issuing from the hills, slowly advancing in
their grave processions to drink at the river. All our amuse-
ments were to be at their expense. An old buffalo bull is a
brute of unparalleled ugliness. At first sight of him every
feeling of pity vanishes. The cows are much smaller and of
a gentler appearance, as becomes their sex. While in this
camp we forebore to attack them, leaving to Henry Chatil-
lon, who could better judge their quality, the task of killing
such as we wanted for use; but against the bulls we waged
an unrelenting war. Thousands of them might be slaughtered without causing any detriment to the species, for
their numbers greatly exceed those of the cows; it is the
hides of the latter alone which are used for the purposes of
commerce and for making the lodges of the Indians; and the
destruction among them is therefore greatly disproportion-
ate.

'Our horses were tired, and we now usually hunted on
foot. While we were lying on the grass after dinner, smoking, talking, or laughing, . . . one of us would look up and
observe, far out on the plains beyond the river, certain
black objects slowly approaching. He would inhale a parting whiff from the pipe, then rising lazily, take his rifle,
which leaned against the cart, throw over his shoulder the
strap of his pouch and powder-horn, and with his moccasins in his hand, walk across the sand towards the opposite side of the river. This was very easy; for though the
sands were about a quarter of a mile wide, the water was
nowhere more than two feet deep. The farther bank was
about four or five feet high, and quite perpendicular, being
cut away by the water in the spring. Tall grass grew along

its edge. Putting it aside with his hand, and cautiously looking through it, the hunter can discern the huge shaggy back
of the bull slowly swaying to and fro, as with his clumsy
swinging gait, he advances towards the water. The buffalo
have regular paths by which they come down to drink.
Seeing at a glance along which of these his intended victim
is moving, the hunter crouches under the bank fifteen or
twenty yards, it may be, of the point where the path enters
the river. Here he sits down quietly on the sand. Listening
intently, he hears the heavy monotonous tread of the approaching bull. The moment after, he sees a motion among
the long weeds and grass just at the spot where the path is
channelled through the bank. An enormous black head is
thrust out, the horns just visible amid the mass of tangled
mane. Half sliding, half plunging, down comes the buffalo
upon the river bed below. He steps out in full sight upon
the sands. Just before him a runnel of water is gliding, and
he bends his head to drink. You may hear the water as it
gurgles down his capacious throat. He raises his head, and
the drops trickle from his wet beard. He stands with an air
of stupid abstraction, unconscious of the lurking danger.
Noiselessly the hunter cocks his rifle. As he sits upon the
sand, his knee is raised, and his elbow rests upon it, that he
may level his heavy weapon with a steadier aim. The stock
is at his shoulder; his eye ranges along the barrel. Still he
is in no haste to fire. The bull, with slow deliberation, begins his march over the sands to the other side. He advances
his foreleg, and exposes to view a small spot, denuded of
hair, just behind the point of his shoulder; upon this the
hunter brings the sight of his rifle to bear; lightly and deli-
cately his finger presses the hair trigger. The spiteful crack
of the rifle responds to his touch, and instantly in the middle
of the bare spot appears a small red dot. The buffalo
shivers; death has overtaken him, he cannot tell from
whence; still he does not fall, but walks heavily forward, as

if nothing had happened. Yet before he has gone far out upon the sand, you see him stop; he totters; his knees bend under him, and his head sinks forward to the ground. Then his whole bulk sways to one side; he rolls over on the sand, and dies with a scarcely perceptible struggle.'[22]

But the buffalo did not always die so quietly, especially when unskilful fingers pulled the trigger. Then the dying struggles of the great beast were painful to witness: the bull resisted the drag of death with all his might, as if he knew that, once down, he was finished. Shot through heart or lungs, with blood pouring from his mouth, protruding tongue, and rolling, bloodshot eyes, glazing with death, he would brace himself, swaying from side to side, stamp impatiently, and lift his shaggy head to bellow out his agony. Still he tries to keep on his feet, spreading his legs as he begins to sway and roll. His head swings from side to side, as if looking for his unseen enemy. Blood spurts from mouth and nostrils, his legs tremble, his body rocks. Then, suddenly, it becomes rigid. A convulsive shudder shakes it, and letting go his last breath in a grunting gasp, the great bull tumbles on his side, with stiff, outstretched legs.

To behold such a battle with death, the hunter had to crawl up gullies, creep on all fours behind hills, or even drag himself on his face over the level prairie, through pricklypear and sandburs. And in the course of his maneuvers, the greenhorn was likely to have the fright of his life.

Webb tells how once, when stalking bison afoot, he suddenly found himself between two herds, both of which stopped to look at him. 'Every bushy head in both herds was turned directly towards me, and so near that I could see their glaring eyes, sharp horns, and vicious appearance. I dropped in the grass and crawled away as carefully as I had formerly approached them. After a few moments they turned their heads and *walked* off on their course. I crawled to my mule, mounted, and started for camp, and calm re-

flection convinced me that I had been badly scared.' [23]
But eventually, somehow, horseback or afoot, the green-horn brought down his buffalo. That was a proud moment. He felt that he had won his spurs, that he was a genuine plainsman, at last. He would walk up and look at that mountain of flesh — and like the bird-dog that caught the rabbit — sheepishly wonder what to do with it!

Butchering was an art for which, in all probability, he had no knack as yet. In his haste to display the triumph of his skill, he might be satisfied to hack off the tail, and tie it to his saddle-horn!

If already well supplied with meat, hunters were often content to take only the choicest cuts. Of these, the tongue was most easily butchered out. Since the buffalo's jaws were likely to be closed, and perhaps rigid, the proper method was to slash out the skin between the prongs of the jawbone, pull the tongue through the opening so made, and cut it off.

The hump might be taken — by skinning down each side of the shoulders and cutting away the meat and chopping off the hump-ribs (vertical projections of the vertebrae above the spine) with a hatchet. The large bones containing marrow were very choice parts. And the *dépouille*, or 'back-fat,' a strip of fatty matter lying along the backbone from the shoulder-blade on, was hardly less appetizing. This piece, if scalded for a few minutes in hot grease, would keep a long time, hanging on a wagon. Slices were cut off from time to time from this tasty 'Injun bread,' and it was never a long time between slices!

Men trained in Indian methods were likely to begin by opening the belly and getting out some of the warm, raw liver. On this they sprinkled a sauce squeezed from the gall-bladder, and refreshed themselves. Buffalo gall was something of a stimulant, and a man could get quite a glow, if he took it straight on an empty stomach. Buffalo-hunters did not wait for the liver to cool; their 'idee was to eat it while it's hot!' If time permitted, they would take also the heart, kidneys, and intestines; first pulling these between their fingers to get rid of the contents, and knitting the long tubes into a loppy chain. This part of the butchering was likely to disgust the greenhorn. He was usually content with the other portions.

Old-timers used to urge the novice to be sure and bring in the liver. A story was common on the plains about three greenhorns who cut open a cow and tried to find this organ — about the size of a saddlebag — but could not, and returned to camp without it!

If meat was needed, the hunters made a thorough job of butchering, and, having propped the cow on her belly by stretching out the legs front and back, cut the hide in two along the backbone, peeled down the hide on both sides, working rapidly, and allowing much of the meat to remain on the hide itself, especially on the belly. These bits of meat, taken off with a dubber, made excellent soup, and when dried looked rather like potato chips.

The hunters then cut away the outer blanket of flesh from the back and sides of the animal; this part was taken off in one piece, and called the 'fleece.' The front quarters were taken off next, the hind quarters removed at the hip joints, the hump removed, and the remaining meat stripped from the ribs. Having cut the ribs free all round, they were chopped off from the backbone in a slab with a hatchet, or broken off with one of the leg-bones used as a club. The insides were put into the paunch (turned wrong-side out) along with the fat. What little remained was left to the wolves. To the Indians, even the content of the stomach was not entirely useless; they used it as a poultice.

When the meat was brought to camp, it did not take long to have the fire ready. Then the men gathered round, and feasting was the order of the day. Tongues were boiled, hump-ribs and marrowbones roasted before the embers, the fat-covered *dépouille* took the place of bread and butter, and yard upon yard of *boudin* (the intestine containing the chyme) were sizzling on the coals like hissing snakes. Kidneys and tongues and hearts baked to delicious tenderness in the hot ashes. The other parts went to contribute their various flavors to make son-of-a-gun stew.

The fleece and muscles generally were not eaten fresh, but were jerked, or dried, in the sun and wind. This process was known as making meat. The flesh was cut into thin sheets and hung on the wagons to dry, like so much washing. Some of these sheets were no bigger than a man's hand; others — parts of the fleece, for example — might be big as a face towel, and stretched upon skewers of plum or willow a foot long and about the size of lead-pencils. Men who understood this art never cut the meat across the grain; they tried to keep the rich juices from escaping, let them dry inside. On the high, dry plains, making meat did not take long; after a few days' travel the skewered sheets would be a dark brown, and stiff as a board. Then they would be stacked in a wagon, where they would be dry, and would keep indefinitely. But, if there was time, even this dried meat would be made into pemmican — roasted and pulverized with a stone hammer to a brown dust, or fibrous shreds, mixed with dried, powdered cherries and melted tallow, and tightly packed in a rawhide case.

But on the evening of the buffalo hunt, such labors had to wait. Then every man was busy chawing on hump-ribs and succulent *boudin*, filling himself with incredible quantities of meat. The hard exercise, the fresh air, the tasty food made everyone cheerful and happy. Buffalo fat, unlike the fat of cattle, could be devoured by the pound without any unpleasant effects. And it was a proverb on the plains that a man could eat his own weight of buffalo meat, and never have a bellyache!

After the first fierce hunger had been satisfied, horse-play and jokes were in fashion, and the greenhorns came in for their share of the fun. Even the men who had succeeded in killing a buffalo were not allowed to forget that others had done it before them. Webb tells how the Captain of his caravan came round and asked the men of his mess if they could furnish guards to sit up with a man who needed watching.

'"What is the matter?" we asked. "Who is sick? How many do you want?"

'"Well, two or three will do. If more are required, you can call. Webb has killed a buffalo cow, and I fear he will become so excited over it that he will get beside himself and keep the whole camp awake all night. I want someone to look after him and talk on other subjects until he gets quieted down, so it will be safe to leave him alone."' [24]

Such jests were common.

But, as the feasting went on, other moods developed. Men full of fresh meat became touchy and combative as the bulls they had killed. Invariably, the night after the first buffalo hunt, the camp was the scene of several fights. The fury of the bison was somehow communicated to their slayers. Maybe there is something in the Indian's idea that the spirit of a creature slain enters into his killer. Certainly, on the Santa Fe Trail, buffalo and bloodshed went together.

When the campfires had died to ashes, and the gorged wayfarers lay in their blankets, they were conscious of other woes than their own, and forgot the snarling of the wolves in the distance. For the buffalo hunt had its note of pathos, too.

Orphaned calves, left behind by the fleeing herd, would take up with the hunters who had shot their mothers, and attaching themselves to the horses, faithfully follow them back to the wagons. These hungry little fellows, udderless and lonesome, blundered among the cattle in the darkness, bawling for their suppers.

PART IV

The Fork in the Trail

CHAPTER X

Pawnee Rock

THE buffalo range was Indian country.

From Walnut Creek, the Trail led southwestward up the left bank of the river over a level prairie usually teeming with buffalo. As each hour's march brought the caravan nearer to the hostile Indians, the greenhorns became more nervous. One alarm followed another. A small party out hunting would come tearing in, chased by a band — of buffalo! As soon as the wagons corralled for the night, three hunters would gallop back yelling that a hundred, probably of the same enemy, were coming on the run. Before people had digested this fearful news, a lone horseman dashed up on his heaving mount, shouting: 'Injuns! Injuns! I've barely got away from a couple of the red devils. They run me clear to camp.'

'"To arms! To arms!" resounded from every quarter — and just then a wolf, attracted by the fumes of broiling buffalo bones, sent up a most hideous howl across the creek. "Someone in distress!" was instantly shouted. "To his relief!" vociferated the crowd — and off they bolted, one and all, arms in hand, hurly-burly — leaving the camp entirely unprotected; so that had an enemy been at hand, and approached from the opposite direction, they might easily have taken possession of the wagons. Before they had all returned, however, a couple of hunters came in and laughed very heartily at the expense of the first alarmist, whom they had just chased into the camp.' [25]

False alarms showing the lack of discipline in the caravan were alarming enough to the Captain. Others might laugh. But next morning, perhaps, someone out looking for buffalo would come upon a dry buffalo wallow. Within its narrow earthwork he would see four small piles of exploded rifle-caps; the ground around would be littered with arrows; and there would be a beaten ring of pony-tracks about the wallow, two hundred yards distant. Even the most careless traveller, after that, was secretly anxious. All knew they had reached the territory of hostile tribes.

Even though no Indian sign were discovered when the wagons corralled at the base of Pawnee Rock, all realized that they were now in the danger zone.

Pawnee Rock, sometimes called Painted Rock, or Rock Point, was the most famous landmark on the Santa Fe Trail. It was a kind of promontory, projecting towards the river (two miles distant) from the high prairies to the north. Its soft sandstone face was abrupt and some forty feet high.

Like Inscription Rock in the Southwest, or Independence Rock on the Oregon Trail, Pawnee Rock served as a register of the names of those who passed by. The soft sandstone invited every man to scratch his name there, and men from the woodlands, accustomed since boyhood to engage in the great American pastime of whittling sticks, found relief from enforced inactivity on the treeless plains by inscribing their names thereon.

From the top of that rusty knob of ferruginous sandstone, the visitor could see the swift, winding river, with its white sand hills to the south, and endless high prairie to the northward, in that clear air imagining distant objects much nearer than they actually were. Old-timers had their jokes up there:

'Do you see that caravan away yonder?'

'Yes.'

'Well, that's the train that passed the Rock yestiddy.

The air's so clear on the Plains, it takes you overnight to see that fur!'

By day the meadow larks cheered the plain with their confident singing, and the river bottoms were alive with yellow-headed blackbirds, cowbirds, and immense flocks of Baltimore orioles. The grass was brightened with prairie indigo, clumps of plum and cherry bushes. At night a man could avoid pools, being warned by the shrill cries of the killdeer which haunted them. Such was the country about the Pawnee Rock.

Various legends were current to account for its name. General Philip St. George Cooke described the Rock as 'a natural monument inscribed with the names of all the fools that pass this way,' and says that it gained its name from the siege of a small party of Pawnees by the Comanches. The rocky mound was impregnable, but the Pawnees were parched with thirst. They let their horses' blood and drank it, then made a desperate effort to cut their way out, but were killed to a man. Afterward the Comanches, according to the General, were filled with admiration for their courageous foes, and erected on the summit of the Rock the small pyramid of stones to be seen there! This story — inspired, as the General suggests, by a supper of two pounds of the fattest cow that ever ran on the prairie — and, quite probably, by two bottles of claret as well — is told of so many buttes in the West that the judicious now give it little credence. Another story is that the Pawnees fought the Cheyennes at this point. Another story offered by Colonel Henry Inman derives the name of the Rock from a false alarm one night when the boy Kit Carson killed his own saddle mule, having mistaken it for a marauding Indian. Inman quotes Kit himself as his authority for the tale, of which there is no other version.

The Pawnees were great fighters, and in the early days of the Santa Fe trade sometimes attacked the caravans, and very possibly near this spot, since their trail from their villages in Nebraska came down past the Blue Hills and Pawnee Rock to Oklahoma, the Texas Panhandle, and New Mexico. Quite possibly, the Rock takes its name from this fact. The Indians would naturally make camp at the Rock beside the river, on their way north or south.

In those days, the Pawnees were very numerous and warlike, but they have been blamed for too many raids of which they were not guilty. Perhaps this was because they ranged along the Oregon Trail in the days of the great migration. Perhaps, too, they were talked of more than other tribes, merely because their name was easy to pronounce!

Certainly their history proves that they seldom made war so far south as the Santa Fe Trail. In old Spanish records, they are not mentioned as making much trouble, and the branded horses they brought home from the Southwest before 1800 were captured or traded from the Comanches.

Most of the later raids for which they were blamed were made by mounted Indians, and this in itself is evidence that those Indians were not Pawnees, for the Pawnees generally went to war on foot, packing their dried meat, extra moccasins, and arrows on one of their wolflike dogs. As everyone knows, the Comanches were great traders, fences, kidnappers, and thieves. They were the gangsters of the Southern Plains, and seldom fought unless for booty.

Sometimes (as in 1832) the Pawnees fought with the Comanches and whipped them on the Arkansas River. Sometimes (as in 1828) the Pawnees raided wagon trains on the Santa Fe Trail. But smallpox terribly reduced their numbers in the thirties, and after 1840 they were generally too busy with Indian enemies to make much trouble for the white man.

Before the Treaty of 1825, they raided to the south more frequently. One thing they went after in those days was captives. One of the bands of Pawnees, the Skidi, sacrificed human beings to Evening Star. This happened as often as Morning Star appeared to a man in a dream and commanded him to secure the victim for this sacrifice. The man who had had such a vision went to the keeper of the Morning Star bundle and was given the warrior's costume and equipment for his expedition. He led the party until he had captured the young girl from the enemy.

The victim was always young and healthy and a maiden. She was kept by herself, fattened on the best of food, and treated with great kindness. Nobody let her know that she was to die.

After four days of feasting and dancing, the Pawnees painted her all over, half red and half black. Then four warriors led her to the end of the village where a scaffold had been set up. This scaffold was rather like a football goal post, except that three cross-poles were lashed across the bottom like the rungs of a ladder, and firewood stacked beneath.

Every woman was there with her digging stick; every man had a bow and arrow. They lifted the captive up and spread-eagled her, tying her hands to the top crossbar, and her feet to the one below.

Then the wood was set afire. But before the flames reached the victim, a warrior shot her through the heart. Then everyone shot into or struck the body. All the people passed their hands through the smoke and rubbed it on their bodies, praying for health, success, and good crops.

In the spring of 1817, a young Comanche girl was led out to be sacrificed. In the crowd stood a young Pawnee warrior, Pitalesharo, or Man Chief. He had told his father that he did not approve of the ceremony, and his father, knowing that his son was a man of valor, foresaw what would happen. The young man had taken great risks on the warpath, so that people, when they saw him, wondered whether he was really living. He seemed as good as dead. Therefore, when he saw the frightened girl lifted to the scaffold, he sang his war song.

> Let me see, is this real,
> This life I am living?
> You gods who live everywhere!
> Let me see, is this real,
> This life I am living?

That morning he had a chance to get an answer to his question. He could not endure that cruelty. He rushed forward and cut down the girl before the astonished warrior with the bow could shoot her or the fire reach her feet.

All the Pawnees were thunderstruck by such unusual daring and stood without moving while he led her away, put her on a horse, and mounted his own. The two rode together until they reached the Arkansas River within sight of the camps of her people. There, Man Chief turned her loose.

The Pawnees, however, claim that she died all the same that summer, having been anointed with the paint of sacrifice.

When Man Chief returned home no one offered to punish him. Everyone regarded his action as one inspired by the gods. They still sing a song in commemoration of his extraordinary courage. The words of the song mention the father's foreknowledge of his son's action.

> Well, he foretold this,
> Well, he foretold this,
> Yes, he foretold this;
>   I, Pitale-sharu,
> Am here.
> Well, he foretold this,
> Yes, he foretold this,
>   I, Pitale-sharu,
> Am here.

Somewhat later Man Chief visited the States, where the young ladies of a female seminary awarded him a medal inscribed to 'The Bravest of the Brave.' One side of this medal shows the Pawnees bringing the girl to the scaffold. On the other side, Man Chief and the girl are shown escaping on foot. This medal, presumably buried with Man Chief, was recovered from a grave about fifty years ago.

It is said that the braided thong used to bind the girl to the scaffold is still in the Morning Star bundle. Coming Sun, the last man to sing the ceremonial songs of this ritual, has said that, sometimes, while he is singing he stops and says, 'Listen!' Then the people can hear a woman's voice singing those songs above his head.[26]

Pawnee Rock today is much diminished, the early settlers and the railroad-builders having used much of the stone. But in old days it was an impressive landmark, topped by a cairn of stones.

On the top of the Rock, near the edge, was a deposit of earth where the remains of some poor fellow had been placed who, after being jolted in a wagon under scorching rays of a summer sun for many days, had been dumped into the shallow hole with only his blanket for a coffin. Just beyond the Rock, Ash Creek flowed towards the river, a stream on which Indian sign, such as discarded moccasins and smoking campfires, often gave proof that Indians were watching from the hills around.

The alarm felt by travellers at this point had a decided effect upon the men of the caravan. Up to this point, the wagons usually advanced in two files only, but from the Rock onward to the mountains the caravan was divided into four files, marched abreast for greater safety. From such a formation, the corral could be formed more quickly for defence, each division making one side of it.

From Pawnee Rock on almost to the Cimarron crossing, the caravans had a choice of routes. The longer followed the course of the river, the shorter, or dry route, ran over the hills and high prairie at a distance of some ten miles from the river. On this route, at least one dry camp was necessary, and the bones of oxen, killed by thirst and abandoned to the wolves, marked the ruts across the level plain. Their sufferings were all the worse for the fact that the river was within sight much of the way. Caravans hastened in order to reach the crossing of the Arkansas before the June freshet, caused by melting snows in the Rockies, could reach the Trail.

Ash Creek, often dry in summer, offered little obstacle. But the Pawnee Fork was another matter altogether. If in flood, it was a difficult stream to cross, and sometimes horses and wagons were swept away, or a man drowned in trying to ford. Then the water came pouring down, bank-full, half-submerging the trees along its margins, tumbling brush and logs in whirling eddies, sweeping the willows up and down by the force of the current, until they looked as if a hurricane were blowing. Only the elms, box-elders, and willows could hold the muddy banks from being washed away. It was the part of wisdom to wait until the stream went down.

In such a time, the men of the caravan might wander over the prairies, noting the prickly-pear which studded them, identify the tea plant or the toothache tree, catch some of the enormous toads abounding there, or dig up the tubers of the prairie convolvulus, known to the Indians as badger's food. Sometimes that tuber was two feet long, twenty inches around. It had a sweetish taste, and was said to be a cure for fever. Swamp grasses abounded along the river, and in the damp spots, the sick gold of the twining dodder smothered the weeds in an inextricable tangle.

Lone wolves loafed around, serenading the camps at night. And a party of naked savages, with painted faces, might appear to inspect the caravan. Then the men would form the wagons in a tight corral, picket their horses close on short ropes, and lie awake all night beside a wagon, with the rifle ready across the wagon-tongue.

Pawnee Fork, when not in flood, was a bold, limpid
stream, with a sparkle that promised a cool drink to the
thirsty horseman. It had a fringe of trees along its banks,
and was known to the Kiowas in early days as Dark Timber
River. Because it afforded good water and fuel for fires, it
was a favorite haunt of these Indians, and of their allies the
Comanches. Raids often were made there, particularly
after the Mexican War began, when caravans were numerous enough to attract marauders.

Raiding was the Comanches' business in life. For centuries they had been in contact with the Spanish settlements, and either fighting for, or against, the Mexicans.
After Texas was settled, they included the Texas settlements in their program, and the Santa Fe Trail they looked
upon as simply another business opportunity. In fact, for
many years they followed a regular program, raiding the
Mexicans at one season, the Texans somewhat later, and
moving up with the buffalo to attack the summer caravans
on the Santa Fe Trail.

Mexico had always been a bloodstained land, where
human sacrifice was common; and when the Spaniards
came, they brought with them the cruel methods of the
Inquisition. According to early reports, they found the all
Comanches a kindly folk. But the Comanches soon learned evil
to be as rapacious and ruthless as their neighbors, and being
better scouts, better horsemen, and better shots than the from
Mexicans, made their lives a nightmare with robbery, tor- Spain
ture, and murder. They lived in a region where temptation
to rob and kill was very great, and some of their Indian
neighbors were cannibals. Torture seems to have come to
the Plains from the Southwest (the Pawnees, with their
human sacrifice, were from the Southwest); and certainly
the Northern Plains tribes had no settled policy of fright-
fulness. The Kiowas, most closely allied with the Comanches, were northern Indians, and in the North had no

reputation for such beastliness. But the Comanches soon taught them, until the Kiowas were almost as bad as their teachers.

After centuries of contact with the Spanish outposts, the Comanches acquired peculiarly repulsive traits. They had no art, no elaborate mythology — like the Arapahoes; no high-minded, instinctive courage, and love of prestige for itself — like the Cheyennes. They did not even have a tribal religion, or hold a Sun Dance. When they raided, it was for booty; and the booty they liked best was a captive — some unfortunate woman or child, whom they could enslave, torment, and hold for ransom. Boy captives, who were strong enough to survive the first rough initiation, were usually well treated, and adopted into the tribe.

Other captives suffered the torments of the damned — and to the tune of Comanche laughter. Most accounts of Indian atrocities have to be discounted, but those of the Comanches are too numerous and well documented to be disputed. This was partly due to their racial stock, and partly to the accident of their location. They belonged to the great Shoshonean group, along with the Utes and Shoshones, and were related to the Nahuatl stock of Mexico.

They were competent — as a wolf or a panther is competent — and admirable in the same way: wonderful horsemen, experts with lance and bow, highly practical in their warfare, but lacking in the more decorative and attractive traits of some other tribes. Their aims and their methods were simply those of gangsters, and their principal business was stealing horses and kidnapping women and children.

What these women captives suffered had better not be recorded. As for the children, even Comanche women would torment them, making them stand on hot coals, or waking the little wretches by applying a burning stick to their noses.

I myself knew an old buck, then a member of a Christian

church, who, in the weekly Experience Meeting, used to testify to his former sinful practices, and relate with gusto how he had tossed captive white children high into the air and caught their falling bodies on the point of his buffalo lance! He was determined to brag of his beastliness, even if he had to join the church to do it.

Some of these women captives, in spite of their harrowing experiences, showed amazing heroism. In the spring of 1867, during the absence of the men, some Comanches raided the home of a settler near the headwaters of the Colorado River. When the Indians came in sight, the house contained the settler's wife, three small children, and a widow by the name of Mary Jane Luster, who was visiting the family. She was a fine horsewoman, about twenty-five years of age, and evidently with a strong constitution. She had been reared on the frontier.

While the women were busy in the house, the two children, playing in the front yard, called out to the mother, saying men on horseback were coming. The mother looked out of the door, and saw to her horror that the strangers were hostile Indians. She called to the children to come into the house, but they were busy playing and did not obey in time. Before they knew it, the Indians had them and were all around the house. Mary Jane Luster ran up the ladder leading to the loft of the cabin and hid there, but before the mother and her youngest child could conceal themselves, the Comanches were in the house.

The mother struggled desperately to save the child from their clutching hands, but they wrenched the child away and beat its brains out upon the floor. Then taking her by the hair, they jerked her head back and cut her throat from ear to ear.

Mary Jane, watching the scene from the loft, gasped in horror. The Indians heard her, rushed up the ladder, and dragged her down. They put her on one horse, the two children on another, and galloped away. For several days and nights they travelled as fast as the mounts could carry them, occasionally halting for a short time to allow the animals to graze. The frightened captives were exhausted by the long ride. But at length, when all chance of successful pursuit was past, the Indians let up and slept.

Mary Jane despaired of saving the children. She could not escape with them, and made up her mind to get away at the first opportunity, and try to ransom the children later. Being a horsewoman, she knew which of the Indians' mounts was the fastest. In the darkness she crept away, caught that pony, straddled his bare back, lying flat on his mane and urging him away toward the north at a gentle walk.

Once out of hearing of the hostile camp, she lashed the horse into a run. All night she rode, halting to look back now and then, to listen for the sounds of pursuit. She heard none.

For all of thirty-six hours she rode as fast as the horse could carry her, half dead for sleep and starving. The second night the wolves followed her, sometimes snapping at the heels of her horse. She had no weapon, and could only whip the tired horse into a faster gait. At daybreak, the horse could only stagger along at a slow walk. But the wolves left her. She felt that she could go no farther. She tied one end of a long lariat to the neck of the horse, with the other end around her waist, and dropped down upon the ground into a deep sleep.

She slept for hours without awakening. Then she was roused by the pattering sound of horses' feet beating the earth on every side. She looked up, and saw a band of mounted Indians. She was once more a prisoner. The Indians were not those from whom she had escaped. This time, they were apparently Kiowas, who carried her to their camp a short distance off.

But Mary Jane was not easily daunted. Her first escape made her hope for a second. One evening a party of warriors who had been gone for six days brought back some ears of green corn. Mary Jane, having been reared on the frontier, knew that buffalo hunters on the Southern Plains did not plant corn. That corn must have come from the field of a white settler, not more than three days' journey distant. She determined to reach that settlement.

One night she repeated her first exploit, and escaped on the back of a fast pony. She rode in the direction from which the raiders had returned, but found no settlements.

The horse brought her to a large river, flowing directly across her path. It was in flood, and flowing swiftly. But she feared the Indians more than death by drowning. Exhausted as she was, she forced the tired horse into the muddy stream, and swam it to the opposite bank.

Beyond the river she found wagon ruts, and followed them along until she met some wagons.

The Captain of the caravan was Robert Bent, and Mary Jane learned that she was on the Santa Fe Trail, and that the river she had swum was the Arkansas. Bent and his men were astonished to meet a lone woman so far from civilization. They gave her food and water, and when she had eaten asked her where she came from. She answered laconically, if not very specifically, 'Texas!'

Then she told of her experiences. After such desperate adventures, Bent and his outfit expected that Mrs. Luster would ride with them to the nearest settlements. But Mary Jane had a mind of her own, and other ideas. When she had rested for a time, she thanked Bent, mounted her horse, and pushed on along the Trail.

At Fort Zarah, Bent halted to call upon the Indian agent, and tell him how he had met the lone woman. The agent, at the time, was in council with the very Indians who had discovered her sleeping, and from whom she had escaped.

At once the Indian agent sent a horseman to overtake Mary Jane, and escort her to Council Grove.

She arrived there safely, and in time, through the efforts of the agent, the two unhappy children were ransomed. Probably that ride of hers was a record for a woman. Mary Jane Luster had ridden bareback and alone five hundred miles to win her freedom.[27]

Not every woman had the qualities, the strength, or the opportunities of Mary Jane. For one who escaped the Comanches, as she did, a score had to endure a long, degrading slavery until death released them.

The Comanches behaved like gangsters: if the prisoner could be sold for a stiff price, well and good; if not, slavery or death was the penalty.

Like gangsters, too, some Comanches — even chiefs — were yellow. On Pawnee Fork an incident occurred which illustrates the character of such men, who could torture the helpless, but dared not face death themselves.

It was early summer, 1847. Red Sleeve and his Comanches were on Pawnee Fork. With them was a party of Kiowas, under Satank (Setangya, or Sitting Bear). Satank was a sub-chief, a hard fighter, member of the Kiowa Dog Soldier Society, and a man feared even by his fellow-tribesmen. The winter before, in a fight with the Pawnees near the Red River in Texas, he had slipped on the snow. After he went down, a Pawnee shot him with an arrow in the upper lip, or as they put it, 'in the mustache!' His lean Mongol face and scrawny mustache, which scarcely hid the scar on his upper lip, were not pretty. But Satank was a courageous man, as he amply proved when he died at Fort Sill, deliberately inviting death, after his arrest by the military.

When Red Sleeve saw the wagons coming, he proposed an attack.

Satank refused. He was hard-boiled as the next man, and

later, in 1871, after the Texans had killed his son, did not scruple to help roast a white man in revenge. But he was a man of his word in 1847, and held fast to his recent treaty with the whites. He said, 'The white men are my friends.'

Red Sleeve laughed, and sneered at Satank. 'You are a woman,' he said. 'You must be afraid. Well, I am going to fight. Come along and watch. Bring all your Kiowas. I will show them how to fight. Watch me!'

Then Satank said: 'Good. We will watch you.'

Red Sleeve made medicine, and then put on his fine war-bonnet, with the lustrous eagle-feathers cascading down his back. He jumped on his war-horse, called his men. The Comanches swept away, circling the wagons . . . not too close at first.

Satank and his Kiowas stopped their ponies on the ridge and sat there, just out of rifle range, looking on quietly. Away went the Comanches. The wagons hastily rolled into a hollow square, and gun smoke foamed out along the high beds. The Kiowas could hear the spiteful crack of rifles, the dull boom of smoothbores. The white men met the charge with a volley.

The first man hit was Red Sleeve. A ball crashed through his thigh, smashed the spine of his war-horse. Down went the chief, with the dead horse on top of him, pinning him to the ground. The other Comanches, several of whom were also hit, disheartened by the fall of their chief, scurried away out of gunshot.

The white men, seeing Red Sleeve twisting and wrenching himself about, trying to free himself, came running across the grass to kill him.

When the chief saw that, saw that his comrades were running to cover, his heart turned to water. He could not free himself, his friends had abandoned him, and the whites were coming, running.

In such a fix, Satank would have met the danger squarely,

as he proved on his dying day, singing his death-song like a man:

> O Sun, thou endurest forever,
> But we who are warriors must die!

But Red Sleeve had no such courage. He was just a raider, who fought for what he could make out of it. He had no pride, no fortitude. He straightway forgot his death-song, if he had one, twisted around to face Satank, and called to the Kiowa to save him.

Satank never budged. He and his comrades remained sitting their horses, looking on, while the ponies switched tails and swung their heads at flies, half-asleep in the warm sunshine. Red Sleeve bawled and yelled until the white men reached him and shot him dead.[28] Then Satank turned his pony abruptly, and rode back to camp. He was ready to fight any Comanche who dared complain. But the Comanches, having run away and let their chief be killed, had nothing to say.

On June 22, Lewis H. Garrard passed eastward with a caravan, and during the noonday halt beside the river, explored the ground: 'I found the skull and skeleton of an Indian. The sinews, well-gnawed by the wolves, were not yet dry, and the skin and hair still graced the head, which, passed from hand to hand by the curious, was at last tossed into the turbulent waters of the Pawnee Fork. The Comanche whose head this was, had been killed a few days previous in an encounter with traders.' [29] If our chronology is correct, this was probably the head of Red Sleeve.

Certainly the Comanches were still in the neighborhood, for the very next day they had their revenge upon Garrard's party:

'On the opposite side of the creek, a train from the States was like ourselves stopped by the risen waters. I accompanied some of our men over to it. We swam across, holding our shirts and buckskins in one hand. At the camp we found a government train, some traders' wagons, any quantity of gaping men, and a white woman — a real white woman! and we gazed upon her with great satisfaction and curiosity. After gleaning the news, we returned in a full run to the creek, and, crossing as before, retailed our scanty information.

'The next day was beautiful, and we waited impatiently for the slowly-receding stream to become fordable. The men scattered on both banks; the grazing cattle and *caballadas*, with the white wagon-tops of the three camps, made a serene and lovely scene. About ten o'clock, an immense drove of buffalo was seen running in the prairie to the southwest. Some of our party set off in pursuit on their horses, while twenty or thirty of us ran down to intercept them as they crossed the creek. A faint cry of "Indians! Indians! Indians!" from the camp reached those nearest the mule-guard, and by them it was repeated and wafted on to us, who, hardly knowing whether to *cache* in the undergrowth or to run for camp, stood for a moment undecided and then streaked it for the wagons. Turning our eyes to the farthest train on the hill, we perceived it in great commotion. Fifty Indians were charging among them with their lances, recoiling from the light volumes of smoke at times and again swallowing up the little force with their numbers and shutting them in from our sight. Others were stampeding the oxen. After a conflict of several minutes they retreated, bearing with them a dead warrior behind the bluff hill which jutted boldly from the opposite shore.

'Our teamsters, during the fight, looked on with mouth and eyes open in wonderment, regardless of their own cattle still feeding in a deeply-fringed savanna. Tall cottonwood timber overgrown with the luxuriant vine and thickset underbrush, impervious to the eye, confined our stock to this secluded spot. The creek, half encircling it with a grand sweep, added its protection. A lightguard of three men watched the grazing herd. We were still congratulating ourselves on our escape, when from the guard we heard the cry that the Indians were swimming the creek and driving off the oxen. More than half the camp started in full run to protect them. As we rounded the angle of the stream, yells were heard, then the dusky forms of a few Indians were seen, and by the time we were within long gunshot, some sixty were among the luckless herd, goading them into a lumbering gallop. The Colonel's party led the van and would have saved the cattle had the teamsters supported them. But, they hanging back, we told them their oxen might go. Hurrying back to camp, Colonel Russell mounted his force and went in pursuit; but in vain we tried to repair the loss that negligence and cowardice had effected. Our ride only rescued thirty oxen and gave us a view of the retreating savages, thrusting their lances into the remainder. In that unfortunate half hour the train lost one hundred and sixty steers; which, at the purchase price — one half less than they were worth on the prairie — was a damage of four thousand dollars, together with a total loss of from five to seven thousand more, in the necessary abandonment of the wagons — the natural result of sending on the plains a set of green men commanded by as raw a director, poorly and scantily armed with government blunderbusses, and meagerly furnished with from eight to fifteen rounds of cartridges each, which were often wasted on game or targets long before reaching the Indian country. And this was not the only instance of miserable economy, as the official reports show.

'Our train was in a sad condition — half a yoke to each wagon. Mr. Coolidge was really to be pitied — nearly four hundred miles from the States, with but two oxen to haul four large wagons heavily loaded with robes and peltries. The colonel carried a few packs (as many as he was able);

he bargained with one of the outward-bound trains to take some back to Mann's Fort, and the rest he *cached*. The government people crowded their "kits" and provision in three wagons; and toward evening of the next day, we crossed the creek which had now subsided, leaving twenty-six wagons and any amount of extras to the Indians and the wolves. Toward sundown, as we were hitching up to travel in the night, a party of dragoons filing down the hill, made camp near. Lieutenant J. Love, commanding, was informed of the outrage and promised satisfaction. We stopped a moment at the train, with which the first fight had occurred. One poor fellow, named Smith, from Van Buren County, Missouri, had been lanced seven times through the neck and breast. He killed the Indian that felled him while on his back and already wounded.' [30]

Lieutenant Love's 'satisfaction' cannot have been very great. Four days later his convoy of thirty traders and eighty dragoons, carrying three hundred thousand dollars in specie (pay for the troops in Santa Fe), was itself attacked, and escaped with a loss of five killed and six wounded. Kit Carson himself was waylaid and lost thirty-five head of horses soon after. The Indians attacked every train on the Trail that year. The loss — chiefly suffered by ill-organized government trains — amounted to forty-seven killed, three hundred and thirty wagons destroyed or abandoned, and sixty-five hundred head of stock run off or killed.

The losses continued, and continued to mount, until after the Civil War. After 1851 Uncle Sam spent some three million dollars a year on this problem. In 1868 the government commission reported their estimate that, during the preceding half century, the loss and expense due to Indian wars amounted to half a billion dollars and twenty thousand lives. Of this, the Santa Fe Trail bore its full share.

For the wagons kept on coming, and in ever greater numbers. Even before the gold rush to California, when a check was made by an army officer (1848) it was found that three thousand wagons, fifty thousand head of stock, and twelve thousand people passed over the Trail. Later years made this migration seem puny.

Small wonder the Indians took alarm, warlike as they were, and tempted by the riches of the white men. Before the Mexican War, caravans had come rarely, and well guarded. Traders and trappers were welcome, for the most part, and the losses in American lives could almost be counted on the fingers of two hands. But after the War, it was another matter.

From the red man's point of view, these organized parties of armed men — generally without women — were simply war parties encroaching upon the Indian's hunting grounds, aggressors. They slaughtered the buffalo recklessly, scared them from their usual haunts, and made no presents to the redskins. Both white men and red feared to trust each other; neither side knew what might have happened on the Trail ahead, to make the other hostile. Both sides indulged at times in ruthless cruelties. White women blanched at the mention of the painted devils of the Plains: Indian mothers hushed their fretful papooses by singing, in effect, 'The white man will get you, if you don't watch out!'

Beyond the Pawnee Fork, the Trail passed through a barren region, crossing two small creeks, known as Little Coon Creek and Big Coon Creek. This was the dangerous part of the Trail, as there was no cover in case of an attack. Here, wild horses were often seen. In the river bottom there was good grass for the animals. Elsewhere it was scanty, the soil consisting of a granitic sand, which was much cut up by washes, offering cover to marauding Indians.

Here, in summer, the heat was intense, and travellers first became aware of the mirage. Buffalo on the skyline would suddenly be magnified to gigantic proportions, and on one side or another false ponds and lakes would appear, blue and inviting. The country was studded with prickly-pear, and the men frequently caught 'horned frogs,' those small, spiny lizards resembling prehistoric monsters which still abound throughout the Southwest, one of the few reptiles sufficiently attractive to be kept as a pet.

So, at last, the caravans approached the Cimarron Crossing, or Ford of the Arkansas, where the Trail divided: the mountain route passing on up the river toward Bent's Fort and the Raton Pass; the other crossing the river to traverse the dreaded *Jornada* and strike more directly towards the New Mexican settlements.

Near the Ford, caravans were likely to encounter the camps of the shifty Arapaho Indians, if they fared no worse before crossing the river into Comanche territory.

On this part of the Trail, one of the regular stopping-places was known as the Caches. It gained its name from an adventure of some traders who set out for Santa Fe in the fall of 1822. Their names were Samuel Chambers and James Baird (Beard). It was a small party, with an assortment of merchandise. They reached the Arkansas River late in the season, and pushed up the stream toward the Crossing. Shortly before they reached the Ford, snow began to fall. It soon became too deep for travel, and they were forced to go into winter quarters. Fearing an attack by Indians, they made their camp on an island in the river, and somehow managed to keep themselves alive during three long months. Some of their animals perished in the snow, others strayed away. When the snow melted in the spring, they had no means of transport.

Knowing that the Indians would steal their property unless it was concealed, they decided to *cache* their goods until they could return and recover them.

Choosing a level bench of firm soil near the river, they

went to work. First the sod was carefully cut out and laid on buffalo robes spread near. Then a bottle-shaped excavation was made, narrow at the top and much bigger below the surface of the ground. All the earth taken out was carefully placed upon buffalo robes, carried to the river, and thrown into the water, so that not a clod remained to show that a hole had been dug. Then the hole was lined with branches and leaves all round, and the tightly packed goods were stowed in it. A covering of poles and grass and earth tamped firm was added, and at last the sod was carefully replaced. When all was finished, no one would have supposed that the grass had been disturbed.

It was the custom to obliterate the marks of digging by tethering horses above the *cache* for a day or two, so that their restless feet would hide all signs of excavation. Sometimes a fire was built on the spot, which charred the space and left it covered with ashes. Unless some prowling Indian had watched their work, they knew that their goods were now in safety.

The men set out, reached Taos, and purchased mules. Then they went back and recovered their goods. For many years after, the holes left in the ground were still visible, and few travellers passed that way without visiting those mossy pits.

[handwritten margin notes: "admittedly", "he doesn't know", "unsure enough", "not way", "guess"]

CHAPTER XI

'Prairie Prison'

depressed

LIFE on the Santa Fe Trail was not always with wagon trains and pack trains. During the Mexican War, when troops and supplies were constantly coming and going between the States and New Mexico, the War Department suffered so many losses in stock and vehicles that it was determined to establish a station between Fort Leavenworth on the Missouri and Bent's Fort on the Plains. The site chosen was near the Caches, on the Arkansas. There was erected a palisade and shelter, at which it was intended that wagons could be repaired and stock recruited 'in safety.' Accordingly, Captain Enos sent one Mann, a wagon-master, with forty teamsters and several yoke of oxen, to build a fort and a blacksmith shop near the Cimarron Crossing.

The fort was simply four log houses, connected by angles of timber framework, in which loopholes were cut for the cannon and small arms. The fort was about sixty feet across inside, with walls twenty feet high. There was no corral for the animals. With a negligence characteristic of the War Department throughout the Indian wars on the Plains, no adequate plant was built, and no adequate garrison ordered out. Since no Mexican troops were anywhere near the fort, and the redskins were supposed to be peaceable, nothing to meet the facts was provided. The thing was called Fort Mann.

No sooner had the Indians seen what was doing than

they ambushed a man fishing in the river nearby, and then stampeded the oxen and mules staked out around the walls. Driving a herd of their own loose animals before them, yelling and waving their robes and shooting, they swept down like an avalanche, and disappeared with all the animals belonging to the garrison. One Indian was hit, but was carried off.

Thereafter, a second stampede — of the white teamsters back to the States — followed. The Captain could find only ten men brave enough to remain on duty, even when the pay was raised to thirty dollars a month. Lewis H. Garrard, in his *Wah-To-Yah*, has given us the best detailed account of what life in Fort Mann was like. It is a picture of pioneer soldiering that is unique, and yet in its way utterly typical. The soldiers were scarcely able to defend themselves, let alone the passing wagon trains. Garrard volunteered for this dangerous service, out of sheer youthful daring and curiosity. He left the wagon train, and joined the handful in the fort.

A guard mounted on one of the houses as soon as the train was in motion. 'As they receded in the distance,' Garrard confesses, 'a slight feeling of fear and loneliness ran through me, decreased not a whit by the sight of our own few members.' The large gates — two ponderous wooden puncheon concerns, a foot in thickness — were to be swung on wooden hinges, which operation, together with relieving the guard, occupied the men until night.

They were now alone; that is, ten well men and three sick ones; 'these last doomed to many a weary hour of unheeded pain not within our power to alleviate by healing medicine, or nourishing food.'

The fighting force was as follows:

Captain, John Simpson 'Blackfoot' Smith. Men: Thomas Sloan, —— Johnson, —— Roy, James Strickler, Samuel Caldwell, L. H. Garrard, Ben Raymond, one Andrew,

William Taylor. Also one six-pound cannon, forty rounds of grape and canister, forty cannon cartridges, six rifles, and seven muskets.

In addition, Smith had his squaw and two children; Raymond his half-breed Rosalie, who, with Smith's seven mules and horses, Raymond's one, Garrard's two, three old government scarecrows, and five broken-down United States steers, was the sum total of all the objects — animate and inanimate, offensive and inoffensive, with the exception of Rosalie's diminutive feist, and an Indian cur, scarce half made-up — left to vegetate in the *Prairie Prison*, aptly so called; for even a visit to the river for water, a hundred yards distant, required the bucket in one hand — the rifle in the other.

They felt this to be a small band to guard a fort in the Pawnee and Comanche range — both tribes noted for their dexterity and willingness to take the white man's 'hair,' or his *caballada*.

Being possessed of writing materials, Garrard was made clerk to keep account of rations issued, and chronicler of events such as passing trains. In addition the office of orderly sergeant devolved upon him, the duties of which consisted in arranging the night sentries. There were ten men including Smith, and calling from twilight to dawn ten hours, he made five watches of two hours' duration each — two men on duty at once; the first, standing until the evening star sank beneath the horizon, which, though more than the allotted period, made not much difference, as it was in the fore part of the night. When the first watch 'guessed' his time had expired, he awoke the next on duty, who repeated the process, and so on through. Smith and Garrard were on first watch; and to avoid contention or dissatisfaction, the first guard was second the next night, the third the next, and so on through — those behind filling up the vacancy.

Two were appointed as day sentries — a permanent office, they doing nothing else. At his own request, seconded by our wishes, Strickler was promoted to the office of cook; and he so exerted his culinary skill as to make the monotonous rations quite palatable. Smith's squaw cooked for him; Rosalie for Raymond and Taylor.

In one day, they built of adobes, on the northwest house and its corresponding diagonal, a breastwork for a defence against the wind as well as arrows. The waterproof roofs were flat, being made of small poles laid parallel, with six inches of mud piled on, and an inclination of one and a half inches to the yard. Standing guard was anything but pleasant, and at night exceedingly dreary. Smith would mount post on the roof for a while, and Garrard, down below, would creep from port to port, now listening for the foe — now seated on the cannon, holding his breath at the least sigh of the winds. In pacing his lonely walk, he was filled with gloomy forebodings. The wind whistled a mournful tune — the damp, fitful gusts nearly overturned him in their suddenness.

Scarce fifteen yards distant, brutal wolves fought over the grave of the murdered man. A large white one, whose faint outline Garrard could see below him, gave a most unearthly howl, which, going out in the stillness, sent back its lonely echo from the distant hills, and met a response from others afar, who, with fiendlike screams, congregated under the walls growling and bristling in fearful wrath, or continuously loped around the fort in hungry expectation. When relieved from watch, Garrard nestled in his warm blankets, and after sending, mentally, the Pawnee and accursed wolves *a los diablos*, he dropped into an inappreciable state of blessed forgetfulness, to be waked at sunrise with the cry of 'Turn out!'

Rain and wind were their uninterrupted visitations for two days. The animals had to be picketed close — the sentry meanwhile keeping vigilant lookout. At night the men brought them inside the fort.

Callahan, a trader, passed on the twentieth of May to the States. He was from Chihuahua and short of provision. Smith, empowered to hire men for the 'fort service,' induced one man to stay who was journeying with the train without leave, license, or provender. Sloan, in his fondness for nicknames, called him Rasamus Cowhorn, a cognomen which clung so tenaciously to the younger gentleman that Garrard never knew his right one.

Sam Caldwell and Garrard were on the same guard. Smith reposed undisturbed through the night. One of the guard fell asleep on his post, for which he received a reprimand, interlarded with expressive terms from Smith, and a no-gentle hint from all that a repetition of the offence would mean the cannon with the accompanying jerking!

In the afternoon succeeding the above transaction, Roy, a heedless fellow, on one of Smith's animals and with two in lead, and Garrard on Bonita, with Diabolique in tow at the end of a rawhide lariat, crossed the river for grass. They rode bareback, with guns in hand, and the slippery mules rendered the possession of their seats uncertain. A gun fired from the fort was to be the signal of danger.

They were a mile off, lying down talking, the mules quietly grazing, when the full heavy sound of the gun was heard. Snatching his blanket in one hand, and with Diabolique's lead-rope and his gun in the other, Garrard started after Roy. The animals, as if interpreting the men's wishes, went in a full run from the start. With rifles ready to fire, they came within a hundred yards of the river, where Diabolique broke away, galloping up the river-bank, head and tail high, neighing and frantic.

'There goes eighty dollars,' thought Garrard, but there was no time for calculation when probably the whole tribe of yellowskins was at his heels. Off flew his hat to the breeze; now they plunged into the water, jamming against each other; when halfway across, Diabolique, with streaming tail, wide-spread nostrils, and wild eye, charged in among them.

Excited friends met them at the entrance; the sentry shouted to hurry. They barred the gate, drew tightly their belts, and fixed their guncaps anew, when the party bearing down on them proved to be only a band of wild horses scudding northward some two miles to the east. After a talk and recovery from the fluttering effects of the false alarm, Johnson and Garrard waded the river, where they picked up Garrard's hat and baited a wolf trap.

With the fore wheels of the cannon wagon, they carried adobes and stiff mud for mortar, to build chimneys to the blacksmith shop and the messroom. Luckily, Captain Mann's party had made enough adobes to last some time; for it was small fun to mould brick. In the evening, a train of wagons corralled at the Caches, much to the men's disappointment, as they wished to meet with them. The next morning they stopped in the road opposite the fort, and the teamsters came to see the garrison.

It was Bent and St. Vrain's company. William Tharpe, an Indian trader, had joined them with his wagons for safety. Mr. Holt, Bent's storekeeper, Ed, the Frenchman, whose squaw Rosalie (then in the fort) had been enticed away by Raymond, and Frank de Lisle, the wagon-master, were all in the train on the way home. Charlotte, the cook (who, with her husband, was set free by the company for the valor evinced by the latter, Dick, at the taking of the Pueblo de Taos), also grinningly showed her ivory, as Garrard extended his hand.

After greeting warmly Edmond Paul and Petout, his two Canadian friends, Garrard gave them the thirty days' rations of flour and coffee he had purchased at Bent's Fort, for which they kindly thanked him. Traders did not provision themselves well, and these clever fellows were feasting on 'poor bull.'

Smith, the Captain, who had been showing, in private conversation with Garrard, a fear of losing his hair, gave notice of leaving with the train, which stopped while he collected his possibles. While on guard together, he had often told Garrard the utter folly, the downright madness, of staying in the fort at the mercy of the Indians, and that his pay would be nothing in comparison to the loss of his animals and the risk of life. To the men his reasons were plausible enough: his animals picketed around the fort were starving, and he would go with the train and let them feed on good grass every night, until he could meet a train to return to Fort Mann.

Knowing this to be his intention, Garrard sent Bonita and Diabolique along with the band, for the risk in keeping them was greater, in fact, than letting them go. It was a trial to part with Bonita; indeed Garrard felt nearer to him than to any of his friends. When he tied the lariat about his neck and gave him a good-bye pat, the little sorrel mule broke away kicking and shaking his long ears joyously, and with head to the ground joined, neighing in delight, the *caballada*.

It was difficult to withstand the solicitations of friends to leave, but Garrard's promise to stay had to be complied with, however earnestly he wished to be with them. The 'brave' commander, his squaw, and his son Jack, were pleased with the change. Little Jack had contributed much to Garrard's happiness; for, although he could not talk American, the sight of him was as an oasis in the desert. Among rough men, and no kind words, Jack, at least, was not void of childish affection, and to amuse and talk to him recalled home and cheerful retrospections.

The loss of Smith all felt, for he was of an agreeable temperament. Sloan was now in command, though from Roy's turbulent disposition they anticipated difficulty. Garrard retained his position, and Sloan was pleased to be lenient in his requisitions on Garrard's time for labor, thus giving him opportunity for enlarging his small journal. He wished Garrard, however, not to incur the ill-will of the rest by abusing the privilege.

The morning following the departure of Smith, the men carried charcoal from the pit to the intended 'shop.' With coffee sacks on shoulders, they lifted until their appearance would have well vied with that of a city *charbonnier*. Dirty work it was, to be sure, but necessity overcame any scruples on the subject, and they began to think thirty dollars and rations rather a poor compensation for so small a sprinkling of adventure, and so much hard work.

One morning, there being a cessation of hostilities on the mudbrick and coalpit, Garrard improved the time by lying full length on a plank in a cool corner of the messroom, rifle within reach (for guns and men were one and inseparable), when the cry of 'Indians! Indians!' from Taylor, the sentry, set him miraculously quick on his feet.

He rushed into the sleeping apartment and back again, before finding his gun, so bewildered was he by the startling announcement. Seizing it, he helped the men run the cannon to the gate. Near were some eight or ten mounted Indians, striving to take the little band of animals. Andrew, with lumbering musket, blazed harmlessly away. A party of warriors dashed furiously up from the plain, and others rode back and forth with glistening lance and spotless shield, while in the narrow strip of wood fringing the river some hundred yards distant, the dusky forms of the foe could be seen gliding hastily forward. Caldwell, understanding more of gunnery than the rest, pointed the piece at the nearest squad, Sloan adjusted the burning match, and Garrard primed the touchhole.

There was a scene! Sam Caldwell, a six-foot, three-inch

man encased in a flaming red-flannel shirt, and in a stooping position, moved the piece carefully, sighting with his fine eye and waiting for the command from Sloan — a little to one side, Sloan himself, with fiery beard and moustache of no small pretensions, intently watching the maneuvers of the savages — then Bill Taylor with his mouth thoughtlessly open, leaning against the *portal*, a long government blunderbuss at rest in the bend of his arm, and nearer the gateway, in attitudes of indecision, stood Rasamus Cowhorn, Cain, and Andrew, not more interesting than usual, except that their perturbed countenances were robbed of the bloom of health at other times apparent. Close to Sam was Garrard — feeling first rate, as he thought at the time.

Imagine this in a flat bottom, wearing away undulatingly to the low hills in the background, and along whose base in the glimmering distance irregular bands of horsemen fast clattered toward the fort; on the other hand the placid Arkansas, winding its tortuous course between lonely and barren banks, with straggling cottonwoods to mark the course; then a small log fort, discernible at no great distance through its insignificance, at the gate of which scarce ten men, grouped around a six-pounder, waited in stern silence for greater demonstration of war from the foe before the commencement of bloodshed.

The Indians were close to the horses, three hundred yards from the fort, and attempting to drive them away. They then charged toward the fort, and the men fell back from the cannon while the match descended; they, seeing the piece, beat a hasty retreat. One presumptuous warrior on a fine black horse dashed at Sloan's picketed mule in desperation; he left again with several balls whistling about his ears. They could have easily killed several of the foe, but warfare once commenced, they might have fared badly in the end; so the whites were amicably disposed. One old fellow, seeing that they had decidedly the advantage, dismounted, and coming within two hundred yards, took the robe from his shoulders, sat down, rose, and shook the buffalo again to show that he was unarmed, and with other signs, meant, as Garrard judged, peace.

Roy, placing confidence in Garrard's knowledge of Indian signs, met the warrior under range of the cannon, telling the men, if the Indian jumped on him, to blaze away and kill both! They shook hands, but could effect nothing, so Roy called for Garrard; with the aid of signs and the Cheyenne tongue, they proved to be Arapahoes. Two others came up, and then two white men. Garrard told them their warriors must go away; the first man arose, and by some fancy manipulations dispersed them.

The spokesman then commenced an excuse for their presence by professing great friendship for the whites; saying that his object in calling was to inform them — that 'the Comanches were in great numbers at a small stream, a day's ride to the east, and were to make a descent upon the fort' (that they doubted not), 'and that had it not been for the Arapaho chiefs, the fort would have been taken.'

This with a lot of other stuff he told, which wound up with a request for tobacco. The whites set before them coffee and bread, and the long pipe, Roy and Gerrard smoking with them on the prairie peace and good-will — the men the while keeping vigilant watch from the fort, to prevent surprise. As Garrard wished them not to spy out the nakedness of the land, the guests were not allowed to approach nearer than fifty yards of the fort. In a short while they left. Though the Indians came undoubtedly with hostile intention, so soon as they found power superior to theirs, they, having confidence in white men, sent a messenger to confer. Reverse the matter, wagh! the white scalp would be off in a hurry. . . .

The next day a buffalo, breasting the breeze, hove in sight on the hill-back — a good sign of the presence of In-

dians, as bison never travelled adverse to the wind in summer, or came to the river but for water, of which there was
an abundance everywhere on the prairie, by reason of the
recent rains — and Roy, with his usual heedlessness, started
in pursuit, killing it. He came to the fort and saddled a
horse to get the meat, but had scarcely reached it when
those who had been watching saw him urging his horse in a
full run on the back track, with three yelling Comanches
at his heels. His comrades greeted him with a shout of glee
as he cut around to the gate.

Supper was at sundown, after which the garrison generally congregated in the sentry's house to smoke and talk,
with guns in repose on the arm, to make shots at the skulking coyotes, who not infrequently took ugly balls with them
in their ignominious flight. The sun, in setting, cast flicker-
ing beams far up on the meandering, broad-sheeted Arkansas, and shone on the numerous verdure-teeming islands.
The slow winging of a forsaken-looking crane, or the more
merry flight of smaller birds up the stream, darting into the
glittering spot, to disappear as if by magic, often excited
Garrard's attentive admiration. But it was his favorite
pastime after a day's work, with plenty within and a pipe
without, to stretch out on the flat roof and listen to the
yarns spun by the different fellows.

Sam Caldwell had been on ships much of his life, and
amused the men in his style and broadly-pronounced 'a's.'
Sloan was a blacksmith, with stories of a prosy, everyday
nature. He had joined a company of horse-soldiers for the
War and Santa Fe, but it was rejected by reason of the re-
quisition being filled before the tender of its services, and
so he started out as extra teamster 'to see the country anyhow.' He received, at Mann's Fort, sixty dollars per month
and rations.

Cain Strickler was a schoolmaster, nineteen years of age
(he and Garrard the youngest) and somewhat green; his

teaching was a good exemplification of 'the blind leading the blind.' He was from Virginia (of the first families, of course), and, being on a tour to Missouri at the commencement of the Mexican War excitement, was seized with a desire to see the oft-vaunted 'elephant,' so he started out as teamster. He was, however, apt, and though he never learned cards before this trip, the way he went ahead of the fellows playing poker put him at once in that class called 'hopeful.'

Roy was rather mysterious, and from circumstantial evidence they found that he had been in a penitentiary. He was heedless of danger, and hardened in feelings; to his former State's imprisonment was attributed his recklessness. When his acquaintances of Captain Enos' company bade him good-bye, they said:

'Roy, we never expect to see you again, you are so foolhardy — the Indians will have your hair yet.' This proved but too true.

Andrew, whose last name Garrard had forgotten, was from the Platte Purchase, in Missouri. He was principal witness in a murder case; and, being of a malleable temperament, had been bribed with a horse and considerable money to perjure himself, and then to leave the country. The men ascertained a few leading facts; and by Sloan's skilful queries, learned the whole state of the case. He had sworn not to return to Missouri.

Rasamus Cowhorn was another genius. He had left the States a year before, as teamster to a trader's train — went to Chihuahua — was at the battle of Sacramento and told great tales of bombshells, cannon balls, valorous Mexicans, and smoke, and was now on his way home *sans* the needful. He remained at the fort some days on trial helping eat rations. The wolf-like appetite manifested for a week was alarming; when his gastronomic demands slackened in a degree, Smith hired him.

On the twenty-eighth of May, they noticed an approaching body of men, and finding them Indians, stopped work, shut the gates, and lounged with guns freshly capped.

Two riding up to the wall, Garrard saluted them in the Cheyenne tongue. They were Arapahoes, and wished to come in, but that was against orders. Garrard asked for Warratoria (the most peaceable and renowned of their chiefs) and was told he soon would arrive. They then wanted *véheo mah'-pe* (literally, 'white man's water' — that is, whiskey). Being negatively answered, they, much dissatisfied, rode off. The sight of the lodge drays, squaws, children, and dogs recalled many thoughts most gratifying. The Indian encampment was three hundred yards above the fort on the river bank.

When Warratoria came, he was admitted, though Sloan much distrusted him. Garrard had made his acquaintance in the Cheyenne village, and knew his friendly disposition toward the whites, and the good effect it would have to treat him with confidence. Shaking hands as old friends, and inviting him into the messroom, they set before him coffee, bread, and the long pipe. The chief wished 'Beardy's' presence, which after a while was granted. He was so called from a tuft of hair growing on the point of his chin, which gave him an odd appearance. His features were coarse, inclining to sensuality. Warratoria's face, on the contrary, wore a benign expression, and the slight furrows of age were so tempered as to give his countenance a cast of deep thought; his expansive brow, slightly receding, was worthy of a statesman. Garrard was filled with reverence for the old man, though he was but an ignorant savage. He spoke in short sentences only (so different from the volubility of most savages, though many persons give them the character of taciturnity), as if conscious of the lasting impression he was making on his listeners.

In an hour the pyramidal lodges dotted the ground at

irregular distances; before the large ones, the stainless shield and medicine bag with blue-enrolled pipestems were supported on the three whitened wands. Where, a short while before, lay a bare spot of turf, was now the site of eighty lodges, nearly three hundred human beings, and eleven hundred horses capering, rolling, and cropping the sweet bottom grass. The girls, from twelve years up to womanhood, waded the river for fuel; some crossing, a few returning laden with sticks, others carrying water, and all laughing, talking, and splashing. Boys played their favorite game of arrows, or astride of ponies ran races over the smooth prairie. This commingled scene of comfort, youth, and hilarity brought back to Garrard, with yearnings for a repetition, his last winter's experience of the Cheyenne camps.

Sam Caldwell and he visited them without other weapon than butcher knives, for they felt little danger while the cannon ranged the village and the two principal chiefs were in the fort. A guard was at the gate to admit or show out the few savages having the freedom of the place, but the garrison were impolitic in discovering their weak force to them. A queer-looking case begged powder and ball, with a load or two of which they satisfied him. He had an old English carbine with 'George' and a crown on the barrel — the property, most likely, of a *pelado* whose scalp was now the decoration of some *coup*-loving Arapaho.

We noticed great commotion on reaching the fort again. The villagers hurried in the direction whence they that morning came — soon returning triumphantly with a young man who had been taken prisoner by a trading party in a skirmish two days before. Garrard now found out that the braves of this village were leagued with the Comanches in attacking trains. To the surprise and great joy of the Indians, the prisoner had been set at liberty — a different fate from that a captive experienced at their hands. The traders had given the young man a new blanket and ornaments; but, as the Indians had outraged the expected wagons, they struck their lodges, pitching them a half mile from the fort.

A train from Santa Fe, in command of Captain Fowler, arrived during the day, corralling a few steps from the gate. A Mexican *ranchero* was in the company — like his brothers, with national peculiarity in features and expression.

Sloan employed a young man, John Nagle by name, for the 'fort service.' His mule he sold to a teamster for forty dollars. The gate was shut at the usual hour; the guard mounted as if alone, being more apprehensive of the light-fingered teamsters, after a winter's sojourn in Santa Fe, than of the Indians. . . .

They hauled wood while there was a large numerical force by the fort, not daring to venture while alone. They fastened the gates, and leaving two on guard, crossed the river astride the coupling-pole of a wagon, holding on with one hand and clenching their rifles in the other. Sloan sat on the fore standard, examining the edge of an ax; Bill Taylor, with bawling voice, and an ox whip, kept up 'steam.' Johnson, who was an adept in the wood line, during the rest intervals told of his questionable feats in cording steamboat wood on the Missouri River. Cain Strickler and Garrard did their best at loading. They threw the wood from the wagon into the fort yard, not caring to give the teamsters a chance to supply their fires at their expense.

The Indians, striving to trade with the wagoners, became quite troublesome; the latter would endeavor to drive the Arapahoes away by cries of '*Bamouse, bamouse,*' calling over the Spanish-Mexican term *vamos*, which they used for 'Leave, get out, go,' and a half dozen similar exclamations. These same fellows had enjoyed the privilege in New Mexico of keeping the 'great unwashed' at a respectful distance from the provision trains; they thought the same ejecting words would serve for the Arapaho.

Among the Indian boys, splashing and riding across the river on the empty wood wagon, was one of thirteen years, whose features wore such a mild and manly air and whose eyes were so intelligent that Garrard took him to his baggage, put on him a clean, bright-blue shirt, and then tied a colored handkerchief around his neck. His hair was neatly combed and the deerskin moccasins fitted nicely. When sent away with some brown sugar, he looked the happiest boy in the country.

The traders with whom these Indians had been fighting arrived about three o'clock. Not a savage was visible. For three consecutive days they had fought these Indians, who, charging, hamstrung the oxen and annoyed them much. This outrageous conduct was the principal theme of conversation, which the sight of the distant lodges increased to such a degree that one well-proportioned six-footer proposed, with the cannon, to 'rake the village.'

Now, the garrison was opposed to this decisive measure for two good reasons. First was the indiscriminate slaughter of women and children that would have ensued. The second was that on their own heads and weak fort would have fallen the speedy vengeance of the tribe. Not choosing to remain the scapegoats of their iniquities, the garrison at once refused the use of the gun — and told them they should take it by force alone.

Nagle, the recruit, and others came in from the hunt, their animals loaded with buffalo. The men were out of available funds, and to accommodate them, as well as themselves, Sloan and Garrard bought a box of chewing tobacco from the traders. Garrard was to open an account with each man and supply them and receive in return drafts on the quartermaster.

Cowhorn borrowed fifty cents, bought tobacco, and

traded it for moccasins, which, sold to the teamsters, gave him three dollars' gain. Sloan purchased six gallons of whiskey, and out of the 'mess fund' the untiring cook, Cain, laid in a store of saleratus and peppersauce, thereby contributing much to the relish for government rations.

The next morning the traders left for Santa Fe, and the United States train, homeward bound, rolled on, with many an agonizing shriek from the rickety, sun-cracked wagonwheels. Garrard drew up a paper for Sloan to sign, showing what had become of the man received into service, so that the Captain of the train on arriving at Fort Leavenworth could satisfactorily account for the nonappearant.

With the train, the invalids left. Poor fellows! they no doubt had a wretched time jolting over the road in springless wagons, and little probability was there of their ever reaching the States. The men shut the gates and cautioned anew the guard. How different the scene within two short hours! Of a busy crowd of one hundred and twenty men and sixty wagons, none save that little force remained.

Toward noon the next day, the sentry shouted, 'Train in sight!' Soon a wagon and horsemen appeared. Turning from the trail, they passed the fort in a long trot and encamped three hundred yards distant. Garrard was glad to see Messrs. St. Vrain, Folger, and Chadwick — old friends; also, E. P. Blair, Jr., Estis (the Taos tavernkeeper); and Fitzgerald, the dragoon. Tibeau, the Canadian driver, and Blas, the Mexican herder, were along, too. A goodly company, indeed! They had twenty-five horses and mules, in prime order. That morning, thinking the Arapaho village to be Comanche lodges, they moved to an island in the Arkansas and threw up a temporary fortification. They stopped two hours and then concluded to run the risk.

Mr. St. Vrain urged Garrard to go with him, offering him a horse to ride; he said it was foolish to stay with so weak a force, and that Garrard would assuredly lose his scalp.

Garrard became scared when such mountain men feared danger, but feeling bound to Captain Enos, he remained.

One night Sam and Garrard were on guard. The rain poured in torrents, the air was damp and chilly; and, as they knew bowstrings and flintlocks would not avail the foe much in an encounter, they merely leaned in the doorway and listened by turns; and, at intervals, floundered in the mud from porthole to gate. Some spoiled buffalo meat, thrown over the wall, attracted the wolves. Garrard watched, not five feet distant, through a port where, in the dim light, the coarse gray hairs of their backs could be seen bristling with rage. At daylight one large fellow remained, slowly retreating and returning. Garrard put the government musket through a loophole (not caring to use his rifle in the rain), and aiming at the animal twenty-five steps distant, fired, killing him immediately. When the gates were opened, the guards, dragging him in, took off the hide and stretched it with pegs to dry.

Again they worked, this time making their own brick. Some dug earth; others, with the fore wheels (tongue and hounds attached) of the cannon wagon and a half barrel, brought water from the river, playing 'hossy,' as their fat commander facetiously observed. They had two yoke of oxen to tramp the mud, and Garrard, being the least strong of the company, with a long stick punched up 'Ball and Bright' when their movements grew tardy.

The seventh of June, according to their reckoning, was Sunday — no work in consequence. *The Three Guardsmen* and Garrard's pocket *Testament* amused them ('can't vouchsafe a great amount of edification') for a while, and in the evening they shot at a target across the fort yard.

The painful necessity of making brick was forced upon them at last, with all its muddy unpleasantness. The molds were sixteen inches long, by eight in width, and four in depth — the facsimile of brick molds on a larger scale.

These were filled with stiff mud and turned out on the smooth ground — the molds brought back, dipped in a barrel of water to free them of earthy particles, filled again, and so on *ad infinitum.* Johnson and Garrard, the carriers, had two molds each, the wet adobes grew heavier as the work progressed. Three hundred and twenty-six were the result of the day's labor.

Mr. Coolidge, with four wagons and five men from the Arkansas Pueblo and the Platte, arrived during the day. He concluded to remain here for a further reinforcement, ere proceeding through the suspicious Coon Creek country.

They made two hundred and ten adobes on the twelfth, and then employed themselves in digging a ditch beyond the fort walls to carry off the accumulated rainwater which might engender sickness the coming summer.

Roy, Nagle, Rasamus, and one of Coolidge's men went for buffalo. Being absent the entire day, much anxiety was felt for their safety. It was late at night. The garrison gave up all hope of seeing them, and were moodily cogitating what to do in regard to fortifying themselves more securely, when a rifle report and a shout not to fire were heard. Rushing up the ladder, Garrard called aloud, and the men whom he had seen scalped in his imagination answered to their names.

'What's the matter? What kept you so long,' he asked, impatient to know.

'Oh! had to go a long ways for meat, then a chase of five miles, hottest kind — were way out on Coon Creeks.'

'See any Indians?'

'Yes, darn 'em, sixteen. They gave chase for a mile; but, after a few shots, one was wounded by Roy, and they hauled off. Rasamus was pretty bad scared — thought his hair was gone; he began to talk about Franklin.'

Sam and Garrard were waked up at midnight to stand post — the rain pouring. They did not leave the messroom.

Thinking the foe would not attack in such weather, they sipped at the hot, lye-like coffee, and smoked until off duty.

No work on the fourteenth by reason of the incessant rain. The men had two packs of cards, and as the specie circulation was limited, rations of beans served as legal tender; the way they changed hands was a caution to hungry men.

In the Indian attack on the trading party, a colt was captured by the latter, which was given to Sloan. In commemoration of the event, he named it Comanche. One night, hearing a strange moaning, the men collected to inquire. Seizing rifles, they found poor Comanche outstretched with a half-dozen wolves at work on him. They drove the brutes away, and carrying the victim into the fort, saw that he was too badly eaten to live; he was shot with a pistol. In the morning a few well-picked bones and strips of sinew were all that remained.

No work on June 15, by reason of the sullen rains. This was Garrard's eighteenth birthday. He says:

'Quite a different one from last — then at home, and nothing particular to do, but to cast enervated glances at dull books — here, in government service, and surrounded by the most hostile Indians on the continent, my scalp in danger of sudden hoisting on some yelling Comanche's lancepoint — my body drenched by the frequent night rains. Well! there is something refreshing in variety, and the comforts of civilization will be better appreciated when regained.

'The afternoon was sunshiny and warm; the swollen Arkansas received our nude bodies in its swift current after a half mile's run up the bank, while the sentry on the fort and another on the river's edge looked sharp for the foe.'

The rest may be told in Garrard's own words:

'In the middle of the day a train hove in sight and camped near the "Caches." Roy started for it, though he might

have been killed before going half way. He soon returned,
with several men. To my surprise Charley M'Carty, with
whom I parted in the spring on the Poinel in New Mexico
shouted: "Why, old fellow, you here! What have you been
doing since I left you? St. Vrain told me you was in Taos,
on guard, when the old *palous* were hung, and that you cut
a 'big swath' generally."

'"In government service," rejoined I. "I wanted to see
an Indian fight, though my curiosity is not yet gratified.
We have come quite near it, however."

'"If they'd see you in the settlements, with those buckskins and old wool hat, you'd pass for one of the mountain
boys — be da-arned if you wouldn't! Do they feed you on
'Old Ned,' as Hatcher called the pork?"

'"Where are you going, and what's your party — government or traders?" asked I.

'"I'm bound for old Fayette County, Kentucky, where
white people live — where you can get cornbread and sleep
sound at night without having screeching yellow devils
skulking around ye; and, old feller, there's a girl that wants
to see me, and I'd give my mule to see her — be da-arned
if I wouldn't — you know I told you about her last winter;
she's the greatest ——"

'"Never mind now, Charley — we'll talk of your girl
after a while. Nobody here cares for her but yourself. I
want to know who is in the train yonder — maybe I have
friends — a scarce *genus* in this region."

'"That's a great old way to bluff a fellow off, when he's
half froze to see his girl, but if you want to know, Colonel
Russell from California, Secretary of State under Fremont,
is in that crowd, with sixteen of the greatest 'boys' you
ever came across. They are of the California Battalion.
The Colonel is bearer of dispatches to Washington, from
Stockton ——"

'"Who are the rest? There are at least thirty wagons."

'"A train of 'Neds,' under command of Captain Bell, of the wagonmasters' department. Any danger of Pawnees here?"

'"Yes, there are a few about, but walk in."

'The fort soon filled with the hard-looking teamsters, and before long Colonel Russell himself appeared, dressed in California buckskin pantaloons open from the knee downward, a light summer coat, white wool hat, and yellow California *zapotes*. Charley introduced me. On hearing my name, he asked that of my father. He then grasped my hand warmly, saying they had been classmates in college. We went to the provision room, and sitting on some floursacks, talked of friends far away.

'"What brought you out here, my boy? Your mother, of course, gave you leave, and how long have you been in the country?"

'Seeing the drift of that and other questions of like import, I replied: "Do not think, Colonel, I came here in an improper manner, for I have letters with me to show to the contrary — this is a trip for fun and health, though I must say it's rather rough fun."

'"I am indeed pleased to hear it, for, at first I feared that you had committed some misdemeanor as many youths do, and run away in consequence; but, my dear boy," said he, laying his hand affectionately on my shoulder, "you are in a most dangerous place; I wonder you have not been killed before this. I never heard of such a thing before. Ten men in a fort in the Comanche range, and you are hardly a man yet, you know!"

'"Oh! 'Our hearts are big,' and we are all center shots."

'"You must go along with me. Only ten men in the fort; it is sheer madness to be here," soliloquized he.

'"I have promised Captain Enos to stay until relieved by troops from the States."

'"Ah, but we must waive all such rash promises! Had I

a son here, no greater kindness could be done by a friend than to take him away — you must go — you must go."

'"Smith has my mules."

'"You can take the best one in my *caballada*. Were you to be killed here, I would never cease to blame myself."

'Through the Colonel's solicitation, Sloan gave me a discharge, entitling me to pay on reaching Fort Leavenworth, and showing that I left with his consent. I made a hasty settlement with him of the tobacco, fort accounts, etc., put my small kit in the Colonel's wagon, my saddle on one of his best mules, shook hands with my tried friends, and with light heart bade farewell to the "Prairie Prison." Cain Strickler, Sam Caldwell, and others, coming in with a load of wood, met me a short distance out. Sam shouted: "What's up now, that you are going to leave — not showing the white feather — if you are, may the cursed Comanches get your scalp!"

'"Hold on, old fellow, take breath and I'll tell you; Colonel Russell, here, is an old friend of the family; and when he found me out, he would not let me stay. Well, good-bye; Sloan will tell you more; the train's gone on and for the sake of my hair I must keep with them."

'"Give us your hand, my hearty," and a warm grasp was our parting salutation.'[31]

CHAPTER XII

The Crossing of the Arkansas

ONLY the absence of a bridge could justify the use of the word *ford* for the usual crossing of the Arkansas River, since one stretch of that monotonously uniform stream was just like any other. Everywhere the sandy banks were steep and low, everywhere the water was shallow, everywhere the bed was quicksand. It was merely a question of a choice, of digging down the banks, doubling teams, and snaking the wagons quickly over. One crossing was much like another — in itself.

But in their haste to get to market, to outdo their competitors, the American traders then, like Americans now, put speed first, and generally chose the crossing which offered the shortest route to Santa Fe. Speed was just as important to men with ox-carts as it is to men with motor-trucks. Men even laid bets on the trip!

Those rugged individuals, as we have seen, frequently left the regular ruts and cut trails of their own, so that today photographs taken from airplanes often show a number of trails more or less parallel, instead of one beaten track. So, likewise, there were several crossings, of which three were regularly used.

The earliest caravans had proceeded up the river to Bent's Fort, and crossed there, or even beyond, or at any rate had preferred the shortest route from the Arkansas River to the top of the bend of the Cimarron River, which left the Arkansas near Chouteau's Island, at the Upper

Crossing. The Lower Crossing was at Mulberry Creek, just west of the present Dodge City. It was dangerous, however, as it led to the longest dry route, 'incommodious of water and timber for fuel,' as Surveyor Brown aptly described it.

The favorite crossing was that known as the Middle Crossing, or Cimarron Crossing, near the present town of Cimarron, Kansas. From this ford, the distance to the scanty water of the Cimarron was all of fifty miles, along a sandy trail without a landmark, a plain crisscrossed by beaten buffalo trails, which — in certain seasons — led to water, but — at others — did not. Whichever trail was followed, the Crossing itself was a bad neighborhood. There is always dirty work at the crossroads.

So it was here. The Ford of the Arkansas had unpleasant memories.

The Texans, after the brutal treatment of their fellow citizens by Salazar when the Texan–Santa Fe Expedition was captured by the Mexicans, made a number of efforts to retaliate. One Warfield, who carried a battle-torn Texas flag, went about in the fall of 1842, and the following spring, recruiting followers on the Arkansas and South Platte, declaring his purpose of attacking Mexican wagon trains. Early in the year, his party assembled at the mouth of the Purgatoire, below Bent's Fort. Shortly after, they rode into Mexican territory, and surprised the village of Mora, where they killed several men and ran off all the horses. On the way back, a body of Mexicans surprised them in turn, and stampeded all their animals, including those which the Texans had captured. Warfield's men had to burn their saddles, and walk back to Bent's Fort, where the expedition collapsed.

That same spring, however, a Texan named Snively marched north through Oklahoma to the Arkansas with one hundred and eighty Texans to attack Mexican trains.

They reached the Arkansas towards the end of May, and went into camp forty miles below the Crossing on the south bank, which he claimed was Mexican territory. From someone connected with Bent's Fort he learned that a large Mexican train was coming from Missouri, and that Governor Armijo, who had invested largely in the venture, was at Cold Springs, a camp on the Desert Route.

Armijo sent several hundred of his men — most of them Indians from the Pueblo of Taos — up towards the Arkansas to meet the train. On June 19, Snively and his men attacked this party in the sandhills south of the river, killing eighteen Indians, wounding many, and capturing some. When the fugitives brought this news to Governor Armijo at Cold Springs, he fled in haste, leaving most of his equipment on the ground, though he had many more men than Snively. This clash between white men and Pueblos had much to do with the subsequent Pueblo Revolt (in 1847), when Governor Charles Bent was murdered with others at Taos.

When the Mexican train reached the Crossing under escort of Colonel Cooke and the United States Dragoons, there was no Mexican escort to meet it, and the wagon-master was afraid to cross. Cooke found Snively and Warfield with one hundred men on the south bank of the Arkansas, below the Caches. There he crossed the river and disarmed the astonished Texans, who claimed they were on their own territory, and not within the territory of the United States. Some of these men were able to conceal their own guns and surrender to Cooke the antiquated fire-locks and *escopetas* which they had just taken from the Pueblos. These men followed Warfield off after the Mexican wagon train, but failed to overtake it, and returned home through the dangerous Kiowa and Comanche country. A number of the Texans went back to the States with Colonel Cooke.

Because of this affair, Santa Ana, by decree of August 7, 1843, stopped all trade between Santa Fe and the United States, and Americans living in New Mexico found themselves in great danger.

At the Ford of the Arkansas, also, Indians, as well as Texans and Mexicans, came to grief.

In 1838, the Kiowas were on the rampage all along the river, and when Captain Blunt brought his ill-manned, ill-armed caravan out from Missouri that autumn, he ran head on into danger. The only man in his outfit that had a speck of gall was a runaway boy of fifteen named Oliver Wiggins, who, wearing a faded uniform coat of the U.S. Dragoons, packing a pistol no bigger than a pop-gun, had come West to hunt Injuns! His job was to herd the cavvy — loose stock at the tail of the wagon train.

A band of mountain men led by Kit Carson overtook the caravan, and the two outfits travelled along through the danger zone together. Blunt was glad to have those fighters with his wagons, and the greenhorns gaped.

One morning these green teamsters were astonished to see all the Carson Men clamber hastily into the wagons, to hide under the wagon sheets. 'This occasioned grumbling and not a few sneers from the teamsters — utterances treated with silent contempt.' [32] Kit and his men made ready.

Immediately after, the Kiowas came pelting out of the sandhills to attack the clumsy train. The wagons hastily corralled, and the Indians charged, thinking they had a sure thing. Then the mountain men poked the snouts of their rifles from under the wagon sheets and cut loose all together.

Powder-smoke hid everything. Reloading swiftly, the mountain men tumbled out of the wagons, jumped on their horses, and took after the Injuns, now on the dead run for their lives. Jumping the dead Indians, they raced away, shooting as they rode. Oliver was right with them, pop-gun and all!

That night, at the Crossing, Kit and his men left the train and made their own camp, intending to head for Bent's Fort and Taos early next morning. About dusk, one of the trappers invited Oliver to join the band, and the invitation did not need to be repeated! When the wolves were howling and the wagon-master snored, Oliver gathered up his scanty plunder and sneaked over to Kit's campfire. Carson liked the boy's spunk. For twelve years thereafter, Oliver Wiggins was his right-hand man. . . .

At the Crossing, also, John Simpson 'Blackfoot' Smith used to lie in wait for unwary *Comancheros*. He was a trader, sometimes for the Bents, sometimes on his own hook, and kept his eyes peeled for bargains. In the fur trade, there were no ethics, and Smith was as free from scruples as a newborn babe. He was, in Garrard's words, 'an unaccountable composition of goodness and evil, cleverness and meanness, caution and recklessness . . . the devil incognito.' He often sang hymns, and as often cursed in three languages, including Cheyenne — though the Indians had a strictly limited vocabulary for that purpose. A versatile fellow.

The New Mexicans often came out upon the Plains to trade with the Comanches, as with other tribes, and these native traders were known as *comancheros* for that reason. They packed their mules with dried pumpkins, corn, and *frijoles*, and visited the Indian camps to swap for robes and buffalo-meat. Smith, being first on the ground, with a Cheyenne wife and plenty of Indian relatives, always demanded tribute. Once, when the Mexicans refused to pay, he called out the young warriors, and with their help emptied the sacks of the cowering Mexicans upon the ground, shouting to the women to come and help themselves. Then he sent the poor *pelados* back to Taos, uttering thanks to Heaven for the retention of their scalps. After that, he had no trouble, and collected his 'customs' with all the regularity of a Mexican governor, mulcting his victims of thirty-three per cent (every third robe) of their trade. At Santa Fe, they put a price of five hundred dollars on his scheming head. But nobody ever collected the reward!

From Fort Mann on up the Arkansas River to Bent's Fort, the Trail passed through the range of the Cheyenne Indians. The Bent brothers at first engaged in trapping and trading with the Sioux Indians in the north, but when the Cheyennes divided into the northern and southern divisions, the Bents followed the Southern Cheyennes down to the Arkansas, where they erected a series of stockades in order to trade with these Indians and with the Arapaho and Atsena, who accompanied them. Yellow Wolf, the Cheyenne chief, gave the four Bent brothers Indian names: Charles Bent was called White Hat, William Bent, Little White Man, since he was still little more than a boy; George Bent, Little Beaver, Robert Bent, Blue Bird. The partner of the Bent brothers, Ceran St. Vrain, was dubbed Black Beard. From that day, the relations of the Bents with the Cheyennes were very close. William Bent married the daughters of the Keeper of the Medicine Arrows, and always referred to the tribe as 'my people.' The first stockades were above the mouth of Fountain Creek, near the site of the present city of Pueblo, Colorado. But as the range of the buffalo contracted, the Bents followed them down and built Bent's Old Fort above the mouth of the Purgatoire, about 1828. In 1852, after Bent's Old Fort had been destroyed by its owner, Bent's New Fort was erected where Old Fort Lyon, the military post, stood later. Because of Bent's management, the Cheyennes remained perfectly friendly with the whites until ten years after the Mexican War, and substantially so until 1864. As a result, much Indian lore concerning this part of the Trail is known to us.

In 1849, the gold rush to California brought cholera to the Plains, an epidemic which swept away half the native inhabitants.

That summer, the Kiowas held a Sun Dance, or medicine lodge, on Bluff Creek, south of Fort Mann, and a great number of Cheyennes, Arapahoes, and Osages gathered to witness the ceremony and take part in the social life of the big camp.

While the dance was going on, one of the Osage onlookers was seized with cramps. Most of the Indians present had no idea what ailed the man, but a Cheyenne named White Face Bull had heard of the plague, and called out, urging the people to break camp and run for their lives.

Immediately, the frightened crowd scattered like blackbirds, struck their tents, and lit out, leaving the dance lodge empty. The Osages fled back towards their own country; the Plains tribes rode southwest, towards the Cimarron River.

All the way people were falling out of the straggling column, dying, wailing, doubled up with the convulsions of that dread disease. Old and young, men and women fell from their horses, died in the Indian drags, rolled gasping on the prairie. The whole rout was in a panic. No one knew what to do, medicine men died like the rest. They reached the Cimarron about noon, and before they could pitch their scattered tents, the living were the dying all through the Indian camp.

In that camp was a very brave war-chief, Little Old Man, who had often fought in defence of his tribe. In the face of this appalling danger, he got out his war-bag, unpacked his scalp shirt and war-bonnet. Having painted his face for war, he fastened his war-charm about the neck of his running horse — a stuffed collar of mole-skin. In countless battles that charm had protected him from bullets and arrows. Then he took his lance and shield of tough buffalo hide, hardened in the fire, mounted, and rode slowly up and down through the camp.

Everywhere the people were dying.

Little Old Man was helpless to defend them. Shaking his lance, he called out, 'If it knew where this thing is that is killing my people, if I knew where it could be found, I would go there and fight it, and die killing it!'

Even while he defied the cholera, it struck him. He was seized with cramps, but managed to stay on his horse. He rode back to his own tent, got off his horse, and fell to the ground. Within a few minutes he died in the arms of his wailing wife. . . .[33]

The Lower Crossing of the Arkansas lay on the route of what most military experts now consider the most remarkable retreat — certainly one of the most successful running fights — in the history of America. This was the flight of the Cheyennes from Oklahoma under the leadership of Dull Knife and Little Wolf.

In the spring of 1877, Dull Knife's band of Cheyennes, which had spent the winter with Crazy Horse on Powder River, surrendered to the United States troops. In that northern country, game was still abundant. The government proposed that Dull Knife should take his people and go down to the agency of the Southern Cheyennes, at Darlington (Fort Reno), in what is now Oklahoma. The Indians agreed and made the trip without trouble in seventy days.

In the south, they found no buffalo and very little other game. Fever and ague attacked them. The beef issued them was all skin and bone, and for three months out of the year they had nothing to eat. They were starving. During the first winter, of about one thousand souls, two-thirds were sick and forty died. Nevertheless, Dull Knife stuck to his bargain through the year.

Then the Cheyennes began to talk of going back to their own high, dry mountain country, where they could be well and eat buffalo. As soon as the grass was long enough in the spring, Dull Knife and Little Wolf decided to return their people home.

Dull Knife was wise in council, Little Wolf a war-chief. From Darlington back to their own country on Powder River, the country was all open prairie, crossed by many wagon trails and several railroads. Part of the country was already settled, and there was no lack of troops in garrison. There were enemies everywhere.

As usual, several young men slipped off in advance of the general movement. When the agent, J. D. Miles, demanded that the chiefs bring back these runaways and give him ten hostages to hold in the meantime, the chiefs refused to obey. They frankly answered that they were going back, that they would not sneak away, but that they preferred not to have a fight at the agency, or make the ground bloody near the camps of their relatives. Some three hundred of them started off to the north. Of these, less than seventy were fighting men. Thirteen thousand troops were under orders to stop them.

Troops from Fort Reno overtook them on Little Medicine Lodge Creek, in the afternoon, before they had gone a hundred miles. The commander sent an Arapaho Indian to call them back. Little Wolf tried to conciliate the official, but refused pointblank to return. The troops attacked. They fired the first shot. Little Wolf loped back to his warriors. The fight continued until dark.

That night both sides remained on the field, and in the morning the battle was resumed. But the Cheyennes stood off their enemies successfully, never trying to retreat. And so about noon the troops withdrew, leaving two soldiers and the Arapaho scout dead. Half a dozen Cheyennes had been wounded.

They pushed on, and three days after, near the Cimarron, a second detachment met them, a gray horse troop, coming from the north. But the Indians, moving forward, had no trouble running this small force ahead of them, and kept moving.

Soon after a third force met them, coming from Fort Dodge and Dodge City. This time the Cheyennes were outnumbered. With the troops was a large number of citizens. But the fight was brief. For some reason, the whites made only one charge. Then, not being able to break the Indian lines, they sounded retreat on the bugles, and pulled out.

Now the Cheyennes were angry. Up until then, they had refrained from depredations upon citizens, only taking some needed horses and cattle as they rode along. But now that the citizens had come out to fight them, they felt justified in attacking all white men whatever.

Late that afternoon, the white men returned, with a number of wagons. Using these as a fort, or base of operations, they fought and fought hard all day.

By this time the Indians saw that they would have to outmarch the troops. That night they left and skipped to the Arkansas River. Before they crossed, they came upon some hide-hunters skinning buffalo. The hide-hunters were scared out of their skins, but the Indians were so glad to see the fresh buffalo-meat — eighteen freshly killed cows — that they let the white men go, only taking their Sharps rifles and long cartridges. Then they hurried across the stream above Fort Dodge.

North of the river, troops again attacked them, but the Cheyennes dug in on a hilltop and stood them off. They had to leave many horses, broken down by the long, hard trip, at this point.

But that night, tired of continual fighting, anxious only to get home, the Cheyennes made tracks. For three days they went on hard as they could go, and almost without stopping. The women jogged along, heavy for want of sleep; the babies rode, silent, heads lolling, in their cradles; old men crouched in the drags, tight-lipped and patient, or singing brave heart songs to cheer their relatives; on the flanks and in rear rode the young men, quirting their jaded ponies; while out in front rode Little Wolf, tireless and fearless as a bear.

They reached Frenchman's Fork of the Republican River, in Nebraska. There again the Cheyennes saw troops, but managed to avoid them. They forded the South Platte, somewhere near Ogallala, and finally made camp for a rest near the mouth of White Clay Creek on the North Platte. The long running fight was over.

Little Wolf wished to push on. But Dull Knife was a gentler soul; he was home now, and that was enough for him. So Little Wolf went on without him. Dull Knife, childlike in his trust, went towards Fort Robinson and surrendered.

There the commanding officer demanded that the band return south to Oklahoma. Dull Knife's people refused. The white officer, determined to break their resolution, shut them all up — men, women, and children — in an empty building, put a guard over them, and told them they could go hungry and waterless until they agreed to obey.

That was a bitter winter. Snow was deep, and the weather was dreadfully cold. The imprisoned Cheyennes had no fire, no water, no food, only scanty clothing. They scraped the snow from the window-sills, ate that. Among them they had the parts of a few guns, a little ammunition, all concealed under the women's dresses, tied in the hair of the children as ornaments. These they assembled — an arsenal of five rifles, a few revolvers, a knife or two — and the floor-boards!

One moonlight night, as the sentry passed their window, a shot rang out. The private dropped dead, and the starving handful jumped from their windows and fled across the frozen snow.

Within a few minutes, before they had crossed the parade ground, the troops were on their trail. Half-clothed, with empty bellies, they fled and fought and died for eleven days, hurrying towards Powder River. More than fifty were taken, thirty-seven killed, the rest surrounded.

But they did not die like dogs. Even at the last ditch, three young men left their shelter and charged the troops, to die fighting. Two of these starving men had knives. One had only an empty pistol.

Little Wolf had better luck than Dull Knife. He did not surrender until the following spring, when 'White Hat' Clark, an officer who understood Indians (he wrote that classic of the Plains, *The Indian Sign Language*) found the Cheyennes near Charcoal Butte on the Little Missouri, and enlisted them as scouts for the Sioux campaign.

After all that needless slaughter, the survivors of both bands were allowed to remain in the north.[34]

That was a memorable march, an epic story, never to be forgotten by those who passed along the Santa Fe Trail. Yet, naturally enough, once the tale was told, the traders were more concerned with their own march across the Cimarron Desert just beyond the Crossing.

PART V

The Desert Route

CHAPTER XIII

The Cimarron Desert

ONCE across the Arkansas, the caravan halted for a day, to let the animals rest and prepare for the dreaded *jornada*, the 'water scrape,' just ahead. Beyond the sandhills was an immense barren plain without wood or water, stretching for fifty miles by the most direct route to the Cimarron River. For four-fifths of the distance, there was not a single landmark, and no trail to be followed. Wagon-masters laid their course by compass on that prairie ocean, level as the calmest sea.

Every teamster was supposed to keep a five-gallon keg in his wagon, and woe to the man who had none. The night before the start, the Captain went around, shouting, 'Fill up the water kegs,' and trying to make his undisciplined crew obey. But every owner of a two-horse wagon assumed as much authority as the Captain, and did not hesitate to issue orders. For the Captain had no legal authority.

Travellers lamented this, and urged that some system of maritime law be set up among the traders. Gregg says, 'For my own part, I can see no reason why the captain of a prairie caravan should not have as much power to call his men to account for disobedience or mutiny, as the captain of a ship upon the high seas.' But no man was ever court-martialed on the prairies by legal authority, or hanged from the yard-arm of a prairie schooner!

That night the cooks of all the messes were busy baking

bread, cooking meat, and preparing supplies for the long trip through the desert. They knew it would be at least two days before they found water or fuel for cooking.

As for the oxen and mules, they had to do without a drink. Their masters therefore took care to see that they had a good rest, ample time to graze, and a bellyful of water before they started.

Unfortunately, the first five miles through the sandhills was very heavy pulling, and by the time the animals had reached the level plain beyond, many of them were already tired, hot, and thirsty. Usually the passage of the sandhills caused a delay of some hours, as wagons were almost sure to be overturned there, and sometimes a man would be injured in trying to keep the heavy craft on an even keel.

On they plodded, and the sun and wind, to say nothing of dread of the desert, made every man thirsty beyond his wont. They prayed for rain, in their hearts. And, not rarely, they had an answer to their prayer — at any rate in June. Then hailstorms beat upon them, forcing the men under the wagons, and pelting the teams to distraction. Terrific thunderstorms and electrical storms came up, stabbing the ground with savage bolts of lightning, sometimes killing an ox, causing the teamsters to marvel that his yoke-fellow remained unhurt. Wild winds swept the plain at times, and even overset wagons with their fury. And sometimes it rained. In that country, it never rained but it poured.

Greenhorns welcomed the rain, and it was refreshing — that first day, if it came that day. But later, when the oxen were half mad with thirst, a rain storm meant disaster. Then, when the creeks filled, the teams would smell the water miles ahead, and take out for it, hard as they could go, in a bee-line, dragging their wagons after them with reckless disregard for any obstacles which they might encounter. Nothing the teamsters could do would check or swerve them. On they lumbered at a clumsy gallop, straight to and into the creek, where they plunged to drink, and the wagon was swept into and overwhelmed in the water.

Then the caravan had to halt, and all hands flocked to the aid of the owner of the damaged cargo. The wet goods had to be unpacked, the bales of cloth unwrapped, and the plain around spread with a motley assortment of articles laid out to dry in sun and wind.

At such a moment, it was sometimes the fate of the caravan to see Indians coming, for this was a favorite range of the worst tribes on the Plains. Comanches, Kiowas, Apaches, Cheyennes and Arapahoes ranged here, and with the Arapahoes, their blood-brothers the Atsena, or Gros Ventres of the Prairie (sometimes called Blackfoot because of their alliance with that tribe in Montana, where they normally ranged). Sometimes the band would approach bearing a flag — generally taken as proof that — at some time — the tribe had made a treaty with the United States. In that case, they might be welcomed, given a smoke, and sent away with fifty dollars' worth of presents. Gregg even met a party of Sioux in the Cimarron Desert, who had come down to raid for Mexican horses. Plains warriors would ride fifteen hundred miles at any time on the chance of capturing a few good horses.

But, even though the first Indians met with might be friendly, they generally gave out the cheering news that hostiles — in much larger numbers — were on the Trail ahead!

After fifty miles of thirst, heat, trouble with refractory animals, frightful storms, and false alarms, the caravan would reach Sand Creek, generally either in flood or perfectly dry, so that water could only be had by digging for it. Then the wagons would roll on towards the Cimarron, another eight or ten miles — a full day's journey in such circumstances. This stream, especially if struck below the usual line of the Trail, was also generally quite dry, so that caravans sometimes mistook it for Sand Creek, and crossed, pushing on into a waterless waste quite away from their true direction.

Plodding on southward in search of the lost river, they would finally bring up spang against a ledge of sandhills, over which they could not drive. Then, if lucky enough to turn westward, they might be heading in the right direction.

Meanwhile, finding no water anywhere, the men would be frightened. They were lost — and knew it — lost in that waterless desert, where so many had met with disaster, died of thirst, or perished at the hands of savages when frantic for a drink. Then the veterans held council, hoping to agree upon a course before men and oxen failed utterly.

The *jornada* was no mere trap for greenhorns. Veteran mountain men died there. Of these, no better man ever stood in moccasins than Jedediah Smith, one of the finest fellows and most competent explorers of the Old West, a gentleman in buckskins, with the courageous heart of a bear. In 1831, when only thirty-three years old, he started for Santa Fe with his own wagons. Three years later, torrential rains made the *jornada* a sea of mud, through which the caravan of that year cut a trail that could be followed. But in 1831 there was no trail to follow, and Smith had no guide. For three blistering days the party was lost on the desert.

The only trails to be seen there were those of buffalo — broad beaten highways, leading — at certain seasons — to water. Knowing the habits of that animal, Smith probably believed the trails would lead to water, though they ran off every which way. But, if so, he was mistaken. There was then no water at the ends of those trails.

He rode alone, leaving the wagons to find succor for his comrades. That was Smith all over. He was a genuine Christian — probably the only one among the Santa Fe traders. With parching lips and tongue, he kept going, and at last he found a stream. Or rather, the dry sandy bed of a stream. The Cimarron!

Smith spurred forward looking up and down the river for a pool. There was none. He dismounted, eager to slake his thirst, so that he would have strength to carry the word to his comrades, back there in the burning heat. Anxiously, he dug barehanded in the sand, scooping out a basin two feet deep. The water began to seep in. Smith watched it, smiling with cracked lips. His comrades were saved, now! He sat and watched the basin fill up, then stooped to drink. When he raised his head, he found himself surrounded by Comanches.

They were horseback. When he tried to mount, they frightened his horse, and shot him, lanced him. Smith jerked out his holster pistols, tried to defend himself. He dropped two of them, but he had no chance. They killed him. All that we know of his death is what they told some Mexican traders, to whom they sold his weapons.

Smith was a good friend to the Indians, and did not approve the cruelty with which some of his companions treated them. He was also a scholar, in his way, loved literature, and had prepared a geography of the Rocky Mountain region. But to the Comanches, he was just a scalp.[35]

Whenever a caravan was in difficulty, Indians were certain to appear. Their appearance was a signal to corral the train, and stung every man into action. The cry of 'Injuns!' caused a mighty cracking of whips, which sounded as if the battle had already begun.

The corralling of a train was a pretty sight. The wagons, which moved in four parallel columns, some rods apart, followed their leaders. The two outside columns swung apart to get the proper distance between, then converged on a point where the two lead wagons met and halted. Each of the following wagons closed up on the one ahead, locking its inside front wheel with the outside rear wheel of the one ahead. This put the teams and poles all outside. The bull-whackers lost no time in unhooking their teams and driving them into the corral.

Meanwhile, the two inner columns kept close together until they reached the point of the rear angle of the corral. There the two lead wagons diverged, heading for the hind ends of the outside columns, and so forming a right-angled quadrangle, with a narrow opening at the rear corner. As soon as the wagons were parked, the men chained the wheels together, blocked the gateway in rear, and prepared for defence.

A strong caravan had little to fear from Indians, once it was in corral formation. But, since there was no water within the enclosure, it could not be held for a prolonged siege. Moreover, in spite of yokes and chained wheels, and every precaution, Indians sometimes so frightened the oxen that they broke out of the corral, and stampeded into the distance. Once started, nothing would stop them. They were, in fact, far worse than mules, though less of a temptation to the redskins.

It was a question whether a hostile war party or a large camp of friendly Indians with squaws and babies and dogs was a worse worry to the harassed white men. The hostiles could be kept at a distance, but the friendlies had to be handled with care. A few thousands of these would make life a burden to the Captain of the train.

They swarmed down, anxious to see the wagons, to see the strange white men, to smoke, to eat, to receive gifts, to talk. At night they serenaded the caravan, riding around, singing their barbarous songs. By day they rode alongside, or camped around.

If admitted to the corral, they pilfered small articles, and even got away with heavy objects like a pig of lead, weighing nearly a hundred pounds. One of them stole a side-saddle, and left its owner wondering what earthly use the Indian put it to. With such doubtful neighbors travelling with the caravan, men did not get much sleep of nights, and every morning thanked God they still had their hair on.

And when, at last, the main camp disappeared, parties of young men were sure to return next day, or the day after, for one more look at the white men, and in the hope of a free meal and some trinkets. Every party had to be placated, since there was no central authority with whom to treat. And every treaty had to be sealed with a gift.

The Captain started his wagons rolling very early in hopes of leaving these pests behind.

At the top of the bend, the Cimarron sometimes showed a rushing torrent of water, and green, grassy glades. The Lower Cimarron Spring, though not good water, was never dry. And those who did not enjoy the water there could refresh their eyes, at any rate, by looking at the cat-tail marsh about it. Here the hills were covered with bright-hued pebbles, the hills themselves being composed of a whitish rock filled with small stones.

On the Cimarron cold, protracted rains were usual at the season when caravans passed. Then the guards would sneak under the wagons at night, leaving the train unprotected, trusting to the wet which covered the plain to the depth of several inches. Even the sure knowledge that savages were lurking around could not make those undisciplined wagoners endure the wet with patience. Daily, the Captain threatened to resign!

The Trail followed the river for a distance of eighty miles, passing the Middle Spring, with its hills infested with tarantulas and rattlesnakes.

All through this region rattlesnakes were so numerous that the progress of the train was accompanied by a continual popping of guns, as men shot them. A lead team would pass over forty of the reptiles in a day's march, though few of the animals were bitten. Men occasionally were struck by the poisoned fangs. One of the soldiers with the troops sent out during the Mexican War was so bitten — on the tip of his index finger. The surgeon gave him all the whiskey he could drink, applied a tourniquet, cut the finger to the bone, and then seared the wound. The patient held his hand down all night, and was as good as ever next morning. Thereafter, so many thirsty men turned up, claiming to have been bitten, that the surgeon was compelled to alter his procedure: he told them he would cut and burn the bite first, and serve the liquor afterwards! [36]

Above the Middle Spring a few miles brought the caravan into the extreme southeast corner of what is now the State of Colorado. Here occurred one of the most dramatic combats in all the history of the Old West.

It was here that Kit Carson, who had only just organized his own band of trappers, had his generalship put to the test. At the time his famous band, known thereafter as the Carson Men, had only six members. Kit and Joe Meek, Bill Mitchell, and three Delaware Indians — Jonas, Tom Hill, and Manhead — had parted with their comrades at Bent's Fort, and headed southeast, to make their hunt in the country lying between the Arkansas and the Cimarron, on the small streams which flow out of the mountains.

That was, of course, Comanche country. Bill Mitchell always hankered to hunt in that country, which he knew very well, having once taken a Comanche woman and lived with that tribe, in which he claimed to have been a famous warrior.

It was new country to Joe Meek, that happy-go-lucky wit and wag from Virginia, one year younger than Kit, with the long nose, full eye, and small, thin-lipped mouth which betrayed his lively temper. He was the youngest, though not a man in the band was over twenty-five. One of the Delawares — Jonas — was not yet out of his teens, though he handled his long rifle with the best of the trappers.

The Delawares were typical members of their tribe, which had taken over the white frontiersmen's weapons and mode of life, differing from them only in speech and blood. Wherever the white man went, there would be found a Delaware acting as guide or hunter. They were well armed, and combined the skill of the white hunter with the sure instinct of the red man. The Plains Indians hated them bitterly because they killed the buffalo in their country, and more than once tried to exterminate a band of Delawares who had ventured upon the prairies. But bow and lance could not match those riflemen, and the Plains Indians were badly worsted. The Delawares were cleanly Indians, proud and industrious in their hard profession, and the mountain men freely accepted them on equal terms. This fact is significant, for the mountain men despised the Spaniards, the Mexicans, the French Canadians, the greenhorns from the settlements, even the soldiers of the Regular Army. Kit knew what he was about when he chose the three Delawares for his band.

One spring morning the six trappers were riding across the bare prairies, heading south. Not a tree was in sight, not a bush. The mountains far to the west showed dimly, blue and vague in the sunlight. The plains undulated gently away and away, one rolling wave like another, far as they could see. But Bill Mitchell knew his way. He rode steadily forward, his red gee-string flagging the wind, his bare buttocks pounding the Spanish saddle.

Suddenly Bill reined up, and Kit, looking where he pointed, saw a round black dot on the hilltop ahead. 'Injuns!' It was the season for war parties. The trappers halted and stared at the Indian scout's dark head, waiting to see what it portended. They had not long to wait.

For the Indians, hidden behind the hill, were at once informed by their scout what had happened. The white men had halted: it was clear that they had seen the Indian scout. Over the hill they came pell-mell — mounted on their best horses — racing to count their *coups*.

All at once the skyline sprouted lances, tossing like grass-blades in the sun, then black-and-white eagle-feather crests, horses' heads, naked, painted warriors. The charge was on. At the same moment the war-whoop, like the quick chatter of a machine-gun, pulsated upon Kit's ears. The whole hillside was covered with Indians.

'Comanches!' yelled Bill Mitchell, and looked to Kit for orders.

'Two hundred of 'em, or I'm a nigger!' said Joe Meek.

The Comanches were magnificently mounted. They always were. They had more horses and better horses than any Indians on the plains, and they 'ate and slept horse-back.' They constantly raided the vast herds of Spanish horses on the *haciendas* to the south of their range — the best animals on the prairies. Kit knew he could not run away from them — and there was no cover within miles. Six to two hundred!

'Fort, boys!' he sang out, and jumped off his mule, jerking out his scalp-knife before his moccasins touched the ground. The mule, with all a mule's instinctive fear of Indians, tried to break away, almost jerking the stocky little man off his feet. But Kit caught the lariat close to the animal's head, and, as it reared back, passed the keen edge of his knife across its taut throat. He jumped clear. While the mule staggered, coughing out its life, drenching the short grass with blood, Kit snatched the cover from his rifle, looked to the priming, glanced round at his men.

They had followed his example. Already three mules were down. Hastily, Kit and his comrades flung themselves prone behind the kicking carcasses, pointing the muzzles of their rifles toward the coming warriors. The ground shook with the beat of eight hundred hooves, the sunlight glittered on the long, keen lance-points, and lit up the garish war-paint upon the naked bodies, the flares and blotches of color upon the spotted ponies. Feathers streamed from lance and war-bonnet. On they came. It was magnificent, and it was war. Kit yelled a warning.

'Bill, don't shoot yit. Hold on, Joe! Let the Delawares shoot fust!' Joe and Bill nodded, grim-lipped, never taking their eyes off the charging Indians. It was hard to die idle, finger crooked on trigger. But they knew Kit was right: it would never do to empty all their guns at once. Three shots against two hundred savages!

Kit was gesturing swiftly to the Delawares. 'You killum, *sabe?*' and Tom Hill, muttering a word to his red companions, grinned knowingly, at the same time drawing a bead across his dying mule on the foremost warrior. Tom looked very strong and competent, lying there, his long body covered to his knees with his straight, black, unplaited hair.

Already the horses were so near that Kit could see the whites of their excited eyes. Ahead rode the chief, his lance wrapped with shining otter fur, his war-bonnet streaming behind. *Crack!* The three long rifles spoke together. The chief tumbled from his saddle, struck the ground on his head just in front of the little barricade, and was dragged away by his frightened horse, having tied his body to the end of the lariat. The charge split, and swept by in a thunder of hooves, the rush of crowding horses, white smoke in clouds from the rifles, a rain of arrows lancing the dust.

Immediately, the redskins turned and charged again, and this time Kit and Bill and Joe swung round, faced the other way to meet them, aimed and fired as steadily as though they had been armed with repeating rifles or machine-guns. Again the charge was split, and the Indians dashed by. Two were left on the ground. Bill let out a war-whoop.

But now, whirling round in a moment, the Indians raced back. The white men's guns were empty, they knew.

The Delawares had not had time to reload. Now they could ride the whites down, lance them with impunity — out of reach of their sharp knives. Back they came, whooping and laughing with expectation of an easy victory. One of them recognized Bill Mitchell and called out, taunting the white man, as he came: 'Lean Bull, your hair is mine. Now I am going to make the ground bloody where you lie!' In a flash the Comanches were upon them.

But the Indians never reached the whites. They could not force their ponies to approach the dead mules. The smell of the blood drove their horses crazy, and the charge ended in a *mêlée* of bucking, rearing animals, circling round the trappers, too unruly to allow their masters to draw bow and shoot. Kit's stratagem had saved his band.

And now Jonas was taking aim; his rifle blazed, and the laugh on the face of the taunter changed as he swayed from his saddle and toppled to the ground. The Comanches saw him fall, saw Manhead aiming, saw Tom Hill strike the butt of his rifle on the ground, too much in a hurry to ram down the charge. They turned, they retreated, and the frightened ponies made the retreat a rout. The trappers stood and cheered.

But the Comanches, in spite of their losses, could not believe that six men could stand off two hundred. Armed only with bows and lances, they re-formed and charged bravely, only to split and retire to the hilltop again. All the while, whenever there was a lull in the fighting, the trappers were busy with knife and hatchet, deepening their defences, and at last they had an adequate fort even against arrows at short range. And as often as the Indians charged, they kept them off, firing in shifts, so that always three rifles were loaded.

Again the Comanches charged and retired. Then their medicine man, shaking a big rattle, confident of his power to turn bullets, led them on. Kit dropped him, and the redskins, finding their medicine no good that day, sat and smoked and talked things over on the hill. During the council, the Comanche women came down to carry off the dead and wounded.

It was scorching hot in the midday sun. The trappers had no shade, no water. Their throats were parched with the heat, the fever of excitement, the dust, the reek of the rifles. Flies swarmed about the dead mules, and stung fiercely. And the women cursed and scolded, shaking their fists helplessly at the whites, threatening vengeance: 'Dog-faces, I throw filth at you. Cowards! Women! Wait till the council is over! I shall dance over your scalp!'

What wonder if Manhead, following the custom of his people, raised his rifle to throw the squaw who screamed out insults? It was an easy shot. And to kill a woman under the eyes of her men was always rated a brave deed — a *coup* — by the Indians.

Kit saw what Manhead was doing, and commanded him to hold his fire. Kit was no Davy Crockett, to have a hand in the slaughter of women. Many a squaw died at the hands of trappers, and even more fell to the guns of greenhorns and men in uniform. But Kit Carson had only scorn for the skunk who would shoot a woman, red or white. Man-head let the squaw go.

All day the Indians sat by and the trappers stood them off. The fighting became rather half-hearted — young men galloping round and round in circles, displaying their marvellous horsemanship, shooting from under their ponies' necks, sometimes dashing up close to the dead mules to throw an arrow into them in sheer bravado. The trappers killed a few horses, but could do little damage to the young men. For every Comanche had a loop of hair rope braided into his pony's mane, and swinging in this, with one heel on the animal's back, was able to screen himself entirely behind his racing horse.

Come night, the trappers were still waiting, hungry, dry, anxious, their shoulders sore from the kick of their guns. They lay low and watched the ragged silhouette on the skyline. At last it melted away. For some time they remained in their fort. Then, thinking the redskins had gone, they got to their feet, stretched arms and legs, moved about. Most of the charges had come from the hill to the south. The bodies of the mules on that side of the fort were so thick with arrows that Kit could not lay the flat of his hand anywhere upon them without touching an Indian shaft. Yet not one of the trappers was seriously hurt. Meek, letting his love of a good yarn smother his better judgment, estimated forty casualties on the Indian side. Kit hammered two brass tacks into the stock of his rifle.

The mountain men had to leave their traps, their possible sacks, their costly saddles, their well-filled packs. Slinging their blankets over their shoulders, and carrying only their hatchets, knives, and rifles, they sneaked away through the prairie starlight. After a mile or two they settled down into a steady dog-trot which they maintained all night. Back to the mountains. Back to camp. Bill Mitchell told them it was many weary miles to the nearest water. . . .

In this region rattlesnakes were so abundant that, whenever camp was made, everybody had to scout over the ground and make sure that the spot selected for his bedroll was free from venomous serpents. A snake, it was said, would not cross a hair rope laid down around a bed. This belief once caused a curious attempt.

In the course of the long trip, some men were bound to take a dislike to one another, and enforced intimacy sometimes developed these grudges into mountainous proportions. One man had come to hate a comrade so bitterly that he determined to make away with him. For a long time he pondered this, and rejected one plan after another. But at last he hit upon a method. He kept referring to snakes, talking of their fangs and poison, until his enemy was nervous about them. Then he casually mentioned the 'fact' that a hair rope was perfect protection. His enemy then purchased a hair rope from one of the Mexican packers with the train, and religiously coiled it around his bed at night.

The would-be murderer then prepared his trap. He managed to catch a big rattler, and hid it under a bucket in some sagebrush until dark. Then, when it was his turn to do guard duty, he brought the squirming reptile into camp, 'riled it' properly, and slipped it down *inside* the circle of the hair rope, where his enemy lay snoring. Quickly, the guard slipped back to his post of duty, chuckling to himself. In the morning, what was his surprise to find his enemy as good as ever after a sound night's sleep, and no snake anywhere around! Thereafter he took delight in killing the deceptive sarpints whenever he met them.

Two days' travel up the Cimarron brought the train to Willow Bar, a ridge or bar of sand covered with a thick growth of willow shoots. Not far beyond lay the bleaching bones of mules, known as the Hundred Mule Heads, which perished there in a blizzard in the winter of 1844–45. The country began to be broken. Gregg tells of an adventure at Willow Bar, which is typical:

'... We took the usual mid-day respite of two or three hours, to afford the animals time to feed, and our cooks to prepare dinner. Our wagons were regularly "formed," and the animals turned loose to graze at leisure, with only a "day-guard" to watch them. Those who had finished their dinners lay stretched upon their blankets, and were just beginning to enjoy the luxury of a siesta — when all of a sudden, the fearful and oft-reiterated cry of "Indians!" turned this scene of repose into one of bustle and confusion.

'From the opposite ridge at the distance of a mile, a swarm of savages were seen coming upon us, at full charge, and their hideous whoop and yell soon resounded through the valley. Such a jumbling of promiscuous voices I never expect to hear again. Every one fancied himself a commander, and vociferated his orders accordingly. The air was absolutely rent with the cries of "Let's charge 'em, boys!" — "Fire upon 'em, boys!" — "Reserve! don't fire till they come nearer!" — while the voice of our captain was scarcely distinguishable in his attempts to prevent such rash proceedings. As the prairie Indians often approach their friends as well as enemies in this way, Captain Stanley was unwilling to proceed to extremities, lest they might be peacefully inclined. But a "popping salute," and the whizzing of fusil balls over our heads, soon explained their intentions. We returned them several rifle shots by way of compliment, but without effect, as they were at too great a distance.

'A dozen cannoniers now surrounded our "artillery," which was charged with canister. Each of them had, of course, something to say. "Elevate her; she'll ground," one would suggest. "She'll overshoot, now," rejoined another. At last, after raising and lowering the six-pounder several times, during which process the Indians had time to retreat beyond reach of shot, the match was finally applied, and — bang! went the gun, but the charge grounded midway. This was followed by two or three shots with single ball, but apparently without effect; although there were some with sharp eyes, who fancied they saw Indians or horses wounded at every fire. We came off equally unscathed from the conflict, barring a horse of but little value, which ran away, and was taken by the enemy. The Indians were about a hundred in number, and supposed to be Comanches. . . .'

CHAPTER XIV

The Canadian River

THE train had only one day's march to make after leaving Willow Bar to bring it to the so-called Battle Ground where Colonel Antonio Viscarra had his conflict with the Arapahoes and Gros Ventres in 1829, before his meeting with Major Riley at Chouteau's Island. Viscarra was encamped on the Cimarron, when one hundred and twenty warriors approached on foot. The American traders did not welcome them, but Viscarra let them come into his camp. They proposed to stay all night.

Viscarra made them welcome, but proposed to disarm them for the night. This may have alarmed the Indians. At any rate, they have generally regarded any such proposal as tantamount to a declaration of war. Certain it is that they delayed handing over their weapons, and at length jumped up, yelling, and fired on the Mexicans. They tried to kill Viscarra, but one of his men, a Pueblo Indian, jumped forward to protect his commander, and received the bullet himself. The Pueblo was instantly killed. Together, Viscarra and the traders drove the Indians into the hills. Three or four Mexicans were killed, and many Indians. . . .

The last camp on the Cimarron, one hundred and forty miles from the Crossing of the Arkansas, was at the Upper Cimarron Spring. This small fountain flowed into a ravine, forming a stream which ran some four miles into the river. The little stream was in a lovely spot, surrounded by towering cliffs, craggy spurs, and deep-cut crevices, and wound through thickets of green-brier, wild currant and plum bushes, mountain cherries ('wild gooseberries'), and grape-vines. The water was good, and though the road passed over the ridge a quarter of a mile from the Spring, travellers generally turned aside to visit it, and taste its really re-freshing waters. Some caravans remained with the Cimar-ron until they reached Cold Springs.

Here Armijo had halted to send troops to meet his wagons under escort of Colonel Cooke, June, 1842. For a long time after, the ground was littered with the equipment he left there, when he skipped back to Santa Fe, after Snively and the Texans had put his men to flight.

Hereabouts, caravans usually halted to celebrate the Fourth of July, in good old-fashioned style. Those traders were Americans, proud of it, and they did not care who knew it. At daybreak, the Glorious Fourth was greeted with salvo after salvo of artillery fire, and rifles were fired by platoons. If the riflemen did not get off all together, nobody minded; the more noise the better. Far from home, on foreign territory, the traders forgot their party differ-ences. As one of them put it, 'nothing intrudes, in these wild solitudes, to mar that harmony of feeling, and almost pious exultation, which every true-hearted American ex-periences on this great day.'

Rolling on, the wagons approached the twin peaks of the Rabbit Ear Mounds, the first hills of any size met with on the Desert Route. Before reaching the Mounds, camp was usually made on McNees Creek. The stream received its name from a tragedy.

In the autumn of 1828, the returning caravan had reached this point on its long way to Missouri. It was seldom, at that early date, that traders were molested by redskins, though the Indians had become accustomed to look for caravans, and knew how many animals were with them. Two young men, McNees and Monroe, riding along ahead, had become tired, and carelessly lay down to rest, on the bank of this stream. They went to sleep, and the Indians found them. Within sight of the caravan, they were killed, shot with their own guns. When the slow-paced oxen came up with them, their comrades found McNees dead, Monroe dying. McNees was wrapped in his blanket and buried in a shallow hole, afterward filled with poles and rocks, to keep the wolves from digging him up. Monroe was put into one of the wagons and carried on to the Cimarron, where he died, and was buried in his turn.

Just as the burial was completed, half a dozen Indians appeared across the river. Probably these Indians had nothing to do with the killings. But the traders did not wait to find out. Seeing their guns, the Indians turned to escape. But the first shot brought down one pony, and the following volleys riddled all but one of the Indians. That one, of course, lived to carry the news to his tribesmen! A few days later, these had their revenge, and swept away nearly a thousand head of horses and mules belonging to that caravan. Not satisfied with that, the redskins lay in wait for others, and seeing a party of twenty men, a pack train with a cargo of Mexican silver, they attacked, killed one man, and stampeded all the animals. When they left, the traders divided their treasure, and plodded on afoot, each man lugging along nearly a thousand dollars. On the Arkansas they cached the silver until they could return and get it.

Small parties were always in danger. Two years earlier, a party of twelve — with only four guns among them — were visited by a band of Indians, probably Arapahoes, who soon saw how defenceless the white men were. They went off, but came back in force, thirty men, each with a lariat. The chief explained that his men were tired of walking, and must have horses.

The white men, fearing to object, asked if one horse

apiece would do, and told the chief to go and catch
them.

Finding the whites so easily robbed, the chief demanded
an extra horse for each of his warriors. 'Well, catch them,'
the white Captain said. The Indians, jumping on the gift
horses, and swinging their ropes, plunged among the stock
with wild yells, and drove off the whole *caballada* — five
hundred head of horses, mules, and burros....

The first caravans passed south of the Rabbit Ear
Mounds, the later ones to the north. Either way, they were
certain to run into parties of Mexican buffalo hunters,
ciboleros. Picturesque fellows, these.

The *cibolero* wore a jacket and close-fitting trousers of
leather, and a flat straw hat. On his shoulder he carried a
quiver, filled with arrows, and a bow. The long handle of
his lance, set in a case, was suspended from a strap from the
horn of his saddle, with the blade high overhead in its scab-
bard, from which dangled a tassel of gay parti-colored stuffs.
If he had a fusil, he carried it on the other side, with a tas-
selled stopper in the muzzle.

It would be hard to say whether the *cibolero* or the
traders were happier at their meeting. Everyone was eager
for news. Traders and idlers crowded around the horseman,
trying their bad Spanish on his patient ears. 'What prospects?' they demanded, 'How are goods?' or, 'What news
from the South?' More especially, everyone wished to
know who was in power at Santa Fe, who the customs officials were: old friends — or strangers!

On his part, the Mexican wished to sell a few *varas* of
jerked beef, bags of oven-toasted loaves, brown and hard
and insipid, but soft and palatable when dipped in hot
coffee, or soaked in water. The bread might not be fresh,
it might be made of coarse meal, and intended for the glut-
tonous Comanches. But to the traders, long out of flour,
it was bread — and bread *was* bread!

Those who went with the stranger to his camp saw his numerous comrades, their heavy carts, with huge wheels of solid wood, and their oxen enduring a heavy yoke lashed uncompromisingly across their horns. All about their camp would be long lines and strings of drying beef, for the Spaniards cut it that way, and sold it by the yard.

The Mexican *cibolero*, like the Red River half-breeds of Canada, was an agreeable fellow. Both hunted buffalo, with carts and families in attendance. Nowhere, I think, has anyone a hard word for these amateur Indians, haunting the fringes of the Plains. Their lances are rust now, their carts silent; they are gone with the buffalo.

Round Mound was the next landmark and camping place on the Trail; a beautiful round-topped cone, rising nearly a thousand feet above the level of the plain. Greenhorns, while yet it was miles away, were tempted to set out and climb it, not realizing how far they could see in that pure air. Even their daily experience of the mirages could not persuade them that the mound was far off.

Once they got to the top of it, they found the view worth the effort. To the south lies a varied country, rolling or level, and dotted with mounds and hills. On the north vast plains, with occasional peaks and ridges. And far beyond these the silver stripe above an azure band — the snow-peaks of the Rockies!

The Trail passed to the north of Round Mound, and camp was generally made west of it. After six or seven miles, Rock Creek was reached, and the Trail became a difficult one in places. Rocks that would not have been noticed in the first half of the journey gave trouble now, because the dry air of the high plains was playing havoc with the wood-work of the wagons.

Tires worked loose, and had to be wedged on again and again; spokes reeled in the hubs, the wheels were loose and shackling, and wagoners were forever bracing, wedging,

and binding their wheels with rawhide — 'buffalo tug.'
Where there was water, the men sometimes left wheels overnight in the creek, to swell them to normal size again.
Daily, during the halts, the corral resounded with the
clitter-clatter of hammers. Sooner or later, some of the
wheels inevitably dished and collapsed.

The Trail passed through the rough sandstones and
emerged upon a less troublesome region. Here lay Point of
Rocks, a small spur striking south, with a good spring below
it. The rocks of the diminutive range were sharply pointed,
rugged, and all pointing southwest.

At Point of Rocks occurred a skirmish which deserves to
rank as one of the decisive battles of the century. In order
to understand the significance of this little-known scrap,
a few words on Plains warfare will prove useful:

Plains warfare was inevitably open warfare. Rarely was
there any cover, or time to dig in. Hostile redskins seldom
gave warning of their presence before an attack, and never
attacked unless they had the advantage of numbers, since
they could usually outrun an enemy on their fleet ponies.
No quarter was given, or expected, on either side. Nobody
took prisoners — unless perhaps women and children. And
the white men believed that, if taken, they would have to
undergo torture. It was literally war to the death. And in
the beginning, the Indian had every advantage: of horseflesh, arms, skill, and knowledge of the country.

The redskin was an expert horseman, accustomed to
killing running animals from the saddle, used to shooting
without aiming, able to loose an arrow every two seconds,
and armed with a quiver filled with forty shafts. At close
range, his lance was more effective than a rifle in the hands
of the average white horseman.

Now, in open warfare, only three things are possible: a
man can run, a man can stand, a man can charge.

To run from Plains Indians was generally fatal. The man

in retreat was not in a position to use his rifle, while his
back made a broad target for the Indians' shafts, or lances.
And, unless he was mounted on an extraordinarily fast
horse, able to race for miles, he could hardly hope to make
his getaway. The Indians could follow, and attack again,
after his horse was winded. If he fired his rifle, they could
kill him before he could reload.

To charge might be equally disastrous. For in charging,
as in running, to fire and hit was difficult. Even though a
man brought down his enemy with the first shot, there
were always others to be dealt with — and his gun was
empty! The charge might suddenly be turned into a retreat — with all the hazards described.

To stand off the redskins was the best way of meeting
them, but even that was possible only to good shots, trained
to load and fire in relays. A lone man on the prairie armed
with a single-shot rifle was in jeopardy. He could hardly
fire and load and hold his restless horse at the same time.
And if the enemy had one man bold enough to ride him
down, or make him shoot, the others would follow and
destroy him.

Mountain men, or Indians from the woodlands trained
to fight on foot, could stand off mounted Indians, if they
were cool, expert shots, and held the fire of half their guns,.
so that some were always loaded. Such a battle occurred in
1854, when the Sac and Fox defeated the combined forces
of the Plains tribes. Thirty Sac and Fox stood in a big
buffalo wallow, and firing in relays, kept their enemies at a
distance, delivering such an effective fire that every feather
in Whirlwind's war-bonnet was shot away. He and his
Cheyennes, and their allies — Comanche, Snake, Kiowa,
Sioux, and Arapahoes — had no chance to use their bows
and lances that day.

What was needed was a weapon which could be fired as
often as the Indian's bow, and as rapidly, a weapon which

could be loaded and fired in the saddle. Colonel Samuel
Colt provided the West with such a weapon in his revolving
pistol, which reached the Plains about 1839.

The Texans claim that the Rangers were the first to
demonstrate the effectiveness of the Colt's against mounted
Indians at the battle of Pedernales, about fifty miles above
Saguin, probably in Kendall County, Texas, in the spring
of 1844. But, if our chronology is correct, as given by Oliver
Wiggins in Sabin's *Kit Carson Days*, the Carson Men first
l'arned the Plains Injuns what a Colt's could do, showed
the white pioneer where his safety lay, and assured the
conquest of the Red Man.

The Rangers tamed the Comanches; Carson's men the
Kiowas. The skirmish took place near Point of Rocks,
where a caravan was besieged on the Santa Fe Trail.

Word was brought to Taos. Carson himself, laid up with
a wound, could not assist. Ike Chamberlain led the party,
riding hard for seventy miles from Taos. He and his men
reached the wagons late at night, and slipped in unbe-
knownst to the cussed Injuns. The teamsters, half dead
with thirst and fright, made them welcome. Ike stationed
his men in the wagons, out of sight. At daybreak the
Kiowas attacked.

The whites fired a few shots in return. Then the redskins,
thinking the whites had emptied their guns, came charging
down like a wolf on the fold. They got the surprise of their
lives, and learned a lesson — too late.

The Carson Men jumped into their saddles, and charged,
shooting left and right, without reloading. Each of them
had two Colt's pistols. 'Saddlepads were emptied, the
astonished Indians broke and fled.... More than a score
were killed, while the whites lost only one man.' [37]

The Comanches had the same experience in Texas. The
Comanches disliked Texans. Now, it is a mistake to dislike
a Texan....

Beyond Point of Rocks, the Trail passed to the Rio Colorado, the Canadian River.

Here, for the first time after more than six hundred miles of travel, the men of the caravan found a genuine *ford* with a bottom of solid rock and an easy approach from either bank. The stream was only a rippling brook, scarcely a dozen paces wide.

Somewhere near the ford, a party from Santa Fe was generally waiting, which consisted of custom-house agents, or clerks, with a military escort, sent to conduct the caravan to the city. These officials came for the purpose of preventing smuggling, and were supposed to keep close watch of the caravans. After some years, the practice was discontinued, since anyone disposed to smuggle found little difficulty in bribing the officials, who would then connive with him against the governor in Santa Fe. The military escort welcomed the caravan with a salute of artillery — a compliment which was immediately returned.

There was no longer any danger from Indians, and those who wished to escape from the surveillance of the Mexican authorities commonly left the caravan here, and rode on ahead towards the capital city. The Captain of the caravan resigned, and every man used his own judgment, and went his own way. In short, the caravan broke up into as many parties as there were proprietors, following the Trail towards the southwest along the base of the mountains.

Here, the wagons were likely to encounter terrific rains, violent hailstorms, and magnificent electric displays. Sometimes, oxen were struck by lightning here.

Having crossed Ocate Creek, the great bulk of Wagon Mound could be seen looming blue in the distance. This was a large isolated butte with two levels, so that it formed the silhouette of a covered wagon and its team. On reaching Wagon Mound, the more energetic travellers climbed it, or visited a semi-circular ravine nearby, where the bones and dried skins of about two hundred oxen lay parching in the sun — oxen run off and killed there by the Indians. Beyond Wagon Mound, the Trail crossed the Mora River, a small, swift, and generally muddy stream. Here the Mountain Route from Bent's Fort united with the Desert Route. From this point there was only one main trail to Santa Fe. The wagons rolled on to Gallinas River, and arrived at the site of the present city of Las Vegas. Here, there was originally only one small hovel, whose owner supplied eggs, chickens, goat's milk, curdle cheese, and mountain mutton, in that day rated as more tasty than venison. In 1835, Las Vegas was colonized, and ten years later had more than a hundred houses.

From Las Vegas, the Trail led through the pinery to Tecolote, with its white church, black cross, and red adobe houses. Beyond this lay the village and spring of Bernal, near the high taper mound known as Starvation Peak, on which a beleaguered party is said to have starved. And so, at length, the caravan reached the Pecos River, and the town of San Miguel, a village remembered for its pretty women. . . .

We have now accompanied the wagons to the end of the Desert Route from the Ford of the Arkansas. But there was another route from that Ford no less interesting and even more historic, which passed up the Arkansas River to Bent's Fort and over the Raton Pass. While the teamsters are refreshing themselves at San Miguel and admiring the brown-skinned girls, let us return to the Cimarron Crossing and take the Mountain Trail.

Adventure still awaits us.

PART VI

The Mountain Route

CHAPTER XV

Chouteau's Island

Because of the dangers of the 'dry scrape' or *jornada* on the Desert Route, many travellers preferred to follow the Arkansas River on up to Bent's Fort, over the Raton Pass, and on along the base of the mountains to the Mexican settlements. General Kearny led his Army of the West over this branch of the Trail on his way to the conquest of New Mexico and California in 1847, and of course all the many wagons bound for Bent's Fort and Taos, and — after the gold-strike near Pike's Peak — many bound for Denver, went this way.

Even those who wished to go by the Upper Crossing of the Arkansas followed the Mountain Route for some distance, though they left it before they reached Bent's Fort. Until the Cheyennes went on the warpath, it was safer from Indian attacks, and the river supplied ample water for the teams. Moreover, greenhorns could hardly lose themselves on that Trail: all they had to do was to follow the Arkansas River.

From the Ford of the Arkansas River on, the country became more arid, the soil gritty with sand and gravel, and grass scanty. Cactus was often seen, and the sandhills on the south bank became a regular range, which extended with few interruptions all the way to Bent's Fort. In places these hills were imposing, and almost without vegetation, showing their white slopes across the stream, sometimes close in, often a mile away, and hiding the country to the south. Behind those hills Comanches lurked, and rushed out to sweep away the animals of careless wagoners. Many a herd of oxen vanished behind those hills, there to be abandoned by the savages, while their scared owners, ignorant of Indian customs, hoofed it back to the States, never dreaming that their animals were alive and sound within two miles of the Trail!

In this dry country, the scanty grass soon cured in the sun, and by August was brown and parched, so that it crunched under the moccasins like snow. Dust storms swept the plain with fury, making the sky one tawny haze, turning the sun into a dull silver disk, paler than the moon.

Antelope became more numerous as they sped away, each one leaving a dusty wake of small puffs where his feet had landed. In summer, few guessed how many antelope — or 'goats,' as they were called by the pioneers — inhabited those plains, for in summer the animals scattered, and were not seen in large bands. But in the winter, when they congregated, no one needed to be told that they far outnumbered the bison. Those hunters who tried to shoot them from the saddle soon learned that antelope were the swiftest things on legs.

Jackrabbits gave better sport.

The hunters would ride a little ahead of the caravan, with their hounds at heel. Suddenly, on the slope of a hill, a jack would jerk into view, running off in quick, erratic jumps, now left, now right, his long ears slanting. Off went the hounds in a pack that could be covered with a blanket, hot on the trail of their quarry. The greenhorn would be tempted to follow, riding his horse to death. But the old-timers would spur to the top of the hill and rein in their horses, knowing that the jack had a habit of running around any hill on whose slopes he was started, trying to get out of sight of his pursuers.

From that ringside — or ring-center — position, the
hunters could see the whole performance without winding
their horses. The jackrabbit would dash round the hill like
a mad thing, until it had left its pursuers far behind, out of
sight. Then it would slow, perhaps stop, until the hounds
came into view. Off went the jack again, and again the
whole performance would be repeated, and repeated, until
the exhausted hounds merely stood and watched in utter
defeat, then came walking, with heads down and lolling
tongues, to lie at their master's feet.

Rarely the hounds would put the jack in danger of his
life. Then the jack would leave his hill, lay his ears back,
and tear off for the river, the brush, a patch of sunflowers,
weeds — anything for cover, where the dull noses of the
greyhounds could not trace him.

Coyotes also gave good sport, though in chasing coyotes
the hunter had to ride hard, that animal not being given to
silly tricks like waiting on his enemies. He was gone to
cover, and generally quite literally 'gone away,' before the
horsemen came near enough to see anything of the chase.
But hounds would not attack a coyote bitch in heat, and
the sport was too severe on the horses to be followed in
summer. Most men on the Trail had a sneaking fondness
for the coyote, anyhow.

When butchering meat, hunters would see the animals
gather to partake of the feast. Gray wolves loped or sat
at a distance, out of range, waiting, watching. But the more
eager coyotes, loping frantically about, came in nearer,
risking their hides to catch scraps of meat flung to them.
The moment one coyote got his piece, away he went,
hustled by all his comrades who had none. This forced him
to run past the waiting wolves, and of course the wolf made
a dash at the bearer of the meat. Then the coyote, afraid of
the big bad wolf, and unable to fight and carry his meat at
the same time, had to drop it. The wolf snatched it then,

and the coyote would hasten back to take a fresh piece of meat from the hunter. This too would go to the gray wolf. In this manner the coyotes fed the wolves as long as the hunter cared to continue the game.

Buffalo were scarce in this region in summer, though sometimes found as far west as Bent's Fort in winter. Of course, in winter, bison could always be found in the Bayou Salade, or South Park of the Rockies.

One day's march up the river from the Cimarron Crossing brought the wagons to Pawnee Fort, the crumbling logs which marked the scene of a siege in the early years of the century. Just here the sandhills had thrown a protecting barrier around a small grove of cottonwoods, so that prairie fires could not destroy them. In this grove, a war-party of Pawnees had taken refuge, felled logs for a fort, and stood off their enemies. During the twenties and early thirties, the Pawnees had been raiding on the Trail a good deal, and also fighting in that valley with their inveterate foes, the Cheyennes and Comanches.

In the first quarter of the century, the Pawnees outnumbered and outfought their foes with steady regularity. The best horses came from Mexico, and all the tribes on the Plains at that time were in the habit of trading, or raiding, to the south in hopes of obtaining good animals. Often they rode all the way from Montana to Mexico for that purpose. It was, comparatively, a short jaunt for the Pawnees from the Platte to the Arkansas.

As soon as the Trail was opened, the whites made haste to make a treaty (1825) with the Pawnees, the main article of which was that the Indians were not to molest caravans. Three years later 1500 Pawnee warriors went to the Trail to rob caravans. The following year, a war with the Cheyennes followed, and the campaign in which the Pawnees captured the Cheyenne Medicine Arrows, taking them in open battle, in the face of the whole Cheyenne tribe.

But the year 1832 put a sudden end to their success on the Trail. Everything seemed suddenly to turn against them.

The Comanches licked them (perhaps at this very spot); one of their chiefs, meeting a caravan on the Trail, advanced with outstretched hand to greet the whites, and was immediately shot down. The Delawares and Shawnees (just established in eastern Kansas by the government) went hunting on the Plains, and being attacked by the Grand Pawnees, retaliated by raiding the village of the tribe while the men were away on the hunt, burning it, and standing to watch it burn.

That same season, a party of Pawnees visited the wagon corral of a Santa Fe trader.

One morning, as the caravan rolled along, a sudden shout of 'Injuns!' threw the men into consternation. Before the outriders could dash back from their position on the flanks, the warriors appeared in force, poised on the edge of the hill in a line that looked a mile long!

'Corral! Corral!' was the order — not that any order was needed. The wagons swung slowly into a circle, rather more irregular than was usual! Before that was done, more Indians appeared on the other side. The oxen milled within the corral, excited by the running about of the frightened teamsters. Many of them had empty guns, having carelessly fired them at jackrabbits, snakes, or prairie-dogs. In their haste to load, the men fumbled, broke their ramrods, or rammed down the lead before the powder, choked the barrel with a ball too large for it, or found that their powder was wet and would not 'go off!' Some tried to borrow weapons; others pressed their own into the hands of better shots. A few ran boldly out and threw themselves down, ready to fire the moment the savages advanced. Others coolly took their places under the wagons, resting the rifle-barrels on the spokes of the wheels.

On came the Indians, at a run, circling the wagons. And, if the caravan had been ready, the battle might have begun at once.

But before the first shot could be fired, the wagon-master began to bellow: 'Hold your fire. Don't shoot yet. I'll handle this!... Bill, here's my pistol. Shoot the first man who fires on the Injuns! I'm a-goin' to talk to 'em.'

Boldly, the wagon-master rode out, reined up his horse, and raised his hand, palm forward, in the ancient gesture for peace.

Instantly the chief began to yell, the warriors fell back. The chief rode forward and sat facing the wagon-master. They conversed in the silent language of signs, the poetry of motion. The men of the caravan, struck with admiration at the courage of their leader, had time to steady themselves. No shot was fired.

Then the chief beckoned to his warriors. Twenty of them galloped forward, and the wagon-master brought them all back towards the wagons. There they dismounted and sat down in a circle. The wagon-master gave orders. The trembling cook of his mess brought a large pan and a bucket of water for the painted guests. Bill supplied the warriors with tobacco for their long pipe.

The Pawnees sat and stuffed themselves, watching everything with curious eyes, talking and laughing among themselves. Had they come in peace, or war? The teamsters wondered. Probably the Pawnees themselves did not know. Meanwhile they ate and ate, and the meat and crackers melted towards the bottom of the pan.

All this time, the wagon-master was busy. He climbed over the tail-gate of the nearest wagon, and began to break out a bale of blankets — red, and white, and blue. The Sergeant of the guard stuck his nose over the tail-gate.

'How come ye brung them Injuns to the wagons? Want to git us all sculped?'

The wagon-master, an old hand, showed no fear. 'Let 'em come,' he said. 'The more the merrier.'

'Bad medicine,' the Sergeant declared. 'I thought you had more sense.'

The wagon-master, kicking in the head of a keg of tobacco, stood with a bottle in his hand, pulling out the cork with his teeth. Then he tilted the bottle, and poured out its slow contents, smearing the blankets and tobacco with the sticky mess.

'Look 'em over,' he urged. 'Your hair is safe this trip, and will be hereafter, I reckon — so far as Pawnees are concerned, anyhow.'

'Captain, what you up to?' the Sergeant demanded.

'Look 'em over. You don't see no pockmarked faces, do ye? My medicine is strong!'

The Sergeant's eyes opened wide. He caught his breath. Then his face disappeared. The wagon-master tossed out the blankets, the tobacco, and jumped lightly to the grass after them. He packed the gifts to the waiting Pawnees.

They had never known a white man to be so generous. Overwhelmed by his liberality, they forgot their warlike plans. Each one wrapped himself in the bright blanket, hugged the twist of tobacco under his arm, and clambered aboard his pony, smiling. Away they went, and the Captain and the Sergeant watched them ride. Two hours later the caravan stretched out on the Trail. They saw no more of the Indians. . . .

That meeting was the end of the glory of the Pawnees. When the party returned to their villages, a strange plague struck them. Nothing could save them. The steam bath and the cold plunge following simply hastened their death: many died in the river, unable to clamber out of the water after their plunge. Medicine men died like others. The tribe, as shown by the official reports, that year lost every living soul over thirty years of age! They blamed the trader. Perhaps they were right.

That trader's bottle contained smallpox virus! ...

The Upper Crossing of the Arkansas River, which offered a much shorter way to the Cimarron River than either of the trails from the two crossings below, was preferred by cautious travellers, though it lengthened the journey to Santa Fe. It had the advantage of greater safety for the animals, wood, water, and more chance of finding game. Wagons crossed some six miles above the present town of Garden City, Kansas, just below the bend, at the lower end of a small island set with trees. The banks there were low, and the river seldom more than knee-deep, though the quicksands made it necessary to keep the wagons moving. Once across, the teams followed the south bank up to Chouteau's Island, where they left the river and headed south.

Chouteau's Island was the largest island of timber on the river. On its lower end and on the south side was a thicket of willows and some cottonwood trees. The island was named after the famous trader and fur-baron, Pierre Chouteau, who once forted there and defended himself against some marauding savages.

Here one of the most significant and colorful events of the Trail took place.

After the atrocities on the McNees party (narrated above) and that on Captain John Means, sentiment in Missouri demanded that the national government send troops with the caravans. In the spring of 1829, shortly after Andrew Jackson entered the White House, Major Bennett Riley took four companies of the Sixth Infantry and proceeded as escort to the traders as far as the Mexican boundary — the Crossing of the Arkansas. He astonished everyone by choosing to take oxen instead of mules and horses. Probably he thought them quite as good, considering that

his forces consisted entirely of infantry. At that date, the
United States Army had no cavalry!

Riley had no trouble until he reached Chouteau's Island
— where, in the nature of things, trouble was sure to begin.
There he went into camp, and the traders moved on into
Mexican territory. Three men rode ahead, among them a
Mr. Lamme, largest proprietor with the train.

Only six miles from the river, the party halted, dismounted, and recklessly stooped to drink. Some Kiowas,
on the lookout, promptly charged them, yelling, from behind the sandhills.

The three whites jumped into the saddle, and turned to
ride for their lives. Two of the men had fleet horses, and it
was every man for himself. But Lamme was aboard a slow
mule, and in a few minutes found himself surrounded by
the painted warriors on their swift ponies. The Indians
shot him off the animal, scalped him, and vanished. His
comrades got to the train safely. It was late in the afternoon.

After sunset, a runner was sent to Riley's camp.

Riley was no stickler for red tape; he was another
McKenzie. Without delay he struck his camp and led his
infantry across the border to the rescue of the American
wagons. The troops tied up their arms to avoid noise, and
marched through the silent sand as quietly as possible.
They reached the wagons after midnight. There they
waited, expecting the attack at daybreak.

But Riley neglected to warn his bugler, and at an early
hour the notes of reveille rang out over the sandhills, warning the Kiowas that the troops were with the wagons. There
was no attack. The wagons rolled on.

Riley kept on with the caravan, as far as Sand Creek.
Then he turned back to the river, and made camp, to wait
for the return of the caravan in the fall. All those weeks
of waiting were made interesting by Kiowa snipers and

horse-thieves, who never would give him a pitched battle, but kept him busy protecting his bulls.

In October, Riley decided to return to Fort Leavenworth. Then he had news that the caravan was coming, under escort of some Mexican troops. Colonel Antonio Viscarra sent word that the train had had no trouble on the way to Santa Fe, but on the way back had engaged the Arapahoes and Comanches — with satisfactory results.

The two commands met and entertained each other at Chouteau's Island. Riley acted as host, but it was a good deal of a joint affair, each contributing what he had to make the meeting a festival. Riley served bread, buffalo-meat, and salt pork — something of a treat to men so far from Army rations. Colonel Viscarra contributed a large New Mexican onion, and there was no end of whiskey in the tin cups. Riley thought he had done himself and the Army proud.

But the cussed Spaniard outdid him in a return dinner. Sixteen officers sat around an actual table in a large tent, ate fried ham and *biscoche* from silver plate, and Viscarra regaled his guests with hot chocolate and Mexican wines!

It was a curious assemblage of men and animals. 'A few Creoles, polished gentlemen, magnificently clothed in Spanish costume; a larger number of grave Spaniards, exiled from Mexico, on their way to the United States, with much property in stock and coin, their entire equipage being Spanish; there was a company of Mexican regulars, as they were called, in uniform, hardly up to the standard as soldiers; several tribes of Indians and Mexicans, much more formidable as warriors, who stood about in groups, along with their horses, each man armed with a lance and bow and arrows; there were many Frenchmen; added to these were the American command of about one hundred and eighty men, hardy veterans in rags, but well armed and equipped for any service; four or five languages were spoken, and to complete the picture was the *caballada* of more than two thousand horses, mules, and burros, which kept up an incessant braying.' [38]

Colonel Viscarra told Major Riley of his adventures on the Trail.

A large band of Indians had approached the caravan in a friendly way, and then, thinking the opportunity excellent, had fired upon the men without warning.

But the traders and their friend Viscarra were not to be taken unawares. They returned the fire with interest. The Indians, who soon ran short of ammunition, had no stomach for a fair fight; they broke and ran. The traders, furious at their treachery, rushed after them. Lamme was terribly avenged. They shot the Indians from their saddles, and treated the wounded with savage cruelty, scalping and flaying them alive, so that even the Mexicans — who were hard-boiled enough — were shocked.

Some of the dead Indians they skinned completely, and nailed their hides to the side-boards of their prairie schooners, like a coonskin on a cabin door. These rawhides were still stretched on the wagonbeds when they reached Chouteau's Island; General Philip St. George Cooke, at that time a young officer with our troops, bears witness to the fact.

After Viscarra's dinner, the Indians paraded the scalps, tied to their lances, singing like demons, stamping on and shooting at the trophies, and wailing at the top of their voices, then bursting forth in an unearthly song of wild triumph and exultation.

After such a demonstration of the fighting spirit of the traders, it was not often thought necessary to send troops along with the caravans, until the outbreak of the Mexican War. On the occasions when troops did accompany the caravans (in 1834 and 1843) the officers had more trouble with the traders than with the savages. Traders had no patience with officers who would shake hands and smoke with the cussed Injuns. In any case, at that time, attacks on trains in American territory were so few and ineffective that no Dragoons were necessary. The traders thought they could take care of themselves. They were all center-shots and their hearts were as big as a mountain.

They would not take orders from a darned Ned, or even agree among themselves how to meet emergencies.

On the Mexican side, escorts were more usual. But the meeting of Riley and Viscarra at Chouteau's Island is unique, a gathering of as strange a collection of men and animals as ever was known on the Santa Fe Trail....

Opposite Chouteau's Island, on the south bank, the grass was very tall. On the bluff there a high round mound was visible, and was named for Chouteau, like the Island. All the way from Pawnee Rock to Bent's Fort, the river fell somewhat more than seven feet to the mile, so that men and animals were continually climbing. And as the road passed the tenth mile beyond the Island, the hills became steeper, and bolder, and at length narrowed the valley, so that grass was harder to find. There was more sand, more gravel, more cactus, and finally soapweed, spraying its sharp green arrows into the air. Occasionally a brackish lake was seen, but trains clung to the river all the way.

In this region, Cheyenne Indians were almost certain to be met with. Sometimes it was a war party, in breechclouts, moccasins, buffalo robes, and long hair, with painted faces and lances, out looking for Pawnees, Comanches, or Kiowas. Sometimes the whole tribe would be on the move after buffalo, or camped in a circle a mile in diameter, while the Keeper of the Medicine Arrows and his helpers put fresh feathers on the sacred shafts in a four-day solemn sabbath, during which nobody was permitted to leave his lodge on pain of being beaten. Sometimes they came together to hold their annual medicine lodge, or Sun Dance.

At such a meeting, the old-timers were sure to have the laugh on the greenhorns, who could not distinguish the braves (with their long hair) from the squaws! But the meeting gave the greenhorn one advantage: he could get rid of his shoes, now slick as glass from long walking on the dry grass, and trade for a pair or two of moccasins. There was no dew on the Plains in midsummer, and a stiff sole was slippery as a ski. But with a moccasin, which fitted the foot like a glove, a man could get along, since his foot could take hold of the ground.

Once a man became used to moccasins, he was very reluctant to wear shoes or boots again. He came to understand why the Sioux called the white man's footgear 'wooden shoes.'

CHAPTER XVI

Medicine Horse

ALL along this part of the trail, from Chouteau's Island to the Big Timbers, travellers had little to interest them. Always the sandhills masked the south, offering cover to the raiding Indians. Always the endless prairies beyond the bluffs stretched away to the northwards. But antelope abounded, and hunters often slipped off alone to toll them within shooting distance.

The pronghorn was a curious animal, and would approach anything which excited its interest, circling nearer and nearer. The hunter, on spying a bunch of the animals, had only to lie down, wave his feet in the air, or display a colored handkerchief on the end of his ramrod, and the wary creatures would come near, marching and halting together with a precision that might have been the envy of well-drilled soldiers. At the first shot they would scamper away in long, graceful bounds, fading from view like scudding cloud shadows, leaving one of their number dead on the ground. One antelope did not go far among the men of a mess, but it was a welcome change from salt pork or broken-down ox-meat, now that buffalo were seldom met with.

It was hereabouts that F. X. Aubrey in 1852 crossed the river on his famous ride. In 1850, Waldo, Hall and Company of Independence received the contract to carry mail once a month to Santa Fe, guaranteeing to make the trip within thirty days. Aubrey, on a bet, rode the distance in eight days' time, establishing a record. He was a small man, and a hard rider. Even so, when he reached the settlements, the saddle was red with his blood!

For many years an abandoned medicine lodge stood beside the Trail a few miles short of the Colorado–Kansas line. A curious story was told concerning it.

The gold rush to California in forty-nine brought Asiatic cholera to the plains, and it swept away half the Indian population between Mexico and the British possessions. Strange tales were told of the desperation of the redskins, and their frantic flight from the dreaded disease. Sometimes they left the dying in their tents, sometimes where they fell on the prairie, prey to the wolves. Friendly Indians implored the help of every passing white man, though most of the emigrants had no better remedy than a solution of cornmeal in raw whiskey.

The plague seems to have struck the Arapahoes when they were all assembled for their annual Sun Dance on the Arkansas River, below Chouteau's Island. Before the dance was over so many had died that the survivors moved camp a little distance above the Island, and immediately performed a second Sun Dance. Two such dances in one summer were without precedent. While the second was in progress, the medicine man directing the ceremony dropped dead within the dance lodge.

Despairing of help from their own dreamers, the Arapahoes sent an embassy north to the Sioux, begging for help. On the way north, all the party were stricken except one old man named Waksenna, the least important of them all.

Waksenna appears to have been a typical dreamer, living in his subconscious mind most of the time, and utterly lacking in shrewdness for practical affairs.

When he arrived in the Sioux camp, driving a string of pack animals loaded with gifts, the Sioux medicine man entertained him gladly, accepted all those rich gifts, and in return gave Waksenna an old broken-down white nag.

Waksenna was so impressed by the Sioux shaman and his hocus-pocus that he failed to look the gift horse in the mouth, and set out for home with his flea-bitten scarecrow, humbly trusting that his mission was successful.

On reaching the old camp of his people, he paused on the bluffs above it, amazed by what he saw. The gnarled cottonwood trees were brown with clusters of buzzards all gorged with human flesh, drunk on ptomaines. At the foot of the bluff lay the bones of men who had leaped upon the rocks in their despair, and a woman's body dangled from a limb where she had hanged herself. As he crossed the river, his horse shied at a withered old woman whose talons still clutched the bail of a brass bucket where she had fallen on her way to the river for water.

As he rode on through the old encampment, he disturbed a cloud of ravens which rose and fluttered down again behind him. Dogs and wolves sullenly gave way before him. The odor of the camp was horrible — a stench like that on a battlefield.

The dead were everywhere: lashed to trees; on scaffolds; in their tents; wherever death had reached them. It had been days since anyone had had the courage to touch the sick — let alone bury the dying. Here and there he saw mourners sitting, crying, bleeding from self-inflicted wounds, or staring at him as he passed with stony, apathetic eyes. He rode on down the stream into the new encampment where the people stood watching him come, hardly daring to hope, discouraged by the sight of the miserable nag he rode.

Waksenna rode into the middle of the camp circle and dismounted before his small sacred tent. His tent was painted all over with the symbols of Arapaho religion: the turtle, the buffalo, the four-pointed star, otters, eagles, suns, and moons, all representing the hopes and fears of the Arapaho dreamer. These paintings were on the inside of the tent, not to be seen by common men. There Waksenna was at home.

Waksenna was a berdache, a man who dressed and acted like a woman. The vision which had led him to adopt woman's customs had arisen from his shrinking nature. As a man he would have been lost in a throng of his betters; as a berdache, he was freed of the obligations of a warrior, free to dream and prophesy. Throughout his long life, he had served the tribe so, divining their dangers, foreseeing their successes. Now, he thought his hour of triumph had come. Soon they would be stroking his face, blessing him, loading him with gifts, for he had come back to kill the cholera — with a dream! The remaining chiefs brought him a pipe to smoke, eagerly awaiting his message. When the old man had finished smoking, they asked him what he had brought them in return for all their gifts.

'That horse there,' said Waksenna, in his senile whine.

They all stared at the glass-eyed white animal, apparently some old woman's pack horse, half asleep in the sunshine. The chiefs looked sidelong at each other. The pipe passed from hand to hand in silence.

'There will be no more dying among the Arapahoes,' Waksenna declared.

Even while he spoke, one of the chiefs stood up, looked around wildly, and said: 'My friends, something terrible is about to happen. I feel it.' The chief doubled up and fell to the ground in convulsions. Before their eyes he died.

Then the Arapahoes were furious. 'Look,' they said, 'the Sioux has deceived us. He has made a fool of this man-woman. Kill him!'

Frantic with fear they closed around Waksenna, and struck him down with their war clubs while the old white nag ran to the end of its tether, snorting. They ripped the tent to pieces. Then they went away. Waksenna lay unconscious under the wreck of his tent of dreams. After a while the white pony began to graze around the tent. There was no one to drive it to water.

That night there was a thunderstorm. Great masses of blue cloud swept over, showing the color of cut lead, and poured down a deluge — while the thunder roared and the lightning flashed and spiked the ground, stabbing savagely at the bluffs, the trees, the tents — flooding the river bottoms, scouring every slope and gully.

The water roused Waksenna at last. He crawled into the tent and sat up. His head rocked. He could hardly tell reality from a dream even then. Only the white horse, garish in the light of the retreating storm, seemed real.

Inevitably the berdache prayed there in the darkness and the storm: 'My Father, Man Above, Giver-of-Food. Take pity on me, Morning Star, my Mother. I belong to you. Be merciful to me. Save my people. Grandmother, Old Woman Night, hear my words. Let the people live. Take pity on your servant.'

He fell down, while his head swam from that great effort.

The night passed while Waksenna cried and prayed, and the white horse paced restlessly outside the ragged tent. It had eaten every blade of grass within reach down to the roots, and now it began to graze within the tent itself; sticking its ghastly long muzzle through the rents, snapping off bunches of grass within. Its lips made a clapping sound, and in the flicker of the lightning the white eyes were very weird.

The man stirred from time to time, and whenever this happened the old nag snorted, blowing in soft surprise upon the upturned face. And so the vision came.

It seemed to Waksenna that the horse was speaking: 'My grandson, do as I tell you. My medicine is strong. Take your paints and paint me as I shall tell you. Then, when it is daylight, lead me into the camp and call the people. Whoever touches my flesh shall live.'

Waksenna got up and staggered around with his paints, smearing a zigzag here, a moon there — whatever his crazy imagination suggested. Afterward, he led the horse into the middle of the camp circle and spoke to it.

'Grandfather, you are strong. You can make us live. That is what you say. Now, *do* it. I promise you that no man shall ever throw his leg across your back. You shall never carry a pack. You shall have four boys to keep the wolves from your heels in winter, and plenty of cottonwood twigs to eat while the snow is deep. Grandfather, be good to us. *Do* as you have *said*.'

The old horse, eager to get to fresh grass, tugged at his lariat. Waksenna took that for an omen and began to call the people together: 'Oooooooooooh! Come, my children. Lay your hands on this horse. Touch it, and you shall live. There will be no more dying. Hurry, my children. Then we can move from here and go where this wonderful horse can get some grass.'

Nobody paid any attention to Waksenna for a long time, but he kept on yelling in his high thin voice. At last he began to lead the horse around the camp circle close to the tents, pleading with the Arapahoes to touch the horse.

The people mocked him. None of them would have anything to do with Waksenna or his wonderful horse.

But at last Thiyeh, an old woman, haggard and decrepit — worn to a shadow by fasting and wailing — hobbled down on her stick and laid a gnarled hand upon the horse's flank.

She felt the better for it, she thought. The sun was out and warmed her old bones.

She told her old man to go and try his luck. He too felt better, it seemed, and soon began to rout out his relatives, greatly relishing his new importance as advisor to the family — which had long ago forgotten him.

And so they came by ones, and twos, and dozens, and

then in crowds, crying, laughing, praying, stroking the white horse, stroking Waksenna, bringing presents, hopeful for the first time in months.

Waksenna gave commands: 'Take down your tents, my friends. We are going to leave this place. You shall all live a long time. This horse is holy.'

Whether the epidemic had spent its force, or the storm had washed away the contagion, who can tell? At any rate, no more Arapahoes died of the cholera that season.

Waksenna was as good as his word. He and the chiefs appointed four young men to look after the wonderful horse, and so long as it lived, it enjoyed complete freedom. Nobody rode it, nobody beat it. It never carried a pack. The Arapahoes took it with them wherever they went and guarded it most carefully.

At last the horse died of old age somewhere in western Kansas. Within living memory, old Arapahoes made periodical pilgrimages to visit the bones of the animal and leave offerings of tobacco, red paint, and feathers.

Finally, after the tribe was placed on the reservation in Oklahoma, the bone-pickers scoured the plains to collect the bones of buffalo to be shipped east on the new railroad for fertilizer, and so carried away the last remains of the medicine horse. The place of pilgrimage was turned under by the plow. . . .

Beyond the medicine lodge, with its dangling buffalo hide and forlorn, sagging rafters, the Trail moved steadily along the barren river banks, until it reached a stream fringed with cottonwoods. The running water, the trees curving across the sandy plain made the spot attractive, and it was known as Pretty Encampment. The caravan was now only some eighty miles from Bent's Fort. If Indians were not too threatening, daring spirits sometimes rode ahead from this point, leaving the wagons to come on at their own slow pace. The Trail had entered what is now the State of Colorado.

The stream on which Pretty Encampment lay was known as Wild Horse Creek. About twenty miles to the north was Dead Horse Lake.[39] These names indicated the presence of wild horses in the region, and travellers often saw them thereabouts. If time permitted, hunters would lie in wait at water-holes and try to *crease* the animal — that is, try to shoot the mustang through the nerves along the top of the neck, and knock him out. If they were lucky enough not to break the neck, and could reach and hog-tie the animal before he came to, they had a captive on their hands.

Such a wild horse was a handful. But men skilled in catching wild horses knew how to tame him.

If an old mare, gentle and well-broken, was at hand, they would rig a rope about her neck, forming a sort of collar, with one end passing back along the animal's side to her tail. They knotted the tail, and tied the halter of the wild horse to the tail (and the end of the rope from the collar), leaving three or four feet of rope for the halter, so that the wild one could graze. Then they let him up.

The wild horse would try to escape, jerking the mare about. But the rope and the collar prevented him from jerking her tail off, and after a while he would settle down and graze and follow where she led. Within a few days, the horse would be so used to following the mare that a man could approach him, gentle and pet him, put a folded blanket on his back, and so by degrees tame him. Eventually, the man would mount, and then dismount quickly — before the mustang could begin bucking. Finally, the man would remain in his seat. The mustang, finding he was not to be hurt, would make no trouble. And then he would be set free. Thereafter, he would follow the mare wherever she went.

Beyond Wild Horse Creek the Trail passed Big Salt Bottom, a lick, or salt marsh, where the ground was spotted with a saline efflorescence, and looked as if flour had been sprinkled on the ground. We have no evidence that Indians used the salt found here, but those who like to argue that Plains Indians, in the native state, *did* use salt, have here an argument in their favor. Undoubtedly, salt was obtainable at this place. Here cannonballs and skulls were sometimes found, tokens of some Mexican affray.

Some miles beyond, the Trail crossed Big Sandy Creek, better known to history as Sand Creek. Where the Trail crossed it, the stream was simply a broad sandy bed, or wash, one hundred yards wide, usually dry. The heavy sand made it necessary to double the teams to snake wagons through.

Higher up, there was water, and the Cheyennes often made camp in the bend, some thirty miles above the mouth. There occurred a memorable massacre, which profoundly affected the history of the whole Plains region, and caused the death of hundreds, both white and Indian. This was the terrible race-riot — there is no other word for it — called Sand Creek: November 29, 1864.

CHAPTER XVII

Sand Creek

T HE gold rush to Pike's Peak sent thousands of gold-seekers across Kansas and Colorado along several trails. The most direct of these cut straight through the best hunting grounds of the Cheyenne Indians. This tribe had been friendly with the whites, with slight exceptions, owing to the influence of William Bent and his partners. But in the early sixties, there was trouble. This was perhaps inevitable. The Minnesota Massacre had hardened the hearts of Americans everywhere towards the Plains Indians, and the endless depredations along the trails ever since the Mexican War had already convinced many people that the Indians were not to be trusted. Herders in charge of cattle and animals which had stampeded found it convenient to lay the blame upon the Indians, and so justify their own carelessness. Young officers, new to the Plains, were eager to fight Indians. Squaw men tried to curry favor with politicians by giving information in advance of alleged Indian raids. Freighters and owners of stage lines tried to damage the lines of other trails, and get the business of their rivals by circulating stories of Indian outrages. Agents appropriated Indian annuities, or connived with traders who sold the annuities to the very Indians to whom the government had sent them. And the Indians themselves were all too ready to seek revenge on the whole white race for any injustices received from parties, however irresponsible.

In the fall of 1863, one Robert North, an illiterate squaw

man, carried a tale to the Governor of Colorado, and warned him that the Comanches, Apaches, Kiowas, and Arapahoes were all planning to go to war as soon as the grass was up in the spring. The Governor knew nothing of Indians, and had too many problems on his hands to investigate carefully. When the Cheyennes found some stray cattle and drove them to camp expecting to claim a reward, an officer named Eayre attacked them. The chief, Black Kettle, prevented war for the time, but other difficulties caused raids up and down the trails in midsummer of '64.

Major Wynkoop, a humane gentleman, made overtures to Black Kettle and other chiefs, promised protection, and sent a delegation of Cheyenne leaders to Denver to talk with the Governor. Nothing very positive was offered the Indians at the conference, but Black Kettle felt that difficulties had been smoothed over, brought his people in, and camped in the Big South Bend of Sand Creek, some thirty miles northeast of Fort Lyon.

Frontiersmen felt it would be an outrage to make peace without first punishing the savages. Some of them were anxious to remain in the goldfields, and, fearing that they might be called into the service to fight the Confederates, were willing to foment an Indian war which would keep them at home. Major Wynkoop's peace policy was not pleasing to his superiors, and he was relieved of his command before all the Indians had come in to surrender.

His successor, Major Anthony, took command of Fort Lyon November 2, 1864. He had no authority to make a treaty, but was willing to accept the surrender of the Arapahoes camped around the post. They gave up their arms and demanded rations as prisoners of war. Major Anthony, not being able to feed them, returned their weapons and sent them off to hunt buffalo. He refused to allow the Cheyennes to come in and camp near the post, and gave orders to fire on them if they came in.

Meanwhile, a regiment of volunteers enlisted for one hundred days was organized in Colorado. This was known as the Third Colorado Regiment, and encamped in the Bijou Basin, east of Denver, in the snow. Colonel Chivington, a man of gigantic stature who had formerly been a parson, led his troops to the mouth of Huerfano Creek on the Arkansas River, and followed the stream down to Fort Lyon, taking care that no one carried the news of his advance to Black Kettle's camp. He reached the Fort on the morning of the twenty-eighth, and left about dark, in very cold weather, for Black Kettle's camp. Major Anthony accompanied him with mounted troops and several howitzers. The force amounted to six or seven hundred men. They moved over the rolling prairie of short grass, guided by Robert Bent, the half-breed son of William Bent, and old Jim Beckwourth, never to be forgotten for his ability to tell tall tales.

The camp of a little less than one hundred lodges stood in the bend, to the north and east of the stream bed, which was there about two hundred yards wide, a bed of dry, level sand with pools here and there. There was no timber. A pony herd grazed west of the stream, opposite the camp. All the lodges were Cheyenne, except ten belonging to some Arapahoes.

In the cool, clear dawn before sunrise, the Indians heard the beat of hooves, and running from their lodges, called out that buffalo were coming into camp. Soon after, they called out that the buffalo were horsemen. The troops came charging from the south. The Colorado Volunteers, on foot, marched up the bed of the stream, while the mounted troops led the way on either bank. The troops began firing almost as soon as the Indians saw them coming. Black Kettle had an American flag which had been given him, and ran this up on a pole before his tent, with a white flag flying beneath. He kept telling the people to be calm, that they were under protection and would not be killed. The people swarmed toward his lodge, which stood in the middle of the camp.

In the camp were several white traders, the principal one being John Simpson 'Blackfoot' Smith, who had come in a day or two before to trade with the Indians. There was light enough for the soldiers to see the flags, but they paid no attention. When the firing began, the Indians, many of them half dressed, and unarmed, rushed toward the up-stream end of the village, and huddled about the tent of Chief War-Bonnet. Some of the young men ran out to catch their ponies. Those who were successful, seeing that there could be no resistance, mounted and sped away to the northeast where another band of Cheyennes was encamped on the Smoky Hill River. By this time, the soldiers had reached the village, and were shooting down everyone they saw. Colonel Chivington saw John Smith and beckoned to him. Smith ran to the Colonel, and followed the troops, hanging on to one of the caissons.

By this time, Black Kettle saw that there was no peace, and turned to fly, calling Chief White Antelope to come along. But White Antelope, feeling that his stand for peace had deceived the people and caused the disaster, or perhaps disdaining flight, stood wrapped in his Navajo blanket in the door of his lodge with folded arms, singing his death song, until the troops shot him down. Black Kettle's wife was shot down as the two of them ran up the stream bed. All around, detachments of troops were chasing the flying Indians, cutting them off, shooting them down, or driving them back towards the creek. The banks of the creek were in places two feet high, and in other places higher than a man's head. The Indians, finding they could not escape the mounted men on foot in that open country, holed up under the sandy banks of the stream and dug in. Around these pits, the troops gathered, and besieged them. They

kept up the fight all morning. The Indians were outnumbered two to one. Most of them were women and children,
and of the men not half were armed.

The Cheyennes fought hard. Major Anthony afterward
wrote: 'I never saw more bravery displayed by any set of
people on the face of the earth.... They would charge on
the whole company singly, determined to kill someone before being killed themselves.... We, of course, took no
prisoners.'

The Indians had been told that white men did not kill
women and children. This encouraged the Indian women
to surrender. Some of them ran screaming towards the
troops, holding up their dresses high to show that they
were not men, hoping for mercy. But the soldiers shot them
down just the same; not content with killing those on the
scene of the fight, they massacred most of the prisoners as
well. It was later testified under oath that certain officers
coolly shot down groups of women and children and scalped
them, blowing out the brains of lost children who had crept
back to their homes among the tents, an hour after the
battle was over. A few half-breeds and women married to
white men were spared. It is said these were seven in number. When Chivington took John Smith over the field to
identify the bodies of the chiefs, they were so badly mutilated that Smith could not be sure and made mistakes. It
was, therefore, believed that Chief Black Kettle had been
killed. However, he survived, to be killed by Custer's
troops in the battle of the Washita, 1868.

After about four hours, the troops left the pits, and the
few survivors crawled out and streamed away up the creek.
Of forty-six Arapahoes trapped, only four escaped. When
the troops withdrew they scalped and mutilated all the
dead.

Twenty-four hours after the battle, the soldiers led out
Jack Smith, the half-breed son of the trader, and shot him

in cold blood. They would have killed Charley Bent, had not some of his friends among the troops prevented it. The pony herd, consisting of several hundred head, was divided 'among the boys.' None of these animals was ever turned over to the officers of the regular Army. Chivington's orders were, 'Kill all, little and big.' His men, with few exceptions, held the frontier belief that the only good Indian was a dead one. They killed the children, saying, 'Nits make lice.'

While the half-naked, bleeding survivors were plodding away through the sandhills toward the Smoky Hill, Chivington led his men back to Fort Lyon, and on to Denver, carrying with them one hundred scalps and three frightened children, two little girls and a boy. These trophies were exhibited in the local opera house between the acts of a theatrical performance. In the Historical Museum at Denver, you can see a Cheyenne woman's buckskin dress. When last I saw it, it was labelled 'Scalp Shirt.' The United States Government made an investigation of this affair, the reports of which anyone may consult.[40] George Bent was present, and wounded in the fight. He told me what he saw.

The whole country was horrified by these atrocities, and some attempt was made to punish the men responsible. But the period of enlistment was over. They were no longer in the service, and nothing could be done.

The Cheyennes on the Smoky Hill sent food and horses to their relatives, and helped them to safety. For some years after Sand Creek, there was no safety for the whites.

It is only fair to say, however, that opinion on the frontier was sympathetic towards Chivington's men. Most of the citizens were newcomers, knowing nothing of Indians, and not realizing what the aftermath must be. But the old mountain men, such as William Bent and Kit Carson, were vehement in their denunciation.

Said Kit: 'To think of that dog Chivington, and his

hounds, up thar at Sand Creek! Whoever heerd of sich doings among Christians! The pore Injuns had our flag flyin' over 'em, that same old stars and stripes thar we all love and honor, and they'd been told down to Denver, that so long as they kept that flyin' they'd be safe. Well, then, here come along that durned Chivington and his cusses. They'd bin out several days huntin' hostile Injuns, and couldn't find none no whar, and if they had, they'd run from them, you bet! So they just pitched into these friend-lies, and massa-*creed* them — yes, sir, literally massa-*creed* them — in cold blood, in spite of our flag thar — women and little children even! Why, Senator Foster told me with his own lips (and him and his committee investigated this, you know) that that-thar damned miscreant and his men shot down squaws, and blew the brains out of little innocent children — even pistoled little babies in the arms of their dead mothers, and worse than this! And ye call *these* civilized men — Christians; and the Injuns savages, du ye?

'I tell ye what; I don't like a hostile Red Skin any better than you du. And when they are hostile, I've fit 'em — fout 'em — as hard as any man. But I never yit drew a bead on a squaw or papoose, and I loathe and hate the man who would. 'Taint nateral for brave men to kill women and little children and no one but a coward or a dog would do it. Of course, when we white men do sich awful things, why, these pore ignorant critters don't know no better, than to follow suit. Pore things! I've seen as much of 'em as any white man livin', and I can't help but pity 'em.'

Some miles up the Arkansas above Sand Creek, stood Old Fort Lyon, on the site of the trading post built by William Bent after he destroyed his Old Fort in 1852. Bent sold his establishment to the government, and it was chris-tened Fort Wise, but afterward Fort Lyon, and finally Old Fort Lyon, to distinguish it from New Fort Lyon not far off.

Here Kit Carson passed his last days, when, after the death of his wife, while suffering from an old injury caused by a fall from his horse, he was awaiting the end. Kit died as he had lived, on May 23, 1868.

CHAPTER XVIII

Kit Carson's Last Smoke

KIT CARSON came to old Fort Lyon
Sick as he could be:
'Make me a bed of buffalo robes
On the floor in the corner,' says he;

'Make me a bed of buffalo robes
Like we used along the trail;
I thought to ha' lived for a hundred years,
But my heart is beginning to fail;

'I ought to ha' lived for a hundred years,
But the strength in my legs is done;
I swelled the veins in them long ago
When the Blackfoot made me run.

'Take care of my children, *compadre*,
I've taken my last ride;
Bury my bones in good old Taos
By my dear Josephine's side.

'I leave you my Cross-J cattle,
My house and ranch, and the rest;
Tell Wiggins, and Tom, and the Carson men
That I always loved them best.

'Now cook me some first-rate doin's —
I'm tired of this sick man's feed;
A buffalo steak and a bowl of coffee
And a pipe are what I need.'

The Army doctor shook his head
And looked Kit in the eye:
'General, now, you ought to know,
If you eat that meal, you'll die!'

'I never was scairt of death,' says Kit;
His eye was cold and blue;
'I've faced it many's the time,' he said;
They knew his words were true.

'There war times when the Injuns bested me;
There war times when I run like sin;
But I never took fright of a square meal yit,
And it's too late now to begin.

'I'd ruther die on my pins,' Kit said,
'With the bull meat under my belt,
Than to die in my bed by inches
Like a beaver trapped for his pelt.'

They brought him a big thick buffalo steak:
He ate it every bite.
He smacked his lips when he drank the coffee,
And swore it tasted right.

'Will you have your meerschaum, General,
Or your Cheyenne calumet?
Will you have the pipe that Frémont gave,
Or what pipe shall we get?'

'Get me my old black clay, Sherrick;
Give me my old dudheen;
It has been over many a trail with me;
It has seen what I have seen.'

He has packed the baccy in the bowl,
Inhaled the smoke so blue;
A happy smile spread o'er his face —
That face so bold and true.

He smoked the pipe out to the end
And brushed the ashes off.
Then Death (whose bullets could not kill)
Killed Kit with a little cough.

The ladies of that lonely post
They loved him one and all;
One gave her satin wedding-gown
To line his coffin-wall.

The ladies on that winter day
For love of one so brave
Pulled from their bonnets all the flowers
To strew upon his grave.

He was happy when he died,
And brave and true alive.
God send the West a many such
To make our country thrive!

CHAPTER XIX

The Big Timbers

THE monotony of the Mountain Route was relieved just here by a fine grove of trees, the first of any size and beauty between Council Grove and Bent's Fort. It was called the Big Timbers.

The Big Timbers was a scattered grove of gigantic cottonwoods, extending up the river towards Bent's Old Fort for a distance of perhaps thirty miles. Some of these huge trees were seven or eight feet in diameter. They stood on islands in the river and along the banks, without underbrush, and at wide intervals, so that travellers on the Trail could see the other side of the river between the trunks without difficulty. This was a favorite camping ground of the Indians, particularly in winter, when the buffalo congregated there. The Grove steadily decreased in length, as wagon trains cut down the trees. The last of them was gone by 1863. The Grove got its start because it was protected by sandstone hills coming close to the river, and the Trail often passed over the spurs of these hills. Even before Bent's Old Fort was destroyed in 1852, William Bent had built some log houses for trading in the Big Timbers, perhaps as early as 1844. The trader, Tharpe, also had a log cabin there, until the Pawnees killed him while hunting buffalo off the Trail, in 1847.

Near the upper end of the Big Timbers, a curious round stone knob, or part of the bluff, standing out in the valley, was one of the landmarks. It was known to the Indians and

old-timers as Red Shin's Standing Ground. An amusing
story accounted for its name.

In 1833, some Cheyennes had camped there for the
winter. Red Shin and another man, a relative of Bull Cannot Rise, had a quarrel over a woman. Red Shin was successful in his suit, and had the better of his rival until the
other man called out his relatives to help. They all ran for
their weapons.

Red Shin, seeing himself hopelessly outnumbered, hurried into his lodge. Soon after, he came out, carrying two
flintlock muskets, a bow and quiver of arrows, two butcher
knives, and a tomahawk. Clutching this small arsenal, he
ran to the stone knob, and clambered up until he stood on
its top, some twenty-five feet above the open valley. There
he harangued his enemies, and challenged them, 'Come on,
if you want to fight.'

The relatives of Bull Cannot Rise quickly accepted the
challenge and advanced to the attack, rushing towards the
knob where Red Shin stood his ground.

Red Shin began with his bow, and sent his arrows among
his enemies with deadly skill. One arrow passed through
the hair of Bull Cannot Rise, and each of the other warriors
had equally narrow escapes. Red Shin's marksmanship
cooled their blood, and they scampered back to cover.

Red Shin remained at his post defying the others, but
before the fight could be resumed, friends of both sides interfered and the battle ended in a treaty.

This warlike demonstration on the part of Red Shin
greatly impressed the Indians. Ever after the knob was
known as Red Shin's Standing Ground.[41]

Not all the combats on this stretch of the river were so
bloodless as Red Shin's squabble over the woman. The
Indians tell another story — this time also concerning a
woman.

Somewhere near the Big Timbers a band of Cheyennes

were in camp in the fall of the year. They had just killed plenty of buffalo and were taking it easy while the women jerked the meat and dressed the robes. One morning while it was still dark a woman lying in her tipi suddenly awakened and felt the beat of galloping hooves against the ground on which she lay. The dogs began to bark loudly. She sat up, then scrambled to her feet just as a war-whoop shrilled at the far end of the camp. She ran out of the tent and looked around her. Enemies were charging the camp, which was suddenly alive.

All around her was confusion. The old men were yelling advice. Young men dashed by to catch their horses or galloped past to meet their enemies. She could see the flash of guns and hear them crashing as the charge swept home.

Women and children sped by her away from the battle, running in all directions to find a place of safety, mothers lugging their babies or dragging older children by the hand, frightened girls clutching their blankets under their chins, matrons puffing for breath, hobbling old women making off as best they could with their sticks. Children cried, dogs yelped, horses reared and plunged, but above all she was conscious of the sound of the shooting.

Already the warriors were among the tents, firing at everybody who came out of them. Some of the Cheyennes were killed before her eyes.

All this she saw in a moment. Then she was running as hard as she could go towards the bluffs, stumbling through the darkness. She could never remember how, but at last she arrived, panting and trembling, among the rocks. As it grew lighter she cowered back among them and found a shallow cave where she could hide.

By that time her enemies had driven her people out of the camp and set the tents on fire. The Cheyennes had been surprised and overwhelmed by numbers. Shortly after sunup, her enemies took the captured ponies and rode away.

In the afternoon when the Cheyennes were sure that their enemies had gone for good, several old men came out of hiding into the valley where the camp had been, and began to call the people together. Over and over again for a long time they kept on calling until most of the people had assembled. Winter was coming on. They had no horses with which to hunt, and all their food, bedding, and tents had been destroyed. Some of the people were almost naked, just as they had jumped from their beds when the camp was attacked. A council was held and they voted to strike out afoot, looking for another camp of their tribe. So the people straggled away to the north.

Before they left, the old men walked around and called again like camp criers, throwing their voices as far as possible. The old men feared that some of the people might still be hidden, and they did not wish to leave anyone behind.

In the cave with the woman was another person, a young boy. They were both frightened almost to death and dared not look out of the cave all day. Even when they heard the old men calling the people, the woman and the boy were afraid to budge out of hiding. They stayed in the cave, and the Cheyennes, who supposed they were dead or captured, finally went away and left them.

All night long the two of them remained in the cave without food, fire, or water. It was cold that night, and they had no buffalo robes to keep them warm. In the morning they were starving and shaking with chill. Everything was quiet. The woman looked out of the cave, She could see no danger. Still they waited there, for they were badly frightened. But at last they became so hungry that they sneaked out, went down into the valley, and prowled around where the camp had stood. Everything had been burned up. The whole place was covered with heaps of ashes where the tents had been. They poked around in the ashes and found a small piece of dried beef charred by the fire. The woman divided it with the boy and they ate it between them.

They were very thirsty then, and went to the spring for a drink. The woman drank only a little water, but the boy lay down on the ground, stuck his lips in the cold water, and filled himself with it. Immediately he took a chill, and in a little while was dead. She tried to help him, but he was puny and almost naked, and the woman had nothing with which to cover him. She was left alone. . . .

Lost Woman had not even a knife.

She took thongs from the fringes of her dress and made snares of them. Next morning she found a rabbit in one of the snares, and ate it raw. This meal gave her fresh courage, and she went to work and made more snares, which she set all up and down the valley. In this way, she captured other rabbits. From time to time she moved her camp a mile or two so that she was always able to catch more. She skinned the rabbits and tanned the skins, using their sinews for thread and a sharp thorn for an awl. In this way she sewed the rabbit-skins together and made herself a fur robe. This kept her warm for the time being. But winter was ahead, and she knew that, without a buffalo robe, she would freeze when the cold weather came.

Buffalo were to be seen all around her, but she could not kill them, because she could not make a bow and arrows without a knife. In her despair, she stood up and raised her open hands to Man Above, praying: 'Take pity on me. Help me to get back alive to my people, and I will make the Sun Dance.'

The very night after she made her vow Lost Woman had a dream.

In her dream she was walking across the prairie, looking for edible roots and small animals which she could eat. As she passed over a hilltop, she saw the whole country with all its streams and hills spread out before her like a great map all dotted with buffalo. She stood on the hilltop and looked at that beautiful country. In her dream, as she passed on over the country before her, she came to a level place between two buffalo wallows. There she saw a knife lying on the ground. Then her heart was glad. She bent down and picked up the knife. That was the end of her dream.

When Lost Woman woke up, she took her robe of rabbit fur, her snares and her root-digging stick, and started off over the prairie on the trail of her people, looking for small animals which she might catch and eat. Suddenly, that afternoon, as she passed over a hilltop, she saw the whole country with all its streams and hills spread out before her like a great map all dotted with buffalo.

She was astonished, for it was the same country she had seen in her dream. Then Lost Woman was encouraged. She went straight to the level place between two buffalo wallows where she had found the knife in her dream. When she came to the place, there was the knife on the ground. Lost Woman picked up the knife and was happy. She held up her hands to Man Above, gave thanks, and renewed her vow.

'*Ah-ho, Ah-ho*,' she said.

A bunch of buffalo was grazing not far from where she stood. The woman sharpened her knife against a stone and sneaked up towards the buffalo. Her mouth watered as she looked at them. She was sick of rabbit-meat, and longed for a warm robe instead of the tattered patchwork of rabbit-skins she was wearing. She went very slowly and carefully, creeping up-wind through the tall grass. Buffalo do not see well, and these could not smell her because of the wind.

There was a cow lying asleep on the edge of the herd. Lost Woman crept on the cow from behind, slipped along to its head, and cut its throat with a swift slash. Then she jumped away.

The cow scrambled up and staggered about, coughing out its life, soaking the grass with blood. After a while it fell down, struggled a little, and lay still.

Lost Woman butchered the cow and ate some of the warm raw liver seasoned with gall. Then she skinned the cow, cut two dozen sharp stakes, and pegged the skin flat on the prairie. While it was drying she jerked the beef, so that she had plenty of meat to eat. She knew it would be very difficult to kill another buffalo as she had killed that one. When the hide was dried, she scraped it clean with her knife and tanned it with the brains and liver of the buffalo. Then she had a warm robe and plenty of meat.

She made a bow and four arrows and found flint arrow-heads for them as she wandered over the prairie. At first she could not hit anything with her arrows, but in time she learned to use the bow and killed other buffalo and made herself a small tent of the hides. She jerked all the beef and had enough to keep her all winter. When spring came, she had seen no human being since the fight in the valley. She made a pack to carry her belongings in and plodded on to the north.

It had been so long since she had seen a person that she did not expect to see anyone.

One day as she was walking over the open prairie, she saw Indians on horseback coming. She was frightened. 'They will kill me,' she thought.

She tried to run, but they were on horseback and galloped straight at her. She was surrounded. They were Arapahoes, allies of her people. She threw down her pack and held up her hands in the sign for peace. They saw that she was a Cheyenne and did not harm her.

She could not speak their language, but told them who she was and all her story in the sign language — all but her dream about the knife. She thought it would not be wise to talk to strangers about the favors of Man Above.

The Arapahoes were friendly and said they would take her with them. They were going on the summer buffalo hunt, but they were not going towards the camps of her people. They could not give up their hunt to take her home at that time. When they did return, Lost Woman had been gone from her people a whole year. They welcomed her as one returned from the dead.

Still she did not tell anyone about her dream. All that winter she kept silent.

The Sun Dance is held in summer. In the fall, Lost Woman fell sick and sent for her sister, who lived with her husband in another part of the camp. Lost Woman raised herself up on her elbow and said: 'Sister, I am going to die. I have offended Man Above. When I was lost and helpless, I prayed to him and vowed to make the Sun Dance if he would take pity on me and bring me back to my people alive. He brought me back. But then I saw that our family was very poor. We had lost all our ponies in the war. I knew that we could not afford to make the Sun Dance. So I said nothing about my vow. And now summer is over and Man Above is angry. I am going to die.'

Her sister said: 'No! It is *not* too late. I will tell my husband, and he and his friends and relatives will gather whatever is needed to make the ceremony. You shall live and be well again.'

Lost Woman shook her head and said, 'Sister, it is too late. I have lied to Man Above. I am going to die. I know it.'

All the relatives of Lost Woman came and talked with her. They told her to take courage, to hold fast to life with both hands. They promised to make the dance. But she always said the same thing: 'I am going to die. I know it.'

At the end of four days she died.

Many years after, when the missionaries and government agents tried to persuade the old men of the tribe to give up dancing, this story was told, and the death of the woman was given as their reason for keeping up the old ceremony. Said they: 'We dare not stop. For, if an Indian becomes afraid of the lightning during a storm, or if he is very sick and makes a vow to Man Above and so gets well or is saved from the lightning, he must make the dance, or Man Above will cause him to die. An Indian is afraid to lie to Man Above. He must fulfill his vow.'

Nowadays, although the Cheyennes are educated, and travel in automobiles, they still hold an annual Sun Dance in Oklahoma. The old men have long memories. They have not forgotten Lost Woman. [42]

CHAPTER XX

Little Chief

O<small>N</small> H<small>ORSE</small> C<small>REEK</small> Kit Carson had his first real battle with Plains Indians, the fight which won him the Indian name by which he was ever after known to the redskins. The story has come down to us in several versions: in the rough notes Kit himself dictated to his authorized biographer, Peters; in Peters' own vague and grandiloquent account; in Cheyenne tradition.

At the time Kit was in charge of a gang of loggers in camp on the stream, where they were cutting timber for the Bent Brothers, whose big adobe fort was building half a dozen miles up-river. The Indians called the stream Short Timber Creek.

While he was there, Black Whiteman and Little Turtle, two Cheyennes, turned up, with a woman, Otter Woman, whom one of them had eloped with from a distant camp.

Anyone who is familiar with old-time Indians will prefer their version of a fight to that of any other eye-witnesses. For the Indian was not only a better and less imaginative observer than the white man. He was also a more interested observer, because war was his greatest and most absorbing sport. More than that, his rating in the tribe depended upon his proven *coups*, and he took good care to claim all he was entitled to, and to demolish any false claims advanced by his comrades. Therefore, in any kind of fracas he had all the keen, clear-eyed alertness of a professional sportsman. And he had the advantage of steady nerves; he was less likely to get excited than most men. He saw just what happened. And as long as he lived, whenever he counted his *coups* in public, he had to rehearse just what he had seen. For these reasons the Cheyenne tradition of this fight is preferable to any of the others. I have it from George Bent, and it has been printed by Grinnell.

One dark night a war party of fifty Crows passed Kit's camp on Horse Creek. As they saw he had only a dozen men and no horse-guard, they quietly rounded up his stock and made off homeward, glad of a chance to ride, since — as was usual in winter — they were all afoot. When morning came, Kit found himself without a single head. But Kit never dreamed of letting them get away with all Bent's stock. He and his dozen men pushed hard along the trail of the thieves, which led off north across the prairie. With them rode two Cheyennes, Black Whiteman and Little Turtle, who had been visiting Kit the night before and had kept their ponies tied up.

'Twilight was falling when Carson's party, the two mounted Cheyennes still out ahead, following the trail in the snow across the prairie, saw a shower of sparks rising from a thicket some distance in front of them. The party halted and held another consultation. Black Whiteman and Little Turtle then rode off alone while Carson drew up his men in a long line, each man several paces from his neighbors on either side.

'As they advanced across the snow a dog barked in the thicket, and a moment later a little ball of white steam shot up from among the willows. The Crows had put out their fire with snow. The Americans quickened their pace and had almost reached the edge of the thicket when without warning sixty Crow warriors broke out of the willows and charged them. So fierce and sudden was the attack that Carson and his men were borne back and almost surrounded; then they threw up their rifles and gave the Indians a volley.

'Carson used to tell how surprised the Crows were when they charged in on his little party and were met by a stunning volley. Back into the thicket went the Crows and in after them went Carson and his men. The Indians evidently intended to mount and either run away or continue the fight on horseback, but when they reached their camp in the middle of the thicket they found that the horses and mules they had left there had disappeared. Right at their heels came Carson's Men; so without halting the Indians rushed through the thicket and out at the far side, making off across the prairie as fast as they could go. The whites, worn out after their long march through the snow and content with the result of the fight, did not attempt to follow farther.

'When Carson had started to advance toward the willows, Black Whiteman and Little Turtle had ridden off to one side, making toward one end of the thicket; then just as the Crows charged out of the bushes the two Cheyennes rode in, stampeded the horses and mules, and ran them down the creek.... In the morning Black Whiteman and Little Turtle returned to the thicket, and there found, counted *coup* on, and scalped two dead Crows.

'The Cheyenne have always expressed surprise that in this fight Carson and his men, all well armed and excellent shots, should have killed only two Crows ... not one of the whites was killed or received a serious wound.' [43]

When Yellow Wolf, that wise old chief, brought his band of Cheyennes in to trade at Bent's fort that moon, he talked over the details of the fight with Kit and William Bent, as they sat smoking together in the council room of the half-built fort. With animated gestures and broad grin he taunted the stocky, sandy-haired little white man with his failure to kill more than two Crows. And Kit, knowing what Indian decorum demanded, sat unperturbed and smiled in turn until the chief had had his joke.

Then Yellow Wolf, after a piercing glance at Kit, rose dramatically and gathered his buffalo robe about his hips. He held his chief's pipe along his left arm, and gestured impressively with his right. The white man was young, he was small, his thin hair scarcely reached the shoulders of his white blanket coat; but he was brave, too, and the Cheyennes respected bravery above all things.

The hissing, choking Cheyenne syllables began, the arm and hand swung more vigorously. 'My son, I give you a new name. You have won it. From where the sun now stands your name is *Vih'hiu-nis*, Little Chief.'

CHAPTER XXI

Bent's Old Fort

FIVE miles march from Horse Creek brought the wagons to Bent's Old Fort, the most celebrated, and for many years the only, building between Westport and the Mexican settlements. The fur trade has always been big business in North America, and in the Old West was for a long time the biggest of all. In this trade only the Astors rivalled the firm of Bent & St. Vrain, who were also interested in trade with Mexico. They had many posts: Fort St. Vrain, near Long's Peak in Colorado; Adobe Walls, on the Canadian River in the Panhandle of Texas; the Log Houses, in the Big Timbers; and the several stockades, above the mouth of Fountain Creek on the Arkansas. But the largest of all, and most permanent, was Bent's Old Fort, erected by William Bent, who made his home there and directed the trade with the Plains Indians. This fort was often called Fort William after him, and known to old-timers as Bent's Big Lodge on Arkansas. It stood on a bench a little distance north of the river.

Coming up the valley, travellers were first aware of a large gray block on the treeless plains, with a flag flying above it. As the caravan crept nearer, the men found themselves facing an extensive gray wall, with loopholes piercing the top at intervals. The wall was fifteen feet high. At the left end, an hexagonal bastion towered up thirty feet high, showing portholes for cannon. At the right end, a second story rose equally high. Above the iron-bound gate was a square blockhouse with windows through which a long brass telescope might be seen. Perched upon the gate-house, a slatted, wooden belfry held two live eagles and a large brass bell. Near the gate, a few graves, protected by living cactus, sheltered the remains of members of the family who had died there.

By the time the men of the caravan had corralled the wagons, the parapet of the Fort was lined with onlookers, standing on the roofs within, ready to welcome the strangers. The faces and figures offered great variety, for Bent's Fort was a large establishment, employing as many as a hundred men, traders, clerks, packers, teamsters, hunters, servants, and their families. In that gallery, one might see Americans, Indians, Mexicans, French, Germans, Negroes, and Kanakas. In summer, many of the men would be gone with Bent's caravan, heading for the States.

If Indians were about, the gates, covered with iron and studded with huge nails, would be closed, only a wicket being opened for purposes of trading and communication. But now these swing open, and the men from the east walk in through the deep, shady tunnel and find themselves within the *placita*, or *patio* of the Fort. This hollow square was spacious and paved with gravel. In the middle stood the robe press, where folded hides were crushed flat and bound together for shipment. To one side, the well-sweep slanted toward the blue sky. All around, the roofs of one-story rooms sloped inward, projecting to form a *portal*, or primitive portico, supported at intervals by upright posts. At the back, a ladder mounted to the roof, now crowded with men, women, and children. After the gloom of the entrance, men blinked against the glare from the white-washed walls. From the rear came the clang of the black-smith's hammer, and the rasp of the carpenter's saw, where wagons were being repaired and horses shod. A cock might be heard crowing, or the gabble of hens, with an occasional

shriek of a peacock. If the traveller were fortunate, he
might see the tame goat belonging to the establishment run
up or down the ladder leading to the roof. Perhaps the bray
of a jackass led the visitor to suspect a corral at the rear of
the building.

Those who explored the Fort found a large number of
rooms with low-beamed ceilings and whitewashed walls of
adobe, and felt their nostrils refreshed with the clean smell
of earthen floors freshly sprinkled with water. These rooms
on the ground floor were used for various purposes. There
was a warehouse containing the goods needed for the Indian
trade. Belts, buckles, finger rings, hawk's bells, tubular
bone beads, steel bracelets, hand-axes, brass kettles, tin
pans, awls, Green River knives, bags of Galena lead,
powder-horns, beaver and bear traps, pins, thread, needles,
combs, and looking glasses, all sorts of fofurraw (*fanfaron*),
as the oldtimers called such civilized trinkets.

Along with these were stored cases of imported edibles —
'State's doings' — bags of coffee, flour, sugar, raisins, boxes
of water crackers, salt pork in barrels, spices of all sorts,
and bottles of peppersauce and *saleratus*. On shelves would
be stacked bales of domestic cotton, blue and scarlet stroud-
ing, flannel, calico, and threepoint Nor'west blankets, red
as blood.

Then, too, there was hardware, frying-pans which the
Indians desired in order to make arrow points, axes, lance-
heads, trade guns, horseshoes and ox shoes, spare parts for
the wagons, and a number of kegs of Pass brandy, rum, and
Taos Lightning, flat to fit a pack saddle. In the corner
was a strong box, banded with heavy strips of iron, in which
men suspected might be silver ingots, gold bullion, or bags
of the curious slug coinage from the California mints. At
certain seasons, bales of buffalo robes and packs of beaver
were stacked high in a dark mound at one end, the swarthy
wool matted with ticks and sand burrs. In the large parlor,

with its polished central pillar, blankets and mattresses were stacked along the walls for seats, and a bucket of water with a gourd dipper stood on a bare deal table.

The Fort contained twenty-two bedrooms, and in addition rooms used by the blacksmith, carpenter, barber, and clerk, two bastions in opposite corners where powder and ammunition were kept, and the walls hung with firearms and buffalo lances. There was a small store with a counter across the middle of the room, so that visiting Indians could not reach the shelves behind.

Best of all to men hungry for civilized food was the kitchen, from whose window floated the welcome aroma of boiling coffee and bread baking. A little flattery of the negress in charge, who called herself 'De only lady in de damn Injun country,' might persuade black Charlotte to part with a pie or some of her delicious biscuits, the only biscuits between Westport and California. Those who were fortunate enough to be invited to dinner enjoyed the unfamiliar luxury of putting their knees under a table covered with a white cloth, and adorned with castors. There a man might remember how a fork was used, and eat from a tin plate like a gentleman.

William Bent and his brothers might wear frock coats and high beaver hats in St. Louis, but in this castle on the Plains, they found it advantageous to dress like chiefs, in moccasins garnished with bright beads and porcupine quills, fringed trousers of deer-skin, and handsome hunting shirts. William Bent, with eyes like augers and a jaw like a steel trap, was lavish in his hospitality. Being a thorough-going Yankee, he had an ice house on the river bank, and those whom he invited to climb the ladder and enter his private rooms on the second floor enjoyed mint juleps served by black Andrew over the bar there. Afterward, if time permitted, a game of billiards was in order — on the only billiard table west of the Missouri. On the second floor also were the offices of the chief clerks and traders. In the bastions were several small cannon, one of which was burst in saluting the Army of the West, when General Kearny arrived at the Fort on his way to the conquest of New Mexico and California. Beyond the Fort proper, an extension of the walls equally large served as a corral for the stock. Here, the parapet was only eight feet high and three feet thick, topped with growing cactus to keep out horse-thieves. A gate led from this corral into the main *patio*.

Nearly every·man of importance in the region, at one time or another, was connected with the Fort. Kit Carson was hunter; Lucien Maxwell was foreman; Old Bill Gary (William Guerrier) was trader. He had a habit of wearing a white blanket coat and a fur cap like a typical *voyageur*. All trails in the Southwest led to Bent's Fort, which was at once the house of refuge, the general store, the bank, and the home of hundreds. Indian women tripped around the battlements in glittering moccasins and long doe-skin frocks. Traders and Indian chiefs sat in the shade of the *portal*, smoking the long red pipe, drawing the precious smoke (tobacco was four dollars a pound) into their lungs with hysterical sucks, then blowing it out through their nostrils; or sat eating jerked buffalo-meat, bread made of coarse meal, and drinking black coffee. Sometimes, the notes of a flute might be heard, or the tuneful scraping of the fiddle.

The Bents seemed never to have had much trouble with Indians, though occasionally these staged a raid upon the *caballada*. This was hardly surprising, since in summer, the season for war parties, thousands of savages were within easy striking distance. For many years after the Bents established themselves on the Arkansas, the Kiowas and Comanches were at war with the Cheyennes. For this reason, the Fort called Adobe Walls was built on the Canadian, so that the firm could trade with the southern tribes more readily. The hostility of these nations increased, until in 1838 a great battle was fought on Wolf Creek, in which most of the best men on both sides were killed. Even Gray Thunder, Keeper of the Cheyenne Medicine Arrows, and father-in-law of William Bent, was killed.

This disaster, coupled with Bent's influence, led the Cheyennes to make offers of peace to the Kiowas and Comanches, and in 1840 a peace was made in the bottoms below Bent's Fort. This was one of the largest Indian gatherings ever known on the Plains, happening as it did before epidemics had decimated the tribes. The story of that peace treaty, and of all the events leading up to it has been told most graphically: how the Cheyennes and Arapahoes almost bought out Bent's stock in order to make presents to their old enemies; how the Comanches, Kiowas, and Apaches begged the others *not* to give them horses, since already they had more than they could wrangle; how the Cheyennes fired off their guns before presenting them to their allies, so that it sounded as if a battle were in progress; how the Comanches invited the Cheyennes and Arapahoes to visit them afoot and sent every person in both tribes home horseback and driving five or six head each.[44]

The Mexican War, the cholera, and other troubles stirred up the Indians later, but the peace was never broken, though on one occasion it was badly bent. This was in the summer of '57. The Kiowas had just completed their Sun Dance, held rather late in the season, when prickly-pears are ripe. The women had gathered a large quantity, and the families had feasted on the sweet fruit. The Kiowas, full of prickly-pears and martial spirit, decided to go on the warpath against the Navajo. Big Bow and Stumbling Bear led the war party, leaving Lone Wolf to direct the tribal buffalo hunt. On such a hunt, the Indians used only light travelling lodges, or windbreaks, as they needed all their pack animals to carry the meat. Every important Kiowa family had a large, painted, heraldic tent, used for state occasions. Being so near the Fort, they asked Bent to keep these large tents for them until their return.

It appears that some of the Kiowa young men, needing fast horses for the warpath, rode away on some of Bent's best animals. Bent was a Yankee trader, and to all intents and purposes a Cheyenne chief, a fearsome combination. When Lone Wolf returned from the hunt, he found the Cheyennes living in the gaily painted tepees of his tribesmen. Lone Wolf went into the Fort to complain to Bent. Bent looked him in the eye and replied, 'I have given them to my people.'

Lone Wolf then tried to replevin the property from the Cheyennes, but found them unwilling to oblige him. A quarrel followed. The Cheyennes shot Lone Wolf's horse, wounded one of the Kiowas, and ran them off, keeping possession of the painted tepees. Eventually, the matter blew over.

Sometimes, a fandango was held in the Fort when a caravan corralled there. In that case, the fiddler mounted the table, and the old hearty square dances filled the crowded room with dust up to the ceiling. Chipita, the enormously fat housekeeper, flopped about with colossal good humor. The Indian squaws pranced, giggling, without a trace of Indian stoicism, and black Charlotte aped the fine ladies whom she had seen pass on their way to California. Women were so few that every one received the most flattering attentions.

During the Mexican War, William Bent received the honorary title of Colonel for the services he rendered as scout and spy, and turned over his establishment to the military for a hospital and depot, without asking any remuneration. The Fort was not equipped to care for invalids, and Bent himself, though he had a small medicine chest, often relied upon an Indian medicine man to care for the family ailments.

The sick soldiers were laid on a buffalo robe on the dirt floor, visited once a day by the assistant surgeon's deputy, who dosed them with calomel, and left them to recover as best they might. Parkman tells how one patient, suffering from brain fever, who was sharing his couch with a fellow sufferer, woke one morning, turned to his companion, and saw his eyes fixed upon the beams above with the glassy stare of a dead man. At this the unfortunate volunteer lost his senses outright.

As the old order collapsed and domination by the traders gave way before the rush of emigration, William Bent decided to sell the fort, and offered it to the United States Government. The War Department would not meet his terms, and Bent, indignant at such treatment after all his services to the Army in the Mexican War, put all his belongings into his wagons, started them down the Arkansas, broke open the powder kegs in the bastions, and blew his fort to smithereens.

Afterward, he built his new fort in the Big Timbers, which the Government eventually purchased. After 1852, Bent's Old Fort was a ruin. It remains a ruin, still to be seen, a few low heaps of gray adobes.

William Bent, like his brother Charles, was a great executive and merchant prince. He was a man among men. Though all his life surrounded by violent men bearing arms, and a man of fierce temper himself, he enforced such discipline over his polyglot employees that no man was ever killed within the walls of his fort. The epitaph of the Bents might well be the phrase used to describe them in Kit Carson's own memoirs: 'Their like were never in the mountains.'

From Bent's Fort several trails diverged. One followed the Arkansas up to the mouth of Fountain Creek and north along the mountains towards Pike's Peak and the headwaters of the South Platte. Another crossed the Arkansas below the mouth of Apishapa Creek, passed north and west of the Spanish Peaks, and on south to Taos. From Taos one could reach Santa Fe by following down the Rio Grande.

Most travellers from Bent's Fort to Santa Fe followed a trail which crossed the Arkansas some six miles west of the Fort. This trail at first passed through a rough, broken country of barren hills, and soon reached the headwaters of the Salty Timpas. The first camp was made at Hole-in-the-Rock, a rocky pool in the bed of this stream, ringed by dark cedars and huge masses of stone on the slopes about. Beyond this was the Hole-in-the-Prairie, where water of a sort could generally be found. Next morning, the far-off mountains were plainly visible. As the caravans advanced the men saw in the distance ranks of stately, dead cottonwoods, gnarled trunks burned bare and black by some old grass fire. These ruined trees marked the course of a clear, swift-running stream.

This river, known to the Spaniards as the Rio de las Animas Perdidas, or River of Lost Souls, had been dubbed by the French Canadians the Purgatoire. Most of the Americans preferred an Anglicized version of the name, and called the stream Picketwire.

The Trail led south and a little west beyond the river. On the right, the Spanish Peaks rose boldly. Towards the left, and ahead, the smaller Raton Peak seemed larger from its proximity, and towered above the Trail. Here a rough mountain trail diverged to the right and Taos. Though the elevation of the Raton Pass is rather less than that of the City of Santa Fe, the approach to it was steep and difficult, until Uncle Dick Wootton, retired trapper, built his celebrated toll-road. Wagons were hauled up with doubled and tripled teams, or even by man power, two slow miles a day over the boulders and through the pines. The high altitude made the laboring men gasp and increased the difficulty of the passage over the range.

However, there were compensations. Wild cherries were abundant in the right season, turkeys and deer were everywhere, and bear steaks sizzled on every mess fire.

The road over the pass was more than twenty miles long. Caravans usually spent a week getting to the end of it, and down to the warm prairies once more. Through that delightful region, the Trail passed over a number of clear, swift streams, tributaries of the Canadian — Vermejo, the Little Cimarron, Ocate Creek — streams which head far up among mountain meadows, where trout and bear abounded, and still abound. It was all plain sailing for the prairie schooners to Mora River, where the ruts of the Mountain Route mingled with those from the Cimarron Desert, all leading towards San Miguel.

PART VII

La Fonda

CHAPTER XXII

The End of the Trail

A̲T̲ ̲L̲A̲S̲T̲ the caravan reached San Miguel, and found itself
at the beginning of a regular road, the Great Missouri
Road, built and maintained by the traders of Santa Fe —
now only fifty-eight miles away. After all those hundreds
of miles of pulling through sticky mud, hot sand, deep ruts,
stubborn rocks, and sucking quicksands, the shrunken,
long-suffering wheels rolled smoothly along over a proper
road. The creaking of the wagons was muted, the tongues
ceased to whip from side to side, and the thimbles rattled
more rhythmically. Both men and animals felt the relief,
the blessed relaxation of effort and unrelenting vigilance,
that might have been theirs on reaching a city pavement.

Their journey seemed accomplished already, and they
began to think of what lay at the end of it. Their road led
up-hill and down-dale along the base of the huge flat-
topped mesa on their left, over gentle slopes for the most
part, and for the most part through scattering evergreen
groves of piñon and juniper. They caught glimpses of
native houses made of mud, saw flocks of sheep and goats,
and met long trains of Mexican men and women riding
tiny gray burros, guided with a jab of a short stick behind,
or a blow on the side of the head, causing a sudden tilting
of the long, fuzzy ears.

The barelegged women paid no attention to the hails of
the teamsters, now ribald and lusty after their long absti-
nence from feminine society, but kept their heads wrapped

tightly in their *rebosos*. The men wore pantaloons button-
ing up the side, but left open to show their white — more
often gray — drawers. Few of the men carried firearms,
but many had a naked sword laid close against their saddles.
They saluted the *Americanos* courteously.

Pueblo Indians also passed, heading out to the Plains
after buffalo, driving their rat mules. Their jet-black hair
was tied up in clubs with bright, hand-woven ribbons.
They greeted the men of the caravan affably, with smiles
and waving hands, and thereby incurred the contempt of
old-timers accustomed to the haughty aloofness of the
warriors of the Plains. Such unearned friendliness seemed
a confession of inferiority. But what could one expect of
these effeminate tribesmen, who had had to run from better
men and hide in barren deserts and mountains, cowering
behind walls raised on cliffs and in caves, where they spent
their days in weaving, painting pots, and gardening? A
lot of old women! The abandoned Pueblo of Pecos was a
sufficient monument to their inability to defend themselves.

It lay just off the road to Santa Fe: a crumbling ruin of
terraced houses perched on a great rock shaped like the
print of a human foot, with the deserted mission church of
the *padres* close by. Built centuries before, it had been the
largest of all the Indian towns, housing thousands when
the Spaniards came. Corn, and trade with the buffalo
hunters, had been its prosperity, until the men of Pecos
made the mistake of matching their might with the Comanches. Then their warriors had been rubbed out, all
but one. That sole survivor the Comanches, following their
cheerful custom, had sent back to carry the news of the
defeat. Afterward, his people abandoned the site, moving
far back into the mountains, and the biggest city in New
Mexico was left to the owls and the pack-rats.

When the caravan corralled down the slope, men climbed
up to see these ruins. The church invited them first. Its

bare, austere adobe walls towered up to the high-beamed ceiling, holding a space of silence and unchanging peace, refreshing in its cool dimness after the glare without. The great doors still swung on their pivots, the altar stood square and solid at the far end, and here and there bits of carven and painted woodwork remained to hint at the color that had been.

Off the main room, smaller ones could be reached through an arched doorway. In one of these, men from the States saw their first small, moulded mud fireplace. On wet nights, sometimes, men camped there. They found the fireplace smoky, until someone who understood New Mexican chimneys showed them how to make the thing draw by standing the firewood on end. Then the firelight danced on the scaling whitewash, and the naked chamber became a living-room. Next morning, all would feel drugged by the close, indoor air.

In the ruins of the Indian town, they found the huge, round, roofless *kiva*. From its round shape, the Spaniards had named the structure *estufa*, stove. This led some travellers to imagine that the walled pit had been used as a brazier, where an undying fire had been kept burning through the centuries. They stood and marvelled at the industry of natives who could have carried logs enough to keep such a conflagration going!

The ruins gave a fine, far view of blue mountains, and now, in spite of the serene skies, bright landscape, and tonic air, men began to feel a certain jumpiness, a quick irritability, caused by the unfamiliar altitude. But their quarrels were of short duration, like a mountain storm, for the blood of every man was tingling with anticipation of reaching the end of the Trail.

On they went, rolling past the Mexican village of Pecos, with its trees, green gardens, and rushing mountain torrent; plodding slowly up the long slopes to the pass at Glorieta;

winding through the colored canyon down to the hovels
and white church at Cañoncito, where the clear rivulet
washed the thin hooves of the oxen as it rippled across the
road. Then they were climbing again through the rough
hills and across the dry arroyos on the last long miles to
Santa Fe.

And so, finally, they reached the top of the rise which
overlooked the Royal City of the Holy Faith of Saint
Francis. To the right were bold, rocky foothills of the
Sangre de Cristo Range, shaggy with evergreens. Below,
on the left, a vast plateau swept away westward, dotted
with green bushes, studded with pointed hills, showing in
certain lights like the bottom of some immense ocean
deep — unreal, mysterious, a setting for the Arabian Nights,
leading the eye to the valley of the distant Rio Grande,
and the far blue ranges of the Sandia and Jemez Mountains.
The city lay straight ahead, due north.

Here, while still hidden among the hills and evergreens,
the caravan halted. The smaller wagons were dismantled,
their parts concealed in the brush, their contents heaped
upon the larger vehicles, now made gigantic by the addition
of extra side-boards taken from the smaller craft. The
Mexican tax on imports was not *ad valorem*, but assessed
so much for every wagonload. Shrewd Yankee traders
therefore made one wagon roll, where two or three had
rolled before.

While this was going on, men took time out to shave,
wash their faces, and 'rub up' generally. Sunday suits
came out of the baggage, and everyone put on his best bib
and tucker for the grand entry, reloaded his weapons,
tightened his girth. Teamsters fastened new crackers to
their long whips, to make society the sweeter welcome. Old
timers babbled obscenely of their prowess with Mexican
women, and smacked their lips at the mention of Pass
brandy or Taos Lightning. All were merry. Yonder, within

sight, were rest, shelter, strange food, and new faces.

Even the animals seemed to feel the excitement. After forty days (which had seemed like forty years) in the wilderness, they were about to enter the Promised Land, a land flowing with the milk of human kindness. Travellers doubted whether the first sight of the walls of Jerusalem by the crusaders could have caused more tumultuous and soul-enrapturing joy.

No such emotion marked a return to Westport. For Santa Fe was not just another town — not just a town at the end of eight hundred miles of labor, danger, and hardship. Theirs was no mere excitement of cowboys at the end of the long trail-drive, or of sailors making port. Santa Fe was not just a town to be painted red. It had a color and a savor all its own. There, everything was strange, different, romantic, and fascinating. As the wagons rolled towards the city, everyone with it was merry, laughing, exhilarated.

Greenhorns, on their first glimpse of the square drab blocks of adobe scattered among the green fields of dwarf corn and shallow wheat along the valley, thought they were looking at brick kilns, and would sing out, "I see the suburbs!" Grinning old-timers would astonish and disappoint them, explaining that the brick blocks were houses, and those houses the town!

They passed down the long winding road, descending the last hill, riding between endless adobe walls high as their horses' heads. Behind those walls were gardens and orchards, from which they hoped to receive peaches, apples, apricots, grapes; *frijoles*, corn, and wine. Under those flat roofs were plump mattresses to lie on, bright fires to sit by, smiles and caresses, and corn-shuck cigarettes. Like so many savages entering a friendly camp, they emptied their rifles and pistols noisily into the blue sky, yipping and whooping, until the very horses reared and pranced.

The citizens shared that enthusiasm, swarming out of their houses into the muddy lanes, calling, '*Los Americanos! Los carros! La entrada de la caravana!*' Lithe young men were there, somber under their big hats, watching their rivals for the women's favors roll into the town, made taller by the narrow colored streak of the *serape* on their shoulders. Untidy Mexican soldiers lounged there, or perhaps a swart Dragoon with enormous mustaches and clanking saber. Shabby *rancheros* watched in tattered, faded *ponchos*, battered wool hats, sandals, and huge spurs. And there were the girls!

A young woman — any young woman — would have thrilled those men. But the dashing *señoras*, in their exotic, colorful costumes, with faces bleaching under a coating of flour-paste, or brilliant with smears of scarlet *alegría*, their blue-black hair and bright, soft eyes, their flashing teeth and friendly manner, proved irresistible. They were females, and seemed not to mind it. Their warm Andalusian-Arab and gentle Pueblo blood danced at the sight of the big, virile *Americanos*, and they made no effort to smother their emotions. As a reception committee, they were a howling success.

They seemed to have an almost continental attitude. They could be haughty and coy, but they knew how to be engaging and flirtatious, too. Coquetry with them was an instinct, apparently, not just a trick. Their smiles seemed to say: 'Men need women, as women need men. There is no use in quarrelling about it!'

The way they dressed was, in itself, exciting to men from the States. They never heard of underwear. Petticoats, bustles, bodices, long sleeves, high necks, hats were all unknown to Santa Fe. The women wore a skimpy *camisa*, loose, abbreviated sleeves, short red skirts, gay shawls, and slippers. They made what then seemed 'a prodigal display of their charms.' And when the prairie schooners made port and slid to a stop on the wide, sunburnt plaza, men and women met and mingled. The fleet was in!

Their greetings did not belie their cordiality. The New Mexican salute was as agreeable as it was novel to the greenhorns. The man swept off his hat. The lady extended her right hand. The man grasped it, shook it warmly, and gently drew her towards him. Then he threw his left arm about her waist, embraced her, and laid his cheek against hers, murmuring his compliments in her ear. Having released her, he put on his hat again. It was as simple as that. Strangers quickly adopted that custom. Home was nothing like this!

The *Americano* went into the bar of La Fonda, the inn at the end of the Trail, emptied his glass, and understood why the trade to Santa Fe was growing by leaps and bounds. Already he had been invited to attend the first of a series of *bailes*, or — as they were called by his friends from home — *fandangos*, that very evening. He gathered that the women of Santa Fe went to a dance every night of their lives.

At the bar he might learn also that, in this paradise, one of the two great banes of human existence did not exist. Death, of course, was certain, even in New Mexico; but taxes did not exist! The natives were a long way from Mexico City, and the central government was supposed to provide the means to finance this remote outpost of Spanish or Mexican power. The natives disliked taxes; any attempt to tax them always resulted in insurrection. The greenhorn was left wondering.

Meanwhile the traders were busy with customs officials. Business before pleasure. The cream of the trade went to the man who first opened his goods to the buyers. Negotiations went forward rapidly. The regulars already had stores rented to receive their goods.

But if the natives paid no taxes, the importers did.

Accordingly, there was 'an arrangement,' an arrangement which depended a good deal upon the character of the governor in power. Usually this was the result of some haggling, influence, and the salving of itching palms. The officials provided the itching palms, the Americans the salve. Legal duties were not infrequently divided into three parts: one for the officials, one for the traders, and one for the Government. This last was likely to be as small as would be acceptable at Mexico City! Trade with the States was the chief source of income in Santa Fe. Sometimes a bullying governor might stop it, but it was too necessary to be discontinued for good.

Once clear of the customs, the merchants displayed their goods to buyers. These flocked into Santa Fe from other communities, and sometimes traders who wished quick profits sold everything wholesale — especially if they had mortgaged their farms and homes in Missouri to finance the venture. Those with larger capital and more local influence could make a better bargain by dealing with the retail trade. And if Santa Fe failed to meet their prices, they could always load up their wagons and push on to Chihuahua — or even to Matamoras!

A month or more might be required to dispose of the cargoes. During that time men of the caravan had opportunity to become acquainted with the city. Some liked the life there, settled down, and stayed on. Others became reconciled to it in time. But there were many who regarded it with disapproval, disgust, even horror.

In those days, Santa Fe was a slum — a small town, huddled hit-or-miss about the bare, sunbaked plaza, which then extended clear to the doors of the Cathedral. The streets were narrow, unpaved, unswept, and unlighted. Water was supplied by irrigation ditches, which brought down streams from the snowpeaks to the gardens: water in which children splashed, animals waded, women washed clothes, and cats drowned. Dogs and burros ran at large, mumbling the garbage in the muddy lanes.

The small houses were dingy and forbidding enough outside, however cool and clean and comfortable they might be within. Everything to be seen looked dirty, untidy, cheap, primitive, and nasty. And though some found every prospect pleasing, most agreed that man was vile.

Rigid Protestants deplored the 'superstition' of the inhabitants, and on being shown the churches, asked to see the schools. Patriots thanked God that such corrupt officials were seldom known east of the Mississippi. Moralists shook their heads at the way women, children, and — in fact — everybody, gambled, drank, danced, and carried on. Nowadays, more often than not, it is the Spanish-American native who is shocked at the revealing costumes of American ladies; but in those days it was quite the other way round. Some regretted that a respectable woman should go half-naked. Others felt equal regret that a half-naked woman should be respectable. It appeared that, either way, in Santa Fe she could afford it.

In the large cities of Mexico good society did not mingle much with the foreign colony, since each group was numerous enough to provide its own social life. The Mexican ladies were 'totally uneducated, and in the presence of foreigners conscious of their inferiority and usually shy and reserved.' [45] In their own houses they were, of course, vivacious, unaffected, and pleasing in manner and conversation, and Mexican women of all classes had warm hearts and intelligence enough to win the respect of all strangers fortunate enough to be admitted to their company.

In Santa Fe, then a small town on the far edge of Mexican territory, no barrier could exist. There was no middle class to introduce a cult of snobbishness, and as a result rich and poor mingled in all public places. There were three social strata: the Americans at the top, the Mexicans at the bottom, and the Indians sandwiched between. But the men with the caravans were eager for feminine society, and most of them were frontiersmen with all of Andrew Jackson's scorn for social distinctions. What they lacked in refinement of manner, they made good in eagerness to join the social whirl. They came with chips on their shoulders, bringing the advantage of an enlightened civilization, very conscious of their superiority, and they were ready to fight any man who offered to oppose their social activities, so that even had the cussed Spaniards been less hospitable and kindly than they were, the Americans might have created hospitality at the point of a gun. It was difficult to resist the importunities of men so direct, forceful, dangerous, and eager for a good time. Santa Fe, always hospitable and even chummy, made them welcome.

The women of New Mexico were not only agreeable, but pleasant to look upon. Ruxton, who travelled clear across Mexico, declares that he never once saw a really ugly woman. 'Their brilliant eyes make up for any deficiencies of feature, and their figures, uninjured by frightful stays, are full and voluptuous. Now and then, moreover, one does meet with a perfectly beautiful creature; and when a Mexican woman does combine such perfection she is "some punkins," as the Missourians say when they wish to express something superlative in the female line.'[46]

Santa Fe was a tiny town in those days, and it did not take the ruthlessly inquisitive Americans long to explore it. The old churches, with dingy mud walls, macabre *santos*, and bells that were rung by banging them with stones and sticks; the long low façade of the Palace of the Governors, with its arcade, and strings of Indian ears festooned between the pillars; the trickling river; the filthy, terrifying calaboose; the walled gardens; the open doors, through which a man might catch a glimpse of a sunny *placita*;

the bare, but neatly kept rooms of the small houses. Life was simple in Santa Fe: people slept and ate on the floor, like so many Indians; there was hardly a plank floor in all the town, and not a single bathroom. Saints, rather than sanitation, predominated; and, as one of the travellers put it, the saints were all of an earlier generation!

With so little to see, so little that roused their admiration, the greenhorns from the States quickly turned to the main attraction: the women.

The strapping Missourians found the handsome brunettes, as they paraded, in their short skirts and gay shawls, smoking cigars, and showing their well-turned naked ankles above tiny shoes with silver buckles, extremely attractive. And the women of those days, who preferred blonds, were receptive to that admiration. Citizens of Mexico then regarded Durango as the last outpost of Spanish culture, and Santa Fe was more than five hundred miles beyond Durango! Therefore the people of Santa Fe, like so many New Yorkers, turned their backs on their own country, and looked eastward towards the States, from which their prosperity derived. They welcomed the fair-haired boys from Missouri.

It is true that many of the natives believed the Americans half savage, perfectly uncivilized, never to be thought as *caballeros*, much less *Cristianos*. Privately they referred to them as *burros* — in plain English, jackasses. They believed them infidels who worshipped the devil, and were indignant at their lack of Spanish courtesy. They were wild men indeed — but perhaps none the less attractive for that. It was true also that some Americans were too prone to drink and fight, but what could one expect?

On their part, the Americans were shocked by the utter democracy of Santa Fe society. There seemed to be less of social distinction than there was in an Indian camp. Work was frankly considered a curse, not a moral obligation, and the natives seemed always ready to play, dance, gamble, and drink every day of their lives. This was all very disturbing to Americans, even to those who in the Mexican War came to bring the blessings of Liberty. The inhabitants of Santa Fe, whether Mexican, Indian, or Spanish, were accustomed to a communal, priest-ridden, almost Mediterranean tradition — the tradition of the *kiva* and the plaza. They loved crowds. The Indians of the terraced towns lived like rabbits in a warren, as the Mediterranean peoples do, as the immigrants in New York tenements try to do. They felt only half alive alone. They were forever getting together. Coming from the lonely plains, the Anglo-American was ready to join the fun.

Here was a small town which — in his opinion — was simply packed with beggars, gamblers, sneak thieves, political bullies, rascals of all kinds; a town without newspapers, schools, theatres, libraries, museums, free government, or religious tolerance; a town full of vice, superstition, and dirt. Yet the people seemed happy and content with their lot. They were constantly singing; music could be heard at all hours. They were forever playing: the cockpit, the gambling layout, the ballroom, were always busy. Life in Santa Fe appeared to be a perpetual carnival. At first, the typical American thought all that gaiety merely a bluff. When he found it was genuine, he was outraged. Nevertheless, the *Americano* was ready to join the fun. He was hell-bent to have a good time, and show the natives a thing or two. He often succeeded in both undertakings, but in the process he was likely to break up the meeting. There were no police to interfere.

All authorities agree that in those days Santa Fe offered every facility for a man seeking a moral holiday.

Justice was not to be had, but injustice was to be bought. The public roads were lined with crosses, monuments to murders perpetrated on travellers. A man had to depend upon his own nerve and bowie-knife, his presence of mind and Colt's revolver.

The sports of the natives were exciting, dangerous, and often brutal. Men loved to display their horsemanship in bull-tailing. This sport required great strength and address. The riders would race to be first alongside the bull. The winner in the race would bend down, seize the animal's tail with his right hand, throw his right leg over it to serve as a snubbing post, then wheel his horse suddenly to one side and so upset the bull. The huge animal rolled over and over in the dust, bellowing with pain and fright.

Another equestrian sport was called *correr el . gallo*. An unfortunate rooster was tied by the legs to a stake driven into the ground, with its head and neck well greased. The contestants started together, raced for the bird, bent from their saddles to snatch it by the neck, break the thongs which bound it, and ride off with the prize. The man who was successful found himself pursued by his rivals, each of whom tried to tear the bird from his grasp. In a very few minutes the poor fowl was torn to pieces, and the scraps of its body were carried in triumph and presented by the winners to their mistresses!

The Anglo-American, with his horror of cruelty to animals, generally preferred the *fandango*. This he frequently converted into a free-for-all fight, in which he could shed blood in his own fashion. The *fandango* was a profitable event for the owner of the house in which it was held, and strangers were not long in receiving invitations. The Americans, now flush with cash and on their spree, were free-handed as anyone could wish and stood treat in potent *aguardiente* to all comers. The clanging of church bells gave warning that the festival was about to begin. The beauties of the town washed their faces, removing the flour paste and scarlet *alegría*, combed their hair, and put on their best clothes, gold and silver bracelets, large earrings, and massive crosses to dangle about their necks. Then, each pretty mouth armed with its cigarette, they coquettishly entered the *sala*.

At one end of the long room, under the eye of their leader, the musicians were already seated, with guitar, *bandolin*, and hand-drum. Gradually, the *sala* filled with men and women in native costume, all smoking, among them American traders and teamsters, in shirt sleeves of gaudy calico, wearing knives and pistols at their belts.

Only the centre of the dirt floor remained open for dancing, most of the room being filled by the crowd looking on. At first, the Mexicans did most of the prancing, engaged in such 'lascivious' dances as the waltz, or in some of their charming folk dances such as the *cuna*, or cradle dance. But as time passed and the whiskey began to take hold of the teamsters and mountaineers, these horned into the performance. Not knowing the figures of the native dances, they interpolated steps of their own, learned on the frontier of Missouri or in the camps of Plains Indians, yelling and whooping, and shouldering aside the lithe young men of the city. At that altitude, only a little alcohol was too much, and the brawlers soon took command, and had the women to themselves. And if a daring Mexican stepped into the ring, he was likely to be shoved back against the wall with a rough warning to quit. Between dances, there was more drinking, the ladies became more coquettish, the Americans more truculent, the Mexicans more jealous and envious of their entertainers. The party became boisterous, the attentions to the ladies warmer, jealousy waxed hot. The fire of resentment was smouldering towards flame.

Yet the behavior of the natives, whether men or women, left nothing to be desired on the score of decorum. The cussed Spaniards were always mannerly. They had none of the American love for smashing conventions.

On such a scene a strapping Missourian, Long Tom, and

his friend Puny came charging. Tom laid eyes upon Dolores; she smiled — and he stopped in his tracks, like a gut-shot buffalo. The gal scared him worse than a whole cavayard of Kioways; he had to swaller three gourds of whiskey afore he could breathe rightly agin.

Her eyes said *yes*, and Tom never had refused a dare. Wading in, he grabbed the girl like an angry bear, and swung her away from her partner. He pranced up and down the room, shouldering the rest aside, like a moose in a thicket. She was warm and alive, she danced with a will. Her little chin poked him on the hairy chest, and his nostrils were filled with the odor of her dark hair. Tom histed her up, and gave her a kiss. 'Yippee!' he yelled, red in the face, 'this *fandango* belongs to me!'

The claim was instantly disputed.

Long Tom, smothering with embarrassment, saw a dark face charging at him. A knife-blade glittered in the light. He dropped Dolores, struck the blade aside, grabbed the rash Spaniard with both hands, raised him high above his head, and flung the stabber against the wall with a thud.

Puny, six-foot against the whitewashed wall, came suddenly to life. His war-whoop rattled on their ears, and he charged to join his comrade in the middle of the room. The war was on, and men who had been too shy to dance with the girls, were happy again at the prospect of taking part in a fight — something they understood better. On every side Mexican knives flashed out, as they rushed the *Americanos*, whose comrades were no less quick in rallying around them.

The squealing women jammed the narrow door in the desperate rush to escape, so that even those men who had no wish to fight were compelled to remain and do battle. The Americans stood shoulder to shoulder in the middle of the room, like so many shaggy buffalo bulls defying wolves, swinging their hairy fists and striking out with the long barrels of their Dragoon pistols. There was no club like a heavy Colt's revolver, and with these the Americans soon cleared a space about them, outnumbered though they were.

But their advantage was brief. From outside, while they stood panting, came shouting, threats, and the rush of feet. Someone shot out the lights.

'Hyar they come, boys,' Puny yelled. 'Give 'em Green River!'

In a flying wedge, the Americans surged towards the open door, fought their way out, down the lane, and across the plaza to their wagons, where they had left their rifles. Grabbing these, they rushed on, and occupied one of the traders' stores.

There they bound up their gashes, wiped off the blood and sweat, and prepared to defend themselves. Officials came and demanded their surrender, and were answered by yells of derision. But, after there had been time to cool off, the Americans made terms, paid blood money, purchased masses to be said for the man killed, posted a guard, and went to sleep.

In the morning, they were greeted by scowling, bitter faces, and itching palms. Ignoring the one and salving the other, they helped the affair to blow over. The only serious damage was to the heart of Long Tom, still smitten by the charms of Dolores, now forever beyond his reach. . . .

After a few of these affairs, the gaiety of Santa Fe palled on the man from the States. He was sick of the place and its people, and his heart swung true once more to the pole of his own tradition — the tradition of the Anglo-American. These aliens, with their dictators and their mobs, their sleek courtesy and vicious habits — what had he to do with them? His feet began to itch.

To such a man there was always something a little indecent about a crowd, something less than human, something offensive and dangerous to his personal identity. The lank boy from the States was no Mediterranean, no Pueblo Indian, but by nature a lonely and solitary creature, a dreamer, wanderer, and adventurer, born to slip the leash of the settlements and go looking for something lost behind the ranges. That was why he conquered and explored and colonized, while the Latin and the Indian were so well content to remain at home. That was why he could sometimes be so ornery to humans, and so tender to dumb brutes; that was why he could not help regarding Society as ridiculous, and fashion as silly. He liked his fellow-men better when they were scattered over a big country. And so, when he got into a crowd, he generally felt like fighting, smashing things. To him, people in crowds were suggestive of maggots.

It was a glorious chance — not to be repeated — which threw open the Old West to the restless feet of such men. It was the irony of fate that such men destroyed the Old West.

They left the States to escape from their neighbors and navigate the plains on their own hook: left the caravan to carouse and scrap on their own hook in Santa Fe; and shook the dust of Santa Fe from their feet to head for the States again. Afterward, many of them spent the rest of their days wishing they were back in the wilds — like Parkman, like Garrard, like Ruxton — like all the rest.

What they longed for was life in the open, the impromptu dangers, the sudden meeting, the handful of old friends (every one an individual — with whom one need not talk), the lone campfire under the stars, the immense and unspoiled Plains. . . .

Torn between his passion for Dolores and his natural craving for the life he loved, Long Tom sat on a wagon tongue, melancholy as a bull in spring. Then the old-timer would heave his weight down upon the pole, slap the greenhorn on the shoulder, and give sage advice, the age-old philosophy of his breed: 'Leave the Spanish wench to her greasers. Thar's buffalo a-runnin' on Arkansas. Cain't ye hear the *boudins* sizzling, and whiff the fat cookin' on the coals yonder? In the mornin' we're puttin' out to the grand prairies, whar thar aint nothin' to bother ye but a passel of screechin' Injuns! Hooray for the Trail!'

THE END

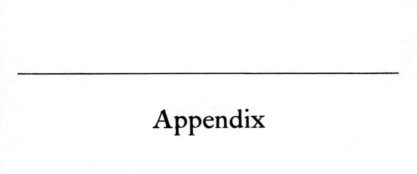

Appendix

APPENDIX

A. Notes

CHAPTER I

1. *Windwagon.* See *The Kansas City Star*, August 6, 1905. See also recent files of *The Southwest Review*, for account of the Indian legend referred to.

CHAPTER II

2. *Robidoux and Lisa.* This tale appears in the *Journal of Rudolph Friederich Kurz*, translated by Myrtis Jarrell, edited by J. N. B. Hewitt. Bureau of American Ethnology, Bulletin 115. Washington, D.C., 1937. See pp. 66–67.
3. *Planters' House.* Information regarding the St. Louis of those days may be found in Ruxton, *Life in the Far West*, Parkman, *The Oregon Trail*, Garrard, *Wah-To-Yah and the Taos Trail*, etc., etc.
4. *Colt's Revolving Pistol.* For the story of Samuel Colt and his great invention, see *Yankee Arms Maker*, by Jack Rohan, published by Harper and Brothers, or consult *A Century of Achievement*, 1836–1936, issued by the Colt's Patent Fire Arms Manufacturing Company, Hartford, Conn.
5. *The Hawkins rifle.* The description is quoted from Ruxton's *Life in the Far West*.
6. *A fine spring.* Known as State Line Spring, at what is now 57th Street and State Line. Wagon trains encamped in what is now the Mission Hills district of Kansas City.

CHAPTER III

7. See *American Anthropologist*, New Series, vol. 40, no. 1., Jan.–March, 1938, p. 112 ff. 'Where Did the Plains Indians Get Their Horses' by Francis Haines.
8. Consult Frederick Remington, 'Horses of the Plains.' *Century Magazine*: 37; 332.

9. *Carafel and Ramsay.* Consult *Kurz*, op. cit., pp. 160–161. For following frontier opinions on Indians, and details regarding equipment, consult *The Prairie Traveller* by Captain Randolph B. Marcy: pp. 211–212, and p. 118 ff.

CHAPTER IV

10. See *The Santa Fe Trail, Letters and Journals of Augustus M. Heslep,* in *Southern Trails to California in 1849.* Edited by Ralph P. Bieber. The Arthur H. Clark Company, Glendale, Cal., 1937, pp. 362–363.

CHAPTER V

11. The passage quoted appears in *Collections of the Kansas State Historical Society,* vol. XIV, 1915–1918. Topeka, 1918, p. 799. 'Diamond Springs: "The Diamond of the Plains"' by George Pierson Morehouse.
12. Garrard tells this tale in his *Wah-To-Yah and the Taos Trail.*
13. See Ruxton, *Life in the Far West.* Chapter III.

CHAPTER VII

14. *Fighting Fire at Diamond Springs.* See Lowe, Percival G., *Five Years a Dragoon '49 to '54, and Other Adventures on the Great Plains.* Kansas City, Mo., 1906, Part 4, pp. 139–140.

CHAPTER VIII

15. John Palliser tells this story in his book, *The Solitary Hunter.* London, 1847.
16. This information came to me from George Bent himself. See also *The Cheyenne Indians,* by George Bird Grinnell. Yale University Press, New Haven, Conn., 1923. Vol. I, p. 271.
17. *Calf-Woman.* See *Warpath, The True Story of the Sioux Wars, Told in a Biography of Chief White Bull,* by Stanley Vestal. Boston, 1934. Chapter IV. Also, W. P. Clark, *The Indian Sign Language.* Philadelphia, 1885, p. 88.
18. *The one-eyed buffalo.* Mentioned in Clark, *op. cit.,* p. 88.

CHAPTER IX

19. See 'The Buffalo Range' by Theodore C. Davis, in *Harper's Magazine.* Jan., 1869.
20. See Palliser, *op. cit.*

21. *In the Far West*, by George Frederick Ruxton, cited above.
22. See *The Oregon Trail*, by Francis Parkman. Chapter XXV.
23. Consult *Adventures in the Santa Fe Trade 1844–1847*, by James Josiah Webb. Edited by Ralph P. Bieber. Glendale, Cal., 1931, p. 51.
24. Webb, James Josiah, *op. cit.*, pp. 53–54.

CHAPTER X

25. Gregg, Josiah. *Commerce of the Prairies*. New York, 1845. Chapter III.
26. Nearly every book on the Pawnees includes this story. See Densmore, Frances, *Pawnee Music*, Bureau of American Ethnology, Bulletin 93, Washington, D.C., 1929, for details added here.
27. *Mary Jane Luster*. The story of this heroic woman will be found in *Border Reminiscences*, by Randolph B. Marcy, Harper and Brothers, New York, 1872.
28. For the Kiowa account of the death of Red Sleeve, see James Mooney, *Calendar History of the Kiowa Indians*, in Seventeenth Annual Report of the Bureau of American Ethnology. Washington, D.C., 1895–1896, pp. 286–287. The death of Satank is also described in that monograph, pp. 332–333.
29. See Garrard, Lewis H. *Wah-To-Yah and the Taos Trail*, Cincinnati, 1850. Chapter XXIV.
30. Garrard, *op. cit.* Chapter XXIV.

CHAPTER XI

31. The matter presented in this chapter has been taken from Garrard, *op. cit.* Chapter XXII.

CHAPTER XII

32. Oliver Wiggins himself is quoted on this event by Edwin L. Sabin, in his two comprehensive volumes (*q.v.*) *Kit Carson Days, 1809–1868*. New York, 1935.
33. My stepfather, one of Bancroft's staff, told me this story when I was a boy. It will be found related in the article by George Bird Grinnell, *Bent's Old Fort and Its Builders, Kansas Historical Collections*, vol. XV, p. 36.
34. See George Bird Grinnell, *The Fighting Cheyennes*. New York, 1915.

CHAPTER XIII

35. Consult *The Travels of Jedediah Smith*, by Maurice S. Sullivan. Santa Ana, Cal., 1934.
36. *Cure for snake-bite.* See 'Diary of Philip Gooch Ferguson,' in *Marching with the Army of the West 1846–1848*, by Abraham Robinson Johnston, Marcellus Ball Edwards, Philip Gooch Ferguson. Edited by Ralph P. Bieber. Glendale, Cal., 1936, p. 311.

CHAPTER XIV

37. Consult Sabin, *op. cit.*

CHAPTER XV

38. See Twitchell, Ralph Emerson, *The Leading Facts of New Mexican History.* Cedar Rapids, Iowa., 1911–1917. Vol. II, p. 23.

CHAPTER XVI

39. *Dead Horse Lake.* The sacred horse died not far off. The story of the Medicine Horse was told to me by my old friend, the late John Homer Seger, author of *Early Days Among the Cheyenne and Arapahoe Indians*, University of Oklahoma Press, Norman, Oklahoma.

CHAPTER XVII

40. See *Condition of the Indian Tribes*, Report of the Joint Special Committee under Joint Resolution of March 3, 1865. Washington, 1867, pp. 26–98. Kit Carson's comment will be found in Rusling's *Across America.*

CHAPTER XIX

41. *Red Shin. Kansas Historical Collections*, vol. XV.
42. *Lost Woman.* This story, told me by John Homer Seger, was first printed in The Oklahoma University Magazine.

CHAPTER XX

43. *Little Chief.* The account of this fight occurs in the Kansas Historical Collections, vol. XV.

CHAPTER XXI

44. In Grinnell, *The Fighting Cheyennes*, Chap. VI.

CHAPTER XXII

45. *Adventures in Mexico*, by George Frederick Ruxton. London,
1848. Chap. VII.
46. Ruxton, *Adventures in Mexico*, Chap. VII.

B. Chronology of the Trail

1541 Coronado returns to New Mexico along the Arkansas River from Quivira.

1804 Baptiste La Lande goes to Santa Fe from Kaskaskia.

1805 James Purcell (Pursley) arrives in Santa Fe.

1806 Don Facundo Melgares goes beyond the Arkansas River from New Mexico.

1806 Zebulon Montgomery Pike starts from St. Louis for Santa Fe.

1812. Robert McKnight passes over the Trail.

1812 Jules de Mun and Auguste Pierre Chouteau traverse the Arkansas route.

1812 Ezekiel Williams follows the Arkansas for four hundred miles.

1821 Captain William Becknell (Father of the Santa Fe Trail) first takes *wagons* over the Trail to Santa Fe.

1821 Thomas James arrives in Santa Fe soon after Becknell.

1822 Jacob Fowler arrives in Santa Fe.

1823 James Baird and Samuel Chambers reach New Mexico, after making the Caches.

1824 Augustus Storrs and M. M. Marmaduke cross the *jornada* and reach Santa Fe.

1825 New Mexicans come to Council Bluffs, and make a treaty with the Pawnees, so that they will not molest caravans.

1825 The United States Government surveys the Trail to Santa Fe.

1826 Kit Carson runs away to join a caravan for Santa Fe.

1827 Independence, Missouri, is founded.

1828 Franklin, Missouri, is washed into the river.

1829 Major Bennett Riley acts as escort to the caravan.

1830 Caravans begin to use the Cimarron Crossing in preference to others.

1831 Josiah Gregg starts with a caravan for Santa Fe.

1831 Jedediah Smith is killed on the Cimarron River by Comanches.

1833 Independence, Missouri, loses its rating as a prairie port.

1834 Heavy rains permit wagons to mark a trail through the *jornada.*

1834 Captain Clifton Wharton escorts the caravan to the Crossing.

1836 Uncle Dick Wootton goes west with Bent's caravan.

1837 Armijo becomes collector of customs in Santa Fe; lays import duty of five hundred dollars on every wagon.

1839 Kansas City is established.

1839 Gregg explores another route — never adopted.

1839 Thomas Jefferson Farnham goes to Bent's Fort.

1840 Santa Fe traders bring specie and save the Bank of Missouri.

1840 Cheyennes and Arapahoes make peace with Kiowas and Comanches at Bent's Fort.

1841 Kit Carson's men demonstrate the effectiveness of the Colt's pistol against mounted Kiowas near Point of Rocks.

1841 Texas Santa Fe Expedition sets out.

1843 Antonio Jose Chavez is murdered on the Little Arkansas River.

1843 President Santa Ana closes northern Mexico to traders from the States.

1843 General Philip St. George Cooke leads escort of caravan.

1844 President Santa Ana rescinds his mandate.

1846 The Mexican War begins. Texas is annexed to the United States.

1846 August 18: General Stephen Watts Kearny occupies Santa Fe.

1847 January 19: Governor Charles Bent is murdered at Taos.

1847 February 4: Taos is retaken.

1847 Indian raids on the Trail increase. Fort Mann is established.

1848 Alexander Majors starts his first caravan over the Trail. Round trip in ninety-two days. Some three thousand wagons pass up the Arkansas River.

1849 California gold rush. Cholera strikes Plains Indians.

1849 Mrs. White is captured by the Apaches.

1850 Mail service is established once a month to Santa Fe from Independence.

1851 Uncle Dick Wootton rides from Raton to Kansas City in seven days.

1852 William Bent blows up Bent's Old Fort.

1853 Windwagon Thomas promotes the Overland Navigation Company, to send wagons to Santa Fe under sail.

1854 Cholera epidemic.

1857 Mail service twice monthly to Santa Fe.
1858 Gold is discovered in Colorado. Cheyenne Indians have first serious clash with whites.
1859 Gold rush. Pike's Peak or Bust.
1860 The railroad reaches Kansas.
1861 Indians compel abandonment of Cimarron cut-off. Travel goes by Raton Pass.
1862 Union–Confederate battle for Pigeon's Ranch and Apache Canyon.
1863 Railroad land grant.
1864 Massacre at Sand Creek.
1864 Fort Zarah is established.
1865 Union Pacific construction is begun, Omaha.
1866 Kansas Pacific reaches Topeka.
1867 Texas trail-drive to Kansas Pacific.
1869 Cathedral in Santa Fe is begun.
1871 Railway to Dodge City.
1873 Railroad reaches Las Animas, near Bent's Fort.
1878 Uncle Dick Wootton helps the Santa Fe Railroad capture the Raton Pass.
1880 February 9: The railway reaches Santa Fe.

C. Mileage and Stops on the Santa Fe Trail (Gregg's Table)

	Miles	Miles
Independence............................	0	
Round Grove (Lone Elm).................	35	
Narrows (Willow Springs, or Wakarusa Point)	30	65
Hundred-and-Ten-Mile Creek.............	30	95
Bridge Creek............................	8	103
Big John Spring........................	40	143
Council Grove...........................	2	145
Diamond Spring.........................	15	160
Lost Spring.............................	15	175
Cottonwood Creek.......................	12	187
Turkey Creek...........................	25	212
Little Arkansas.........................	17	229
Cow Creek..............................	20	249
Arkansas River (Big Bend)...............	16	265
Walnut Creek (up Arkansas)..............	8	273
Ash Creek..............................	19	292
Pawnee Fork............................	6	298
Coon Creek.............................	33	331
Caches.................................	36	367
Ford of the Arkansas....................	20	387
Sand Creek (leave Arkansas River)........	50	437
Cimarron River.........................	8	445
Middle Spring of the Cimarron...........	36	481
Willow Bar.............................	26	507
Upper Spring...........................	18	525
Cold Spring (Leave Cimarron River).......	5	530
McNee's Creek..........................	25	555
Rabbit Ear Creek........................	20	575
Round Mound...........................	8	583
Rock Creek.............................	8	591
Point of Rocks..........................	19	610
Rio Colorado (Canadian River)...........	20	630

D. The Commerce of the Prairies
Gregg's Table

Year	Cost of Goods in the U. S.	Proprietors	Total Number in Party
1822	$15,000	60	70
1823	12,000	30	50
1824	35,000	80	100
1825	65,000	90	130
1826	90,000	70	100
1827	85,000	50	90
1828	150,000	80	200
1829	60,000	20	50
1830	120,000	60	140
1831	250,000	80	320
1832	140,000	40	150
1833	180,000	60	185
1834	150,000	50	160
1835	140,000	40	140
1836	130,000	35	135
1837	150,000	35	160
1838	90,000	20	100
1839	250,000	40	250
1840	50,000	5	60
1841	150,000	12	100
1842	160,000	15	120
1843	450,000	30	350

E. Bibliography

Bancroft, Hubert Howe. *Works*, vol. 12. Arizona and New Mexico. San Francisco, 1890.

Becknell, Captain William. *Journal.* (In *Missouri Historical Review*, vol. 2, no. 6, p. 56.)

Bieber, Ralph P. *Some Aspects of the Santa Fe Trade*, 1848–1880. (In *Missouri Historical Review*, vol. 18, no. 2, p. 158 ff.)

Bradley, Glenn Danford. *The Story of the Santa Fe.* Boston, 1920.

Chittenden, H. M. *The American Fur Trade in the Far West.* New York, 1902, vol. 2.

Clark, W. P. *The Indian Sign Language.* Philadelphia, 1885.

Conard, Howard Louis. *' Uncle Dick' Wootton.* Chicago, 1890.

Cooke, Philip St. George. *Scenes and Adventures in the Army.* Philadelphia, 1857.

Cooke, Philip St. George. *The Conquest of New Mexico and California.* G. P. Putnam's Sons. New York, 1878.

Cordry, Mrs. T. A. *The Story of the Marking of the Santa Fe Trail by the D.A.R. in Kansas and the State of Kansas.* Crane and Company. Topeka, Kansas, 1915.

Dellenbaugh, F. S. *Breaking the Wilderness.* New York, 1905.

Duffus, R. L. *The Santa Fe Trail.* New York, 1930.

Dunbar, Seymour. *History of Travel in America*, vol. 4. Indianapolis, 1915.

Emory, William H. *Notes of a Military Reconnaissance from Ft. Leavenworth in Missouri to San Diego in California* (with Report of Lt. J. W. Abert of the Examination of New Mexico in the Years 1846–1847; Report of Lt.-Col. P. St. George Cooke of His March from Santa Fe, New Mexico, to San Diego, Upper California; and Journal of Capt. A. R. Johnston). Washington, 1848.

Farnham, Thomas Jefferson. *Travels in the Great Western Prairies. See* Thwaites.

Fowler, Jacob. *Journal*, 1821–1822; edited with notes by Elliott Coues. New York, 1898.

Garrard, Lewis H. *Wah-To-Yah and the Taos Trail*. Cincinnati, 1850.

Gregg, Josiah. *Commerce of the Prairies*. (The classical account of the early history of the Santa Fe Trail.) Eight editions in English and one in German between 1845 and 1857. Reprinted in Thwaites, *q. v.*

Grinnell, George Bird. *The Fighting Cheyennes*. New York, 1915.

Grinnell, George Bird. *Bent's Old Fort and Its Builders*. In Collections of the Kansas State Historical Society, 1919–1922, vol. XV, p. 28 ff.

Grinnell, George Bird. *The Cheyenne Indians*, Yale University Press, 1923.

Hughes, Colonel John T. *Doniphan's Expedition and the Conquest of New Mexico and California*. Cincinnati, 1847. (Reprinted in Connolly, William Elsey: *War with Mexico, 1846–1847*. Topeka, 1907.)

Inman, Henry. *The Old Santa Fe Trail: The Story of a Great Highway*. (Picturesque and atmospheric but inaccurate.) New York, 1897.

Journal of Rudolph Friederich Kurz, translated by Myrtis Jarrell. Edited by J. N. B. Hewitt. Bureau of American Ethnology, Bulletin 115. Washington, 1937.

Kendall, George Wilkins. *Narrative of the Texan Santa Fe Expedition*. 2 vols. New York, 1844, 1846, 1847, 1856. London, 1845, 1846.

Lowe, Percival G. *Five Years a Dragoon '49 to '54, and Other Adventures on the Great Plains*, Kansas City, Mo., 1906.

Magoffin, Susan Shelby. (Ed. Stella Drum.) *Down the Santa Fe Trail and into Mexico: The Diary of Susan Shelby Magoffin, 1846–1847*. Yale University Press, New Haven, Conn., 1926.

Marcy, Captain Randolph B. *The Prairie Traveller, a Handbook for Overland Expeditions*. Harper and Brothers. New York, 1859.

Marcy, Captain Randolph B. *Border Reminiscences*. Harper and Brothers. New York, 1872.

Meline, Colonel James F. *Two Thousand Miles on Horseback. Santa Fe and Back. A Summer Tour through Kansas, Nebraska,*

Colorado and New Mexico in the year 1866. New York, 1867. London, 1868.

Mooney, James. *Calendar History of the Kiowa Indians.* Seventeenth Annual Report of the Bureau of American Ethnology. Washington, 1895–96.

Palliser, John. *The Solitary Hunter.* London, 1847.

Parkman, Francis. *The Oregon Trail.*

Pattie, James O. *The Personal Narrative of James Ohio Pattie of Kentucky during an Expedition from St. Louis through the Vast Regions between that Place and the Pacific and Back through the City of Mexico,* ed. T. Flint. Cincinnati, 1831. (*See also* Thwaites.)

Pike, Zebulon Montgomery. *Expeditions,* ed. Elliott Coues, vol. 2.

Rister, Carl Coke. *The Southwestern Frontier,* 1865–1881. Cleveland, 1928.

Rohan, Jack. *Yankee Arms Maker.* Harper and Brothers.

Ruxton, George Frederick. *Adventures in Mexico,* London, 1848.

Ruxton, George Frederick Augustus. *Life in the Far West.* New York, 1859. (Also published as *In the Old West.*) New York, 1915.

Ryus, William H. *The Second William Penn.* Kansas City, 1913.

Sabin, Edwin L. *Kit Carson Days, 1809–1868.* 2 vols. New York, 1935.

Stephens, F. F. *Missouri and the Santa Fe Trail.* (In *Missouri Historical Review,* vol. 10.)

The Santa Fe Trail, Letters and Journal of Augustus M. Heslep, in *Southern Trails to California in 1849.* Edited by Ralph P. Bieber. The Arthur H. Clark Company, Glendale, Cal., 1937.

Thwaites, Reuben Gold. *Early Western Travels,* 1748–1846. See index for narratives of Gregg, Farnham, Pattie, Long and others. Cleveland, 1904–1907.

Twitchell, Ralph Emerson. *Leading Facts of New Mexican History..* (Not always minutely accurate but the best and most complete history of New Mexico.) Cedar Rapids, Iowa, 1911.

Vestal, Stanley. *Kit Carson, the Happy Warrior of the Old West.* Boston, 1928.

Vestal, Stanley. *Warpath.* Boston, 1934.

Webb, James Josiah. *Adventures in the Santa Fe Trade 1844–1847.* Edited by Ralph P. Bieber. In *The Southwest Historical Series.* The Arthur H. Clark Company. Glendale, Cal., 1931.

Webb, Walter Prescott. *The Great Plains.* Ginn and Company. Boston, 1931.

Williams, Ezekial. *Letter.* (In *Missouri Historical Review,* July, 1914.)

Wislizenus, Adolphus. *Memoir of a Tour to Northern Mexico, Connected with Col. Doniphan's Expedition in 1846 and 1847.* Washington, 1848. (Also a German edition, 1850.)

Index